SOCIAL JUSTICE
AND THE CONSTITUTION

SOCIAL JUSTICE AND THE CONSTITUTION

Edited by
AJIT BHATTACHARJEA

INDIAN INSTITUTE OF ADVANCED STUDY
RASHTRAPATI NIVAS, SHIMLA
1997

First Published 1997

Published by the Secretary
for
Indian Institute of Advanced Study,
Rashtrapati Nivas, Shimla

Typeset at the Indian Institute of Advanced Study, Shimla
and printed at Replika Press Pvt. Ltd., Delhi

Contents

Introduction

AJIT BHATTACHARJEA

Perusing the proofs of the presentations to the seminar on Social Justice and the Constitution more than a year after it was held, I am even more impressed by the extensive range of urgent, topical issues that were discussed. At the time, it was not always possible to appreciate the extensive research, field study and personal experience that had gone into the presentations, together with their implications for governance and society, at one listening. To see them in print, and be able to turn back when needed to take in the finer points of an argument, is to realise and appreciate the extent and importance of the ground that was covered.

What is missing in the reading, however, is the verbal disputation. Unfortunately, the taping and transcription facilities proved inadequate to the task. But the quality of the presentations makes up for this lack. What cannot be made up in print is the ambience of the setting of the seminar at Dhvanyaloka, Professor C.D. Narasimhaiah's picturesque retreat-cum-literary study centre on the outskirts of Mysore, and the hospitality of his family. The happy decision by the Indian Institute of Advanced Study to hold the four-day seminar in Mysore, so far from Shimla, also enabled a wider number of participants, some of them social activists, to be present.

The concept of the seminar took shape in 1994 under the guidance of the then Director, Professor J.S. Grewal. The idea originated in a suggestion made by members of the staff to the Chairman, Dr. S. Gopal, that the Institute discuss issues concerning the Dalits and the under-privileged to observe the centenary of the birth of Dr. Ambedkar. A group of Fellows was associated with the project; they felt that a seminar focussing on social justice and the Constitution would be appropriate in view of Dr. Ambedkar's outstanding role in formulating the Constitution and his leadership of what were then known as the Depressed Classes. I was asked to prepare a concept paper for advance circulation to the participants. It is reproduced below.

I was to learn that not everyone accepted my approach. In his welcoming remarks at Dhvanyaloka, our host, Dr. Narasimhaiah, confessed that he had drafted his inaugural address before receiving the concept note. This proved fortunate. In his polished, literary manner, he proceeded to introduce a different approach in which the State, and therefore the constitutional requirements on it, played little part in the pursuit of social justice. He strongly believed that inequalities should be obviated by individual and community effort; indeed to depend on the government could be degrading.

Dr. Mrinal Miri's prefatory remarks were also a warning against using the word 'justice' lightly. He traced the different meanings of the concept in history and in different civilisations. Currently, too, the objective of the concept could be divergent. For the Dalits and other disadvantaged groups it could lie in the obliteration of social differences; for ethnic and language groups social justice could mean protection and retention of cultural differences to enable them to retain their identity.

Most of the participants were deeply concerned and involved with the issues raised by the concept note. The general opinion was that the Constitution had failed to provide the social justice promised in the Preamble and in the Directive principles. The promises had been treated as political assurances rather than commitments and this had been made possible by imprecise wording. Taken together, the presentations amounted to a wide-ranging indictment of the constitutional system.

It was argued that the Constitution-makers had imbued the document with their own commitment to an elitist status quo; that the Gandhian blueprint had been abandoned, leading to marginalisation of large sections of society; that the system of elections had corrupted the polity; that minority and ethnic rights had been subordinated to excessive centralisation, creating serious unrest. On the economic front, the policy of structural adjustment was being pursued though it was contrary to the Directive Principles of the Constitution.

The language policy of the Constitution was criticised on the ground that it discriminated unfairly between different groups. It was strongly argued that retention of English was a root cause of social injustice. The damage caused to the culture, language and economy of the scheduled tribes was also set forth in detail, backed by field studies. Here it was not always the Constitution that was to blame, but neglect of the safeguards it provided. The significance of the mode of enumeration of castes and communities in achieving constitutional objectives was also analysed.

Not all the presentations were critical of the constitutional system. One differed by providing a detailed account of court judgments and amendments to the Constitution that, it was maintained, had provided social, political and economic stability.

Three presentations focussed on the police and bureaucracy: the machinery designed to maintain constitutional rights and execute policies. One was by a serving and another by a retired police officer. They were remarkable for the frank analysis of the problems facing the services, but there was disagreement over whether continuance of the colonial structure, as reflected in the Constitution, was beneficial or injurious.

Dr. Ambedkar's thinking on economic and social issues was described in detail. It was explained that for him democracy was meaningless without the achievement of economic and social equality. For this reason, he believed that the constitutional provisions for Fundamental Rights and Directive Principles were organically interlinked. To reduce inequalities, he proposed that State ownership of land and key industries be classed as Fundamental Rights, but was unable to persuade the Constituent Assembly to accept his programme.

The concept of the 'creamy layer', as undeserving of the benefits provided to the backward classes, was discussed in another presentation. According to one participant, the upper class rulers of India had wrecked the Constitution, which was imperfect and had been rejected by Dr. Ambedkar himself. The situation had led to virtual war. A more peaceful expression of Dalit anger in the form of plays was the subject of another presentation.

THE CONCEPT PAPER

The Preamble to the Constitution commits it to the pursuit of social justice more specifically than any other single objective. It assures to all its citizens: JUSTICE, social, economic and political; LIBERTY of thought, expression, belief, faith and worship; EQUALITY of status and opportunity; FRATERNITY assuring the dignity of the individual. This commitment is reinforced by the chapter on Directive Principles of State Policy. Among the stated objectives are: all citizens have the right to an adequate means of livelihood; the operation of the economic system must not result in the concentration of wealth; within ten years the State shall provide for free and compulsory education for all children upto the age of 14; the State shall promote with special care the educational and economic interests of the weaker sections of the people, in particular the Scheduled Castes and Tribes, and shall protect them from social injustice and all forms of exploitation.

This was the original document that was adopted on 26 November 1949 and came into force on 26 January 1950. The verbal thrust towards social justice was further elaborated by subsequent amendments. Indira Gandhi introduced the word 'socialist' in the official definition of India. The Janata Government expanded the Directive Principles to direct the State to promote justice, social, economic and political (as already promised in the Preamble). More specifically, the State was directed to minimise inequalities in income and in status, facilities and opportunities, not only among individuals but also amongst groups residing in different areas or engaged in different vocations. Free legal aid was to be provided. Panchayats established. But neither the Preamble nor the Directive Principles are legally enforceable; at best they amount to statements of intent.

Instead of serving as beacons to light the way of governments, as they have been described, these provisions have served only to highlight the gulf between promise and performance. The gap between rich and poor, in the facilitation available to the privileged and to the deprived, has been steadily widening. More than 30 per cent of the population, or more than 30 crores, are estimated to subsist below the poverty line, which means they do not get enough to eat. India has the highest number of illiterates in the world and its placing in world development statistics is near the lowest. Recent economic policies have enhanced the gap between the standard of living of the middle and upper classes and the rest. The assurances concerning right to work, free and universal education upto 14, free legal aid etc., have been virtually ignored.

Those who have occupied government office must bear the primary responsibility for non-implementation of the promises made in the Constitution. But what we should examine is whether there are elements in the document itself that obstruct, or make it easier to obstruct, their implementation. Did the framers of the Constitution sabotage the idealistic objectives from within? They were not elected in any meaningful sense of the term; they were indirectly elected by provincial assemblies in British India, which were themselves elected on a limited franchise from which the poor were excluded. Many were men of property. Their cultural moorings were Western; they had little time for the Gandhian stress on indigenous institutions of democracy. In the name of national development, they debased the values of groups outside the mainstream.

Subhash Kashyap, former Secretary-General of the Lok Sabha, makes the point: "It was, however, perhaps the class character and elitist composition of the Constituent Assembly that was responsible for distribution of basic human rights into the enforceable fundamental *rights* and non-enforceable directive *principles* of state policy. The poor, illiterate, hungry masses had no use for most of the rights like the right to property, freedom of thought and expression, equality of opportunity in matters of public employment etc. In any case, they were in no position to claim any benefit from these rights. The rights they needed were those of freedom from hunger, right to a living wage etc. All these were relegated to the non-enforceable principles".[1]

The key question that arises is to what extent was the Constitution designed to enable the colonial administrative machinery, with its repressive status quo approach, to function in independent India? Much of the 1935 Act was imported into the Constitution. The undemocratic powers wielded by and through the inherited office of Governor and the steel frame provided by the entrenched civil services have much to do with devolution of power remaining suspended above the grass roots. In contrast, neither panchayats nor local bodies enjoy the same constitutional protection. Yet, we must bear in mind that Dr. Ambedkar believed that a strong Central government could do more for the deprived sections than grass-roots institutions which, he believed, would be dominated by the privileged castes.

Even so, it is noteworthy that such basic measures needed to secure social justice as land reform were denied constitutional sanction. Nor were provisions made to remove the elitist character of education and suit it to the needs of the people. This points to the biggest single flaw in the Constitution: elaborate provisions were made for elections on the basis of adult suffrage, but not for the rapid spread of literacy and public awareness without which the electoral process has become a fount of corruption.

[1] *Reforming the Constitution*, ed. Subhash C. Kashyap, U.B.S. Publishers' Distributors, New Delhi, 1992.

The Meaning of Justice

MRINAL MIRI

It gives me great pleasure to welcome you this morning to the inauguration of the Seminar. The Seminar, as you can see, has been made possible by the generosity of Professor Narasimhaiah and his dedicated team in Dhvanyaloka. It is a great privilege for us at the Institute to be associated, in this, with Dhvanyaloka. I hope that this is just beginning of our association, and we shall continue to collaborate in the collective pursuit of academic research and debates.

The guiding force of the Seminar has been Mr. Ajit Bhattacharjea, who conceived the idea and pursued it until its realization here in Mysore. I, on my part, would like merely to make one or two remarks about the general concepts around which the debate in this Seminar will turn.

First of all, the concept of justice. As you know, there has been a long debate about justice both in the West and in the Indian intellectual traditions. I think the debate about *dharma,* about *yuga dharma,* about the relationship between *dharma* and *karma,* is, in a central way, a debate about the concept of justice. In the West, there is not one, but several traditions of thinking about justice: the Homeric or the heroic tradition, the Platonic-Aristotelian tradition, the Christian tradition and the Thomist tradition. This last, some say, is a happy and, some others say, an unhappy combination of the Platonic-Aristotelian and the Christian traditions. And then, of course, you have the modern liberal humanist tradition – we are all part of this modern liberal humanist tradition of thinking, whether we realise it or not.

It is not often easy to relate these different strands of thinking about justice to one another. For instance, I do not know how to bring the Indian thinking about justice about *karma* and *dharma,* to bear upon some of the Western traditions of thinking about justice. Or, if you take some of the Western traditions, it seems very difficult to reconcile, say, the Aristotelian thinking about justice with the liberal humanist way of thinking about justice.

So, there are different concepts of justice – different justices – if you like, corresponding to different rationalities, different ways of articulating the various conceptions of justice (a view which has been argued for in great detail by Alasdyre McIntyre in his book *Whose Justice Which Rationality*). In its most common usage, the word justice is almost synonymous with the word fairness : to do justice to another person is to be fair to him, to give him his due, or to give him what he deserves. The idea of desert or merit is an important constituent of the idea of justice. Of course, the notion of what somebody deserves will be different from tradition to tradition. For instance, in the context of the *karma* theory, the notion of what one deserves is very different from the idea of desert in the context of the liberal humanist theory. One way of reading the karma theory is that there is nothing that one does not deserve, everything that happens to one is by one's merit. And this is very different from the liberal humanist way of thinking about deserving.

But what is this liberal humanist conception of justice? It will be impossible for me to try and answer this question here, even if I had the necessary intellectual resource for doing so. I shall merely mention one crucial aspect of this conception which I think may have a bearing on the theme of the Seminar. This is that for the liberal humanist theory, an individual human being, just because he is an individual human being, a being definable, characterisable independently of society, tradition and culture deserves to be treated in a certain way – treated by the society, by the state or by other individuals in a certain way. Of course, there is no unanimity about what this individual being is – an individual who is essentially characterisable independently of society, culture and so on. We have the utilitarian idea, just as we have the Kantian view of the autonomous moral agent; there is also the Nietzchean view and the post-Nietzchean elaboration of it.

When you think about social justice, things are a little different. Social justice is presumably opposed to individual justice. One of the things that the idea of social justice obviously implies is that one can be just or unjust not merely towards an individual but also towards a community or a society – a community or a society just because it is a community or a society of a certain kind – definable or describable in a certain way.

I think there is a kind of, not incompatibility, but a basic contrariety in the liberal tradition of thinking which makes it difficult for us to articulate this conception of social justice. What does the notion of social justice presuppose? It presupposes many things. But at least one of them is that a community as a whole, and not just an individual human being, can be a moral entity, that it can be the object of moral assessment or moral sympathy as a community. Also, a community insofar as it is a community can be treated as a moral agent and is, therefore, capable of being held responsible for what it does or does not do, what happens to it or what does not happen to it. Now, one might ask, how is this possible? In the liberal way of thinking, it is the individual – the individual, characterisable independently of a community, society etc. that has deserts and merits, that is the object of moral judgment and sympathy. How is it possible for an entire community to be a moral agent or an object of moral judgment or sympathy or hostility? I do not think sufficient attention has been paid to a clarification of this notion of social justice – justice to a community. The liberal humanist debate about justice has been almost entirely a debate about justice to an individual, to an individual human being. And there is a great deal of unclarity about how the conception of justice to a community can be incorporated into this debate. It seems to me, on the face of it, that within the liberal framework, the two conceptions of justice are incompatible. About this, I shall say something in a moment.

Now, given that we can coherently talk about justice to a community, just because it is a community of a certain sort, I think, at least as far as the contemporary situation in our country goes, we can talk about two radically different kinds of communities here. And it is very important that we realize the difference between the two.

One of these kinds of communities is such that to be just to such a community is to begin a process, the end result of which is that the community loses its mark of identity as that kind of community. If it does not lose its mark of identity, then the process of justice has not been completed. Such are communities like, e.g., the scheduled castes, the community of child or bonded labourers. To be just to the scheduled castes or to complete the process of being just to them is for them, at the end of the day, to lose their identity as scheduled castes. The same is true of the child or the bonded labourer.

The second kind of community is such that to do justice to it is not to initiate a process, the end result of which will be such that the community loses its mark of identity as that kind of community. For instance, we have linguistic communities, ethnic communities and, may be also racial communities. And to do justice to a linguistic community is not to see that it loses its mark as a linguistic community of that kind. Similarly, to do justice to an ethnic community again is not to see that it loses its mark as an ethnic community of that kind. And perhaps to be just to a racial community is to see that it retains its character as a racial community of that kind.

There are, of course, communities which cannot unambiguously be put in either of these two classes of communities. Thus take the poor of our country. To be just to the poor would also, I suppose, mean that the end result of it is that they lose their identity as poor, that they are no longer poor. There will be no difficulty about this if the poverty that one is speaking of is such that it crushes the man both bodily and mentally, so that there is, in practice, no possibility of his working towards realising any of his human potentials. But there is a tradition of thinking about poverty which is such that poverty, not in its extreme form, but yet poverty that is recognizably so, is the basis, the infrastructure, as it were, of the pursuit of the good life. Thus you have the Christian, the Hindu and the Buddhist traditions, much of which would regard poverty in this sense as the foundation for the pursuit of the good life.

I think it is one of the marks of modernity that we do not make this distinction. We do not make the distinction any longer between these two types of poverty, that the second notion of poverty has been allowed to collapse into the first. But there are perhaps still people who live by the old notion of poverty and obviously, to try and remove their poverty will be to do injustice rather than justice to them.

Another example that may be ambiguous is that of women. What is the feminist conception of justice? Is it that as a result of the process of having done justice to women, they should lose their mark of identity as women? This is something about which there has been considerable debate. I shall not go into it.

But to return to the two clear examples of two radically different kinds of communities in relation to social justice: one, where to do justice to a community is to help it obliterate its mark as a community of that kind, and two, where justice to a community consists in enabling it to flourish as a community of that kind: flourish in the Aristotelian sense of flourish. Scheduled castes or dalits cannot possibly flourish as long as they are truly describable as castes of a certain kind or dalits. Dalits cannot possibly flourish as dalits. As long as slaves are truly describable as slaves, they cannot possibly flourish as slaves. On the other hand, to be just to a linguistic community will consist in enabling that community to flourish as a community of that kind. The same may be true of ethnic communities of different kinds and even racial communities.

So much about social justice. Now, I would like to say a word or two about the idea of responsibility which goes obviously with the idea of justice. Once again, the liberal notion of responsibility goes with the liberal notion of the human being as independent of all those things that I said that it could be imagined as independent of. This is the notion that I, the individual self, am responsible for what I have done or have not done. Of course, sometimes I can be held responsible for what my students have done or what my children have done or maybe what my wife has done. But this is because what my students have done, or what my children have done, or even what my wife has done seems to be either a direct or an indirect result of what I have done. Given this notion of responsibility, how can I, in this way of thinking, be held responsible for what I have never done or what cannot be seen as either a direct or an indirect result of what I have never done? For instance, how can I be held responsible for the plight of the scheduled castes? How can I be held responsible for the plight of the bonded labourers? I have done nothing either directly or indirectly which could be said to have resulted, even in a partial manner, in their plight.

The neo-Nazis use two kinds of arguments in their attempt to free themselves from the responsibility of the holocaust of the second world war. One argument is that they did not do anything as horrible as they are painted to have done to the Jews. But the other argument is more serious. And this is that even if all these horrible things happened, how can I, a German living now, be held responsible for what those other people have done? I had nothing to do with the horrors, nor are they direct or indirect consequences of what I have done or what I have not done. Therefore, I cannot be held responsible for what the Nazis did.

Now, we have obviously discarded this notion of responsibility in our Constitution, because in the Constitution, we hold ourselves responsible for the plight of the scheduled castes or the plight of the dalits. How can the notion of responsibility be articulated in such a way that, e.g., our responsibility to the dalits is accounted for, our responsibility to linguistic minorities is accounted for? And this is something that this Seminar will hopefully go into. I think it is very essential that we are clear about the idea of responsibility that is implicit in our constitutional mandate.

It seems to me that the basic debate about the Constitution has to be a moral debate. In this debate, we can, of course, take different stances, but we should be clear, at the same time, that we are doing so. One of the difficulties about taking a moral stance is that frequently we are not at all clear about why it is that we take such a stance.

It seems to me that the notion of responsibility that is inherent in our constitutional imperatives can begin to make sense only if I can relate myself to my tradition, to my past, in such a way that a deep understanding of myself necessarily involves me relating myself to my past in a way in which I can own up my past – I can acknowledge it as my past. It is only if I can own my past, or rather own up my past, in this deep kind of way that I can be held responsible for what is happening now as a result of things which were done not by me but my ancestors. So, this debate about responsibility must also be a debate about my relationship to my own past, about my relationship to my history, about what it is that I owe to my past and what it is that makes it necessary that I acknowledge my past as my own past. We feel proud about our past and we also feel ashamed of it. How is it possible for me to be either proud or be ashamed of my past? I think these are questions which the Seminar will have to go into.

Mr. Bhattacharjea has pointed out that there are moral ambiguities in the very language of the Constitution, that frequently the language of the Constitution is a mask for motivations which are not very noble. This again is essentially a moral debate. And whenever we are talking about the changes in the Constitution or possible changes, we must ensure that we do not once again put them in a language which masks motivations of different kinds which may be ignoble in different ways. So, the entire exercise of contemplating changes in our Constitution is in a large measure an exercise in moral thinking.

I am sorry that I have put before you these stray unconnected thoughts. We have, among the audience, constitutional experts, acute legal minds and scholars of distinction from various disciplines. Many different aspects of our problems with the Constitution and social justice will, quite naturally, be brought out in the Seminar. I would like to end, again by thanking Professor Narasimhaiah and thanking all of you.

Social Justice or the Destruction of Initiative

C.D. NARASIMHAIAH

The Institute's statement on the theme of the seminar concerns itself with specific issues such as the maldistribution of wealth, social discriminations against certain groups, denial of educational and employment opportunities to large sections of our people and gaps between government's promise and its performance. My preoccupation has been not with what a government or a Constitution can do to set right inequalities and injustices but what individuals and groups could do on their own to virtually obviate the very need for governmental action to redress existing ills. Government's help, I hasten to add, should come only to qualify them to gain confidence to feel equal to others, though some preference must still be shown to the poor wretches handicapped for centuries. Predictably, I have my fears, anxieties and even strong reservations on the way social justice operates in government and other public bodies. I should even be happy if government's main emphasis is on adding to the inner resources of the backwards and not place them at the mercy of social justice. To me it is almost degrading to their self-esteem as individuals and groups. I suspect I find myself ineffectual in the present ethos. But I have on my side one of the profound thinkers of the age, Simone Weil, who lists degradation of the sentiment of justice among the four obstacles to the pursuit of a civilization that is of any worth.

I shall therefore make bold to adhere to my note, not only because I have put in some little effort to prepare it but strongly believe – to repeat myself, that social justice as conceived and administered by government destroys initiative in individuals and groups – initiative is life, its absence death: I fear social justice's first assault is on life propelling initiative. I seem to see it, besides, as utterly unfair and demoralizing to those who have to bear the brunt of the effects of social justice for the imaginary sins of their forefathers. It breeds a strong sense of injustice among them in the very act of rendering justice to some others. It is tantamount to correcting, like the wars fought in history, one injustice by another injustice through unjust means – hence John Stuart Mill's unequivocal observation long ago that social justice is not justice. One doesn't know where it lands the country and so seen I thought the seminar is seminal to the present and of profound significance for the future of the country.

The Institute's note rightly cites the mouthful phrases written into the Constitution and government's failure from time to time to remove disparities between the actual and the ideal, between promise and performance inducing cynicism which I myself wholly share. And so I hope you will bear with me while I am not so naive as to think my address will not amuse you by its irrelevance.

II

Is social justice a contradiction in terms? For, while it sounds affirmative it carries with it a negative implication as it suggests that something has gone wrong somewhere and calls for radical measures like legal remedies with political overtones, if necessary, written into the Constitution. Shall we suspend our preoccupation with social justice for a while and coolly contemplate the inner workings of Nature and Man to look for possible analogies and gain a larger perspective? I submit imbalance appears to be the governing principle of life in Nature as well as Man, though mercifully it is simultaneously accompanied by a built-in self-regenerating mechanism which exponents and beneficiaries of social justice would do well never to forget, for there is in it a lesson for them. Nature is a standing example of the cyclical process of light and darkness following each other. The sun, that great bridegroom, must strain to appear on the resplendent eastern horizon day after day. When trees dry up in autumn there must be hectic activity in Nature's workshop before they put on fresh foliage, flowers and fruits. So do rivers and lakes when under the sun's heat send up vapour to form clouds and bring down rain to the parched land. Why, look at the snake which sheds its skin from an inner necessity because a new one forms itself underneath and so must cast off the old one. The underlying principle in human society is the same though it cannot be either so smooth or simple because thanks to his meddling intellect, man no longer lives as a child of nature; our ancestors who lived on Nature's terms or approximated to her ways have left us a legacy of the cyclical view of life and history. I have in mind two myths. Consider the myth of Parvathi giving up her barest physical subsistence of leaves of plants, and become *Aparna* in her indefatigable pursuit of Siva for her spouse. So is Ahalya, an inert stone under a curse but kept throbbing for aeons to sense the touch of Sri Rama's feet. Both are examples of *Nirvritti* in Indian thought but both paradoxically are charged with a divine aspiration, *Pravritti* which sustains them.

> Old order changeth yielding place to new
> And God fulfils himself in many ways
> Lest one good custom should corrupt the world

is glib generalization, if also poor poetry. But that was by a tired and ruminating Tennyson. Perhaps the reason why Goethe felt prompted to enact the struggle between opposing forces in dramatic form which held the attention of Toynbee as he was reading Goethe's great work *Faust* on a plane journey. The professor perceived in the confrontation between God and the Devil, Mephistopheles, a well-wrought divine plan with Faust symbolising the vital force capable of responding to the challenge of Mephistopheles. Toynbee wondered if this was not true of historical epochs as well. Only those civilizations have endured, he observes, which have successfully responded to the challenge posed to them; others have gone down. Apart from the Mayan, Phoenecian and Egyptian civilizations of an earlier day, two notable examples are those of Greece and Rome, both civilizations of the top few with vast numbers of the population kept at the bottom rung of the social ladder. If the Indian historian missed his chance of anticipating Toynbee and enunciating this spectacular theory it is just that he failed to apprehend the vitality and continuity of his own civilization, also impressively enacted in the story of Harishchandra, an Indian counterpart of Goethe's Faust who responded successfully to the challenges of Viswamitra. The story is told to our common people ('suno Janamejaya') who often feel aggrieved against what they consider unmerited suffering. It is narrated to bring them some solace and build the sinews of their spirit by demonstrating there are others who have suffered more and for no valid reason. The implicit lesson is: Do not exaggerate your own troubles but learn to understand and find in the story stimulus to go on living. Literature, I keep repeating, must have a *prayojana* and *purushartha*.

Anyhow, the historian's failure was the poet's opportunity. In a remarkable essay on his 'Vision of India's History' Rabindranath Tagore sees his way straight to the primordial myth to make it yield a new meaning and effect a transfusion of the blood into weak veins. The poet's trade demanded it of him, because it is the collective unconscious of a whole people. Actually Western historians today speak of history as myth. Tagore saw in the myth the four vedas falling from the four mouths of Brahma which the Brahmin held firmly in his clasp and wouldn't share it with others. There started the initial mistake, or, so many of us think with our hindsight. But the Kshatriya emerging from Brahma's shoulders compensated for it and went on expanding, conquering and consolidating. In the process there was, as Tagore sees it, confrontation, a prolonged one, between the Brahmin and the Kshatriya or the Sattvic and Rajasic ideals. Brahma must have willed the cosmic design thus as being conducive to creativity in life lest society, it is paradoxical to say, stagnate in a state of harmony. For perfection is not an unmixed blessing and must be even illusory. Imagine a state in which the ripe fruit never falls. Is a stable society, then, a dull society? It's not necessarily a dynamic one, though only a powerful current causes eddies and pools. Plurality of religions, even castes, with their own rituals, food habits, variety of costumes, jewelry as well as linguistic dialects, far from being a curse, can make for a colourful tapestry, if we can look at it all in serene detachment. One can't miss, though, the stitching and unstitching on the seamy side of a colourful surface. 'Social justice' may well have found its fertile ground precisely there.

A psychologist friend, now no more, one day held before me two cardboard figures of a man and a woman and started with his accustomed casualness: You see, when they are apart there is tension which makes for creativity – the truth of it subsequently brought home to me when my Cambridge tutor's wife sent me a picture of her with her husband F.R. Leavis, inscribed on its back 'Engaged in creative quarrel.' To return to my psychologist friend, he continued, if they are apart for long it results in frustration. Likewise, if they come together there is repose in union but if it lasts long it results in stagnation. And so, neither staying apart nor coming together should last too long. They better alternate as they do when the wheel turns. Is that why a 17th century poet in England thought on the eve of European Enlightenment

God ordered motion
Ordained not rest
– George Herbert

Was it divine strategy that Buddha was foiled in his wish to stop turning the wheel so as to attain Nirvana? It seems the gods themselves implored him to resume his task at the wheel as chaos had descended on the world. Buddha relented and went back not only to keep the wheel turning but to enjoin on his chief disciple, Ananda, never to cross the threshold of this life if even a blade of grass was caught in distress. It had to be rescued. Which means there shall be no cessation from action. Which was also the message of the Upanishads and the Gita, '*Charaiveti, Charaiveti,* March on, March on, o ye traveller'. Which the Buddha absorbed into his compassionate personality as he had visualized mankind like fish in a pond which was drying up and so imparted a terrific personal urgency to it by his Great Departure – from wife, child and palace. It is seen the Buddha virtually set out to correct the malady of Creation at large – shall we call it cosmic injustice? the cause of all the *Dukkha* of the world? – which moved even a monk like Vivekananda to feel impelled to say he will be a servant of the servants of the Buddha, but was constrained to comment adversely on his utopian ideal. He said Buddha hypnotized the country by his voice, didn't influence it. Is it surprising that Buddhism squeezed itself out of the country what with the abiding appeal of Hinduism which meant everything to everyone – *Advaita* to the man of intellect, *Bhakti Marga* to the man of faith and *Karma Marga* to the man of action and disarming respect for all religions as different ways of experiencing Reality. Its priests even invited the Charvakas to preach godlessness from the precincts of our temples and subsequently included Buddha himself as an *avatar* in its pantheon of gods. The Buddha story found its poetic justice but social justice is still a far cry, because the social and the spiritual in Indian tradition are inextricably intertwined and can't be separated. Buddha himself like all great rebels was enriching the tradition while revolting against it.

It is surprising that so intelligent a man as Dr. B.R. Ambedkar became a Buddhist, presumably to spite the caste Hindus who had humiliated him and his kind and not for any known inner compulsion. Would it be embarrassing to ask if he lived in a manner becoming of a Buddhist, himself? Did his concern as a reformer extend to the entire society, and not stop with a particular section, because that is after all a part of the larger organism which is perilous to ignore. How many of his followers were moved emotionally to embrace Buddhism? Did he exhort them as the Buddha did 'O bhikkus, work out your salvation with diligence!' T.S. Eliot made his psychiatrist advise a broken young woman 'My daughter, work out your salvation with diligence'. Most political leaders from backward castes said, in effect, 'my followers, come, I'll give you a *mantra,* – social justice, in this case. Chant it whenever trouble assails you. That will give you deliverance. I see government and the ubiquitous fake swamis have a meeting ground here – they seem to need each other. What society at large needed was the healing touch of the compassionate surgeon behind his wounded knife. In this case the followers only warmed to their leader when he offered material benefits, but couldn't enthuse themselves either in the matter of commensurate responsibility on their part or what the new religion entailed. It should invite its own comment and it is pointless to labour at it. It is hard to change a man's religion, especially Hinduism for all its shameful failings, for it is less a religion than a way of life which means all things to all people. It has taken kicks and remained a milking cow, as Vivekananda observed. I call attention to Mulk Raj Anand's novel *Untouchable* in which inspite of himself the novelist couldn't help presenting Bakha, the untouchable, and his father as offering resistance to the subtle entreaties of the Christian missionary. Why change a religion which was good enough for our forefathers? they argued. It is ironic that after his death the Buddha began to be worshipped as a god with all the attendant rituals on which he had frowned. Interestingly the Buddha was a Kshatriya like his ancestor Viswamitra who while he aspired to be a Brahmarshi, only paved the way for Kshatriyas like Rama and Krishna to be worshipped in temples while the Brahmin Parasurama has yet to find an opening into temples as object of worship. The circle is complete and the lesson isn't missed. Material benefits which are the gift of social justice without spiritual foundation are like a house built on sand. Understandably, Camus, the sceptical French thinker, acknowledged that if with all the ravages of invasion India has preserved itself it is because of a spiritual principle deeply embedded in it. Precisely what endeared Buddha himself to millions of people, of all religions and countries – at a personal level, that is, with nothing beyond, but they have, at that level, found in him fulfilment of a deep spiritual need.

Where does all this lead to in our concern with social justice? It reduces things to brave clearness. It calls for spirited striving – you see it so evident in the meanest worm in the way it seeks to attack you if it can or swerve to a side to protect itself from any threat to its life. He is a beggar without self-respect who cringes for alms without giving some good in return – in that sense there were no beggars in Indian society. He was a *dasa,* devotee of God who sang His praise and made an honourable living. Mature leadership should exploit the good things that have come down from the past including its popular practices like common festivals, rituals, ceremonies at weddings, birth, death, house-warming and even superstitions. A radical Australian nationalist, P.R. Stephenson, has written: 'Where there have been fewest changes . . . the race survives. Where there have been most changes, there it perishes. Experience shows that change of habits among natives can be bloodier than a bombardment'. A sense of right and wrong, thanks to the concepts of *dharma* and *adharma* is ingrained into the conscience of an Indian and an appeal to it can shame him when there is a breach.

There is a place called Melkote, hardly 25 miles from Mysore, a famous Vaishnava centre associated with Ramanuja, the propounder of the philosophy of *Visistadvaita.* The seer was one day taken in procession by his devotees when one of his two chief disciples, Dasarathi, sighted at the head of the procession an untouchable woman coming in the opposite direction and shouted at her to get away from the path of the Master. The poor woman wailed 'Where shall I go? Before me is the Master, behind me is the temple; to the right is the river Cauvery, and to the left are the dwellings of the disciples.' The other disciple, Kuresha, reprimanded him for hurting the poor woman, for being a brahmin he could go and have his bath in the river and change his sacred thread, but the inhuman hurt!

It was such a master who made public his Guru's *mantra* intended only for him even if it meant Hell for him and successfully fought against orthodoxy as early as 12th century and had his way in throwing the temple doors open to the untouchables. Today you can't reach to the shrine without paying obeisance to the images of his untouchable disciples at the entrance. Not only he, but the entire country threw up from the lower castes noted saint-poets, the *Sivasarnas* in Karnataka, the *Alwars* in Tamilnadu, *Nayanmars* in Kerala and the *Sants* in Maharashtra. Hence the saying, 'don't ask the past of a saint, nor the origin of a river.' Farseeing Indians of an earlier day structured the four-fold Hindu society vertically to suggest the limitlessness of possibility, for it was open to anyone to reach to the top by inner striving. Even in this age of ours there is the supreme example of Gandhi, who was neither a Brahmin nor a Kshatriya and, could become the supreme leader of India and move the hearts of millions without force, position or money. As Jawaharlal Nehru says this is 'as good a test as any of a nation's cultural background'. Will our leaders today realise they have abdicated their leadership by throwing away the primary condition laid down by Gandhi and Nehru and thus exposed to the people's contempt. What our public men do not realize is the central idea of Aryan culture was Dharma which was more than a religion. It was a conception of obligations or of duties to oneself and others. They haven't emphasized rights too much. They feared that security could only be purchased at the cost of ultimate progress. Our ancestors have left us the legacy of *Abhaya,* fearlessness, which is the product of selflessness. The poet T.S. Eliot put this notion to splendid use when he wrote in *The Waste Land.*

London Bridge is falling down, falling down, falling down.

But by implication, he sees no cause for alarm or despair, for the protagonist says, 'shall I at least set *my* lands in order? Gandhi put it more arrestingly when he said 'Add zero to zero, it is still zero. Add zero to one it is 10 and goes on increasing with every zero. Indian thought commended individual salvation by way of working for *Lokakalyana* or *Lokasangraha.* There is the notable instance of Sri Ramakrishna admonishing Vivekananda while he preferred to be lost in a state of *Samadhi* – he wanted him to awaken the slumbering sections of our people. That is what led T.S. Eliot to look to the Indian myths for stimulus in writing that seminal poem of the age *The Waste Land.* In the Rig Vedic myth the *Sapta Sindhu* was tied up by the demon Vritta and the land was wasted. The gods and men implored a mendicant sage, Dadhicha to help them out. Not having anything else to offer he gave them his backbone which they used as *Vajrayudha* to smite the relentless clouds with and make them yield the rain: Eliot reinforced it with another myth in which Bhagiratha did penance for 1000 years to bring the Ganga down. The poem's implicit message to modern man is that old sources of regeneration are still available to him. But does he have the will? Does he have the wisdom to tap them in answer to a present need? Which is the only way to take us out of the Waste Land of modern life. By this and this only we have existed, says Eliot, not by our obituaries and monuments to which shall I add 'social justice'.

The poem's call is most pertinent to those who give and those who receive. It should be salutary to think of the social and economic disparities of 19th century France and the French Revolution together with its consequences. While the revolutionary thinkers gave the exploited people slogans of liberty and equality, both legalistic, they were thoughtful enough to add fraternity or brotherliness as they well knew legalities would not take them far. Indeed, they didn't. A revolution devours its children. This child of the Revolution, Napoleon, became a General at 24 and looked upto by the Army as a young Father, *petit padre* but ended up by placing himself on the throne as Emperor with ambitions of perpetuating dynastic rule. What a dangerous precedent!

We are today faced with a wilderness of Napoleons in India wanting to devour each other, like monsters of the deep but the tragedy is they will in the process devour the people at large.

How different was Gandhi! He went on prolonged fast to exhort the caste Hindus to look into their hearts and realise the grievous wrong done to the untouchables. He adopted an untouchable girl as his child and even wished to be born an untouchable if there was a rebirth. The country's Independence for which he had fought all his life when it came, wouldn't attract him to Delhi to join in the celebration. He ultimately met his end at the hands of a Hindu for championing the cause of the Muslims. Ironically neither the Harijans nor the Muslims look upon him as a friend or well-wisher; on the contrary, he is in their eyes a reactionary, even a hypocrite. Gandhi sought to give them what they 'needed', not what they 'wished for '. 'Needed' and 'wished for' are quotes from Ruskin's *Unto this Last* which he read on a train journey in South Africa. He was moved, in his own words, by the magic spell of the book: 'I couldn't sleep that night.' He says, he arose with the dawn and set out to establish the Phoenix Settlement. It called for maximal self-effort; Gandhi evoked it in the Indian community and he succeeded where Ruskin and Tolstoy had failed in their own countries. It is possible, though, that Ruskin's book had fertilized the Labour Party's philosophy in England. Hence the Labour Government's stand towards the worker' 'Dig a pit and earn a wage, fill the same pit, also earn a wage.' It makes for self-respect. Not until our leadership puts it to practice will social justice bring us the desired result. It's the most pragmatic approach.

But backward caste leaders in India gave what their followers wished for – if Gandhi's handling was meant to raise them, the other would bring ruin to them, again, the words 'raise' and 'ruin' are from Ruskin. When he started the National Movement, Gandhi warned his followers, it will be a terrible struggle and a prolonged one, because it is against a powerful adversary and called for great suffering and sacrifice. In that celebrated controversy with Rabindranath Tagore this great sentinel exhorted: Let the poet bring his bucket of water, because India is a house on fire. This was the man whose insistence was on suffering as the elevating principle of life: the mother suffers so the child may grow, the seed suffers so the tree may grow. Which the Australian Nobel Laureate Patrick White used as epigraph to his first novel *Happy Valley* with all his subsequent novels celebrating the theme of suffering in its different variations. When the uncle in his novel *Voss* asks his niece in anguish over her adoption of a convict's child and tongues were wagging about its parentage, 'Laura, what of your future?' her touching reaction was 'My future, it is in the hands of God'. This is giving and the kind of giving which social justice worth the name should evoke from those who bear the brunt that social justice entails. It ennobles the giver as well as the receiver.

As for Jawaharlal Nehru, he starts writing *The Discovery of India* with the urgency of someone engaged in rescue operation of a house on fire. He asks himself 'What is this India that I seek to serve? How well do I know her? What did she represent in the past? Has she lost it altogether? Does she still have that vitality? For if the Indian people have lost it all our efforts would end in patch-work and make-believe solutions. His final message was 'This generation is sentenced to hard labour'. My friends, I had to traverse a long way to bring you to an encounter with Gandhi and Nehru and visualize the white heat on their faces which sensitized and shamed our fathers into correcting our age-old wrongs in acts of expiation. The pomp and splendour of princes looked vulgar; wealthy people were ashamed to flaunt it and took to simple living. Hence the supreme heights to which our leaders of the day before yesterday rose in public esteem and were absorbed into the affections of the people because they were made men out of dust.

Aldous Huxley in a sharply worded critical essay titled 'Where Gandhi Failed to See' nevertheless concludes by remarking as an implicit tribute to Gandhi, 'A politician who eats a good dinner makes a poor leader in India'. We have been robbed of the sense of sacrifice, *Vairagya* which alone can ultimately save a people, certainly the Indian people who have built it into a *purushartha* and its absence provoked one of our tallest patriots, Acharya Kripalani, to despair 'I sometimes wish the British would come back to rule us'. Do we reject Gandhi in his own country while the rest of the world looks upto him for a lead – they did it in South Africa and in Black America. We might soon be heading for a state of society in which our leaders would even incite people from behind to pull down Gandhi's statues and erect any others for their own survival. Leprosy is eating into our vitals as a people because the good men have lost their hold over the leaders.

Look around the world to see how a dispossessed people can recover themselves. In the West Indies when the invading white man exterminated the original inhabitants, the Caribs, and left no trace of their language, their Nobel Laureate of two years ago, Derek Walcott, wrote, 'You can't be a poet and believe in the separation of people'. Not for him to say like Caliban, 'You taught me language and I know how to curse you'. If your history is destroyed, said Walcott in effect, start making history. It is like Vivekananda saying 'If your coat is stolen a hundred times that is no cause for despair, buy yourself a new coat.' As a boy Walcott approached his mother, a school teacher, sitting in window sill sewing for the West Indian equivalent of our $200 to print his poems. He hawked the copies in the streets and realized the cost. He learnt to spill blood for ink in his poetry and earned greatness. In a much anthologized poem of his, 'Sea Chanty', the poet presents a sailor boy who bathes in sunlight and salt water and keeps a conch close to his ear to say 'he hears nothing, he hears everything': The unsuspected maturity of thought and heightened imagination of the sailor boy is a standing rebuke to those who have deprived his people of their valued inheritance. And the sailor boy has the pride of making a beginning in the writing of history where it had been annihilated by the white man. Here is an example for Dalit writers to emulate.

There is something more from Australia. The aboriginal poet, a woman to boot, Kath Walker, has written.

> No more gammon
> If you have to teach the light
> Teach us first to read and write.

Her poems have been frequently reprinted.

Another writer, Wilson Harris from Guyana, writes a novel called *The Palace of the Peacock* in which a ship-wrecked crew drawn from many countries encounters an old Arawak woman. She is seen making an embroidred quilt out of patches of discarded rags. The many coloured quilt is a symbol of reconstruction of the future from the wasted past. This is the way purity of motivation and interest will work, ought to work, for the larger good. The reformer's business, if his interest is in the enduring advancement of backward castes, is to expand the scattered sources of self-reliance and hold them up for the edification of large groups of the deprived and dispossessed.

I was pleasantly surprised to learn that the Government of Andhra Pradesh runs special schools in rural areas for talented children. How they function in practice I don't know. But I do know an industrialist, Jindal, has opened on the Bangalore-Bombay Road a well-equipped school with committed teachers and well-stocked libraries where children study under supervision. Admission to this school is restricted to rural children within a radius of 5 K.M. The free facilities and the style of functioning are worthy of emulation by prestigious institutions which are philistine at bottom and demoralizing in their competitiveness, not Socratic. Socrates, it seems, demonstrated that knowledge is *a priori* and has to be drawn out by a teacher worth the name. He made a slave boy work out a theorem in Geometry – all on his own; he only guided him – in our language, like a true guru, he held the lamp. Hence Buddha's call to his disciples 'Be you a lamp unto yourselves'.

We have destroyed the Gurukula and haven't found a substitute for it, but think social justice is the magic formula. It has no feeling, no concern, for the wretched of the land, it only ends in projecting immoral political leadership for its advocates, and opportunism among those who follow them.

Beneficiaries of social justice are today entitled to free hostel, free tuition and handsome pocket money to pick up habits unbecoming of students. They marginalize their studies but poor progress is no bar to the privileges. They are the ones that lead demonstrations for non-vegetarian food for seven days in the week in free hostels, postponement of exams, and higher class in exams regardless of what they have put in; their leaders think that is the concern of educational institutions whose fabric they have undermined. I am reminded of an incident in a Cambridge college where a young man returned from war service emptied his tea kettle and blocked the wash basin. Repetition of it against the servant's warning brought from the Tutor a note in the following words: 'Please note there are instances of students having been sent down for lesser offences.' It seems comparable discipline was enforced 2000 years ago at the University of Nalanda.

Yet another instance from the English academic scene. I recall reading in British papers in 1947 of a meeting of vice-chancellors called by Chancellor of the Exchequer to sort out a crisis arising out of the return of young people from war-service under conscription. The number of universities had remained the same, with facilities the same as before the war. And the question was how to accommodate fresh aspirants from schools and those with war service after interruption of their studies. It was a moral dilemma. The Chancellor naturally pleaded the case of those who had served on the war front. And at one point brought in the question of government grants to universities as a threat. The Vice-Chancellor of Oxford was reported to have said, 'If by giving grants the Government thinks it can dictate terms to the Universities I shall fling the grant back on the face of the Government.' His voice prevailed as the British still believed 'Destroy Oxford and Cambridge, destroy British civilization.' Poor man, it seems while he was returning by a night train, opened the exit door mistaking it for the toilet, fell from the train and was killed. That's by the way. But I mentioned the British example for comparison with our unbridled opportunism and sheer anarchy that prevails in our universities. Their remedy was the Open University, where, by the way, it is more difficult to get a degree than in the others.

One or two examples from the domestic scene before I resume my seat.

Some 12 years ago a young man with a bare Second Class in M.A. became a college lecturer under reservation. Not unfair if he was found promising. Before he hardly taught the under-graduates with any sense of earnestness he became lecturer in a post-graduate department of the University under reservation. He had to be protected from students who, not unreasonably, expected him to teach. And so he was seconded as lecturer and placed as warden of a university hostel. Three years after he applied for a readership in the reserved category, became a reader, subject, it was said, to the condition he would acquire a Ph.D. in three years' time. Again he chose the easy way. Why not? The University went all out to oblige him. He became Dean of Social Welfare in the reader's grade and in less than five years he applied for a professorship under the reserved category and got it with the same qualifying clause regarding Ph.D. Ten years elapsed since registration for a Ph.D. and rules required he apply again for fresh registration which he did and it so happened the supervisor under whose guidance he worked was a reader in the same department, obviously holding a rank below him. Preposterous! At the end of twelve years after registration since he had made no progress he was awarded the rare privilege of sabbatical meant for those engaged in advanced research, here to help him complete his Ph.D. The sabbatical made no difference to him, except that it not only exposed him to ridicule but the entire backward class, and its denial to someone who was internationally known was wholly subversive of academic ideals. Sir Ivor Jennings as Vice-chancellor of Colombo University, Sri Lanka in the late forties, sent for a young lecturer in history to say he was shocked that there was no publication against his name for two years since his entry into service. The young man's plea was he couldn't find a proper subject, 'No proper subject, for a historian!' he felt outraged and said 'Look, collect a few old coins and write a paper,' if you are interested in earning your increment, with more serious consequences to follow in the coming years.

In another University his counterpart was appointed pro-Vice-chancellor since he was denied a readership by the selection committee. In a third University, a young lecturer appointed last year, still on probation, brought eight sets of applications for readership under reservation to the Chairman to be forwarded to the Registrar, and a week after an additional eight sets for a professorship, also under reservation. The Chairman who was obliged to forward the applications felt outraged but there was no help. He at least held a lectureship which was not so bad as when 23 out of 24 professors' posts were advertised in the reserved category while the University must have known there weren't as many qualified for lecturers' positions. Did the Vice-chancellor think he discharged his responsibility to the unfortunate by displaying reservation in all the newspapers? And this utter lack of concern can be traced to a government whose Prime Minister's Secretariat had no Scheduled Caste officer and a President's Secretariat that had just one as revealed by a survey of 25 years ago.

My friends, I wasn't trying to be sarcastic at the expense of these young men. Sharing their humble origins of village, caste, class, myself, I am less callous than that. Actually it hurts me they should have been so misguided and held to contempt. I thought we were here at the seminar to go into the question of social justice thoroughly, not as representatives of castes, political parties or ideologies which we are not but as disinterested individuals with a concern for the future of the unfortunates who have been denied the good things of life for centuries, and our commitment to those at whose expense we seek to render social justice shouldn't be any the less. We have to strain every nerve to find a fair solution not by starting from the wrong end of recruitment and promotion but from the grass root level, keeping in view the history and destiny of this country. And speak the truth, speak all the truth though in the speaking of it you may do it with a slant, but not cheat ourselves and cheat the people. There's the verdict of history to care for.

Window-dressing the Constitution

AJIT BHATTACHARJEA

When the Constitution was being drafted, K.M. Munshi, no great socialist but with an established reputation as literateur and Congress worker, objected that certain provisions 'created an unwarranted impression of progress and freedom'. Another member of the Constituent Assembly, K.T. Shah, complained of 'needless fraud' and 'window dressing'. Several other members also expressed unhappiness. They were participating in the Sub-committee on Fundamental Rights considering the draft of the Directive Principles of State Policy. The question that arises today is whether their fears were not applicable to the entire Constitution.

I

Judging from the language of Constitution, India should have been the most egalitarian country in the world. No similar document promises so much. No people merit what it promises more than those of this country: exploited, impoverished, caste-dominated over the centuries. But like politicians composing a party manifesto, the Constitution-makers knew what to promise the people to achieve power without committing themselves to effective social change and procedures that limit the exercise of power.

The Preamble to the Constitution, which is supposed to constitute its basic philosophy, could hardly be more eloquent. The pursuit of social justice would seem to be its primary objective. It assures to all its citizens: Justice, social economic and political; Liberty of thought, expression, belief, faith and worship; Equality of status and opportunity; Fraternity assuring the dignity of the individual. Some of these objectives are guaranteed as Fundamental Rights. Among them: equality before the law; prohibition of discrimination on grounds of religion, race, caste, sex or place of birth; equality of opportunity in public employment; abolition of untouchability, and abolition of titles. Yet other Fundamental Rights assure such personal freedoms as to speech, life, liberty and religion.

That is not all. Social objectives are prescribed in the Directive Principles. The State is instructed to direct its policy towards securing a wide range of measures, some essential to the achievement of social justice. Not all are of equal merit. Some amplify what is already guaranteed by the Fundamental Rights; others satisfy individual whims and sound good. The State is required to provide equal justice and free legal aid, which seeks to flesh out a Fundamental Right. It is asked to honour the citizen's right to work, education and public assistance. It is specifically enjoined to ensure a living wage to all workers.

Then there is the key recommendation for provision of free and compulsory education for all children below the age of 14. Unlike other Directive Principles, this was given a specific time limit: ten years from the commencement of the Constitution, which reflected the realisation that mass literacy was central to an informed democracy and that ten years was a realisable target.

With these important Directive Principles, however, were clubbed: better organisation of agriculture and animal husbandry and protection of monuments. If this seems to reflect on the seriousness with which the Founding Fathers viewed essential steps towards social justice, such doubts are magnified by the specific provision that Directive Principles 'shall not be enforceable by any court', unlike Fundamental Rights. Having made the Principles toothless, a cosmetic touch was added with the promise that they are 'nevertheless fundamental in the governance of the country and it shall be the duty of the State to apply these principles in making laws'. The condition that these objectives were to be fulfilled 'within the limits of its (the State's) economic capacity' provide a further excuse for inaction.

The patronising phrasing of one Directive Principle, which should have occupied a central place in the Constitution, is revealing. It instructs the State to 'take steps to organise village panchayats and endow them with such powers and authority as may be necessary to enable them to function as units of self-government.' This was an inadequate sop to the Gandhians. According to them, the higher organs of the State draw legitimacy from basic units of self-government, not the other way around.

In fact the Gandhian approach reflects the basic philosophy and legitimacy of the Constitution. The opening line begins: 'We, the people of India.' It is they who 'adopt, enact and give to ourselves this Constitution.' It could not be otherwise; power and authority to rule was no longer a function of the British Crown; it could only vest in the people. The whole approach of handing down power from above was, therefore, outmoded. But it was this imperial inheritance that influenced the Constitution-makers and inhibited the empowerment of the people.

The acknowledgement of popular sovereignty is an essential element of the Constitution but it does not balance the centralised political and top-heavy administrative structure detailed in the document. Some commentators have suggested that this gives the Directive Principles supremacy over Fundamental Rights because the Rights protect individuals whereas the Principles are meant for the improvement of society as a whole.

II

More than forty years after it commenced, the Constitution is a testament to betrayed hope. That India continues to be among the poorest countries in the world is serious enough; that it is also among those in which the national income is the most unfairly distributed reflects on the stated purposes of the Constitution. This is true not only in the sphere of income; effective political power and social equality remains out of the reach of the millions.

The expanding gap between rich and poor has become politically acceptable. It is seen in the fact that more than thirty per cent of our people subsist below the poverty line – in other words, thirty crores do not have enough to eat. This means there are more hungry people in India than in the rest of the world put together, and the number is increasing. Figures for life expectancy, infant mortality and literacy – the quality of life index – also indicate unequal distribution of the national income. Inequality is bound to rise further with what can be described as the Rao/Manmohan Singh amendment to the Constitution which ensures that the cult of the market shall supercede Fundamental Rights and Directive Principles.

It is not necessary to look only at figures to realise what is happening. The contrast between the luxurious style of living in proliferating five-star hotels (a seven-star hotel is planned for Bombay) and the hovels alongside in which daily wage workers survive is harsher evidence. More significantly, it is seen in the huge gates being raised to protecting areas in which the affluent live and the increasing employment of private guards before private houses. Attempts by members of the non-privileged castes to secure the rights promised by the Constitution continue to be opposed by force and by social humiliation, as seen in the stripping and public parade of a woman in a UP village recently, while the forces of law and order looked on.

The saddest evidence of the failure of Constitutional promises is the growing army of children on the streets, looking for any kind of work. If the Constitution had been taken seriously, they would have been at school. Their parents, too, would have been literate and able to contribute much more to the social and political well-being of the country. This was why, presumably, the Constitution required the State to provide free and compulsory education for all children within ten years of its commencement, and that was on 26 January 1950. The excuse of inadequate resources is unacceptable after so many decades, especially when more money is being spent on higher education and elitist schools. The desire to exploit child labour in homes and so-called cottage industries, when adult labour is becoing relatively expensive, is an obvious factor.

The reason that poor families would be worse off without the money their children bring in is questionable. Surveys have shown that child labour increases adult unemployment because children can be paid less and exploited more. A society then continues to permit children to labour in the most cruel and dangerous conditions can hardly claim to be concerned with social justice. The prolonged lack of concern for literacy suggests that those elected to the seats of power prefer the bulk of the people to remain ignorant.

Because the elementary right to universal education for children is non-justiciable, it cannot be taken to court however sternly the Directive Principles may insist that they are "fundamental to the governance of the country." In any event, the poor can expect little from the courts. They are the worst victims of prolonged delays and mounting legal costs.

III

Even before Independence the Indian National Congress was accepted as the leader of the freedom struggle and secured mass support by emphasising the need to remove poverty and ignorance and to put an end to economic and social exploitation. After the general elections in 1937 Jawaharlal Nehru said:

> We went to our people and spoke to them of freedom and the ending of their exploitation; we went to that forgotten creature, the Indian peasant, and remembered that his poverty was the basic problem of India; we identified ourselves with him in his suffering and talked to him or how to get rid of it through political and social freedom.

Earlier, in 1928, the All Parties Conference adopted a list of fundamental rights which included free elementary education and suitable laws for the health and fitness for work of all citizens, a living wage for every worker, protection of motherhood, welfare of children and assistance in old age, infirmity and unemployment. In 1931, the Congress itself adopted a Declaration on Fundamental Rights which stated that "in order to end the exploitation of the masses, political freedom must include real economic freedom of the starving millions".

In many respects, the detailed Congress manifesto for the elections in 1945, when it was known that Independence was near, anticipated the Constitution. Again, the focus was on "how to remove the curse of poverty and raise the standard of the masses". The purpose of development was defined with more concern for removing inequalities than it is today.

> Industry and agriculture, the social services and public utilities must be encouraged, modernised and rapidly extended in order to add to the wealth of the country and give it the capacity of self-growth without dependence on others. But all this must be done with the primary objective of benefitting the masses of our people and raising their economic, cultural and spiritual level, removing unemployment, and adding to the dignity of the individual.

Employment of every able-bodied person, social security for all, minimum wage, decent standard of living and adequate arrangements for education of the masses figures specifically in the manifesto.

The following year, Congress resolved to join the Constituent Assembly established after discussions with the British Cabinet Mission. Once more, it pledged itself to seek "immediate independence and the opening out of avenues leading to the rapid advance of the masses economically and socially." Before the first meeting of the Assembly on 9 December 1946, the Congress adopted a resolution declaring that it stands for "an independent sovereign republic wherein all powers and authority are derived from the people, and for a constitution wherein social objectives are laid down to promote freedom, progress and equal opportunity for all the people of India."

But who were the individuals who would breathe life into these aspirations? In 1938, Nehru had stated that the Congress "has proposed that the constitution of free India must be framed, without outside interference, by a constituent assembly elected on the basis of adult franchise." In the hurry in which the final arrangements were made, however, there was no time for such elections. So the members of the Constituent Assembly were indirectly elected from provincial legislatures. And the members of these pre-colonial-period legislatures had been elected on a highly restricted franchise in which tax, property and educational qualifications limited voting rights to the top ten per cent of the population. The elections were held before partition.

Shiva Rao's monumental work on the framing of the Constitution provides an interesting analysis of the membership of the constituent Assembly: ten members of the (then) Central Government; five ex-presidents of the Congress; seven ex-members of the Congress Working Committee; eight members of the Muslim League Working Committee; eleven presidents of provincial Congress committees; two presidents of the provincial Muslim League; four ex-members of the Viceroy's Executive Council; eight premiers of provinces; ten ministers of provinces; seventeen ex-ministers of provinces or ex-members of Governors' Executive Councils; 34 members of the Central Legislature; three ex-members of the Central Legislature; 155 members of provincial legislatures; four ex-members of provincial legislatures; one Speaker and one ex-Speaker of a provincial legislature. In addition there were a sprinkling of lawyers, doctors, educationists, industrial and commercial magnates, journalists, authors and an unstated member of working class representatives.

IV

When Nehru moved the historic Objectives Resolution on 13 December, 1946, the focus was on the territory and powers of government inherited from the British. Since the Crown was pulling out, it stated that the power and authority of independent

India was derived from the people. Another phrase that would be echoed in the Constitution was to guarantee and secure to the people of India:

> Justice, social, economic and political; equality of status, of opportunity, and before the law; freedom of thought, expression, belief, faith, worship, vocation, association and action, subject to law and public morality.

The proceedings of the Sub-Committee on Fundamental Rights, however, indicated that social justice did not occupy as high a priority as previous pronouncements had suggested. It was the Constitutional Adviser, B.N. Rau, who advocated the distinction between Fundamental Rights and Directive Principles on the model of the Irish Constitution. He was of the view that the right to work, for instance, could not be guaranteed but personal rights could. Another consideration put before the members was that the State should not guarantee what it could not afford.

Several members were unhappy with the concept of non-justiciable rights. K.M. Munshi wanted right to work to be fundamental. K.T. Shah feared that this would reduce them to "pious wishes". Rajkumari Amrit Kaur and Mrs. Hansa Mehta urged provisions that would commit the State to fulfil the Directives within a specific period. But they were unsuccessful except for verbal changes.

The Advisory Committee reviewing the sub-committee's report made the most serious change in its recommendations. The clause concerning free and compulsory education for children was demoted from a Fundamental Right to a Directive Principle, which was the form in which it was finally adopted.

During the general discussion, B. Das voiced the views of a minority of members. He said:

> I am not satisfied with the opinion of the legal savants and great authorities of law in this House who interpret the functions of Government as justifiable and non-justiciable. They have said that we cannot include in the Union Constitution of India what the Government has to do for its people. I think it is the primary duty of Government to remove hunger and social justice to every citizen and to secure social security. . . . The teeming millions do not find any hope that

the Union Constitution will secure them social justice, will ensure a minimum standard of living and a minimum standard of public health.

The primary concerns of the majority of the Constitution-makers is evident from the inordinate space given in the document to the distribution of the political power that was soon to be inherited. Even more indicative are the detailed provisions to protect the public services, the machinery of Government. No other Constitution in the world contains such a feature. The system was adopted in entirety from the British-devised Government of India Act of 1935, meant for a highly-centralised form of administration.

The reason given was that the smooth working of an infant democracy might be jeopardised unless the constitution went into detail about matters left to ordinary legislation elsewhere. The Centre's control over the All-India Services was justified, though conflicting with the principle of provincial (State) autonomy, on the ground that those in charge of the provinces had accepted it. The problems created by partition accentuated the desire to strengthen the Centre and its machinery.

V

The process through which independence was gained gave stability and tradition priority over social change, despite the pronouncements of the Congress leadership. The British Government described the process as a Transfer of Power, which was accurate. It was far from a revolution. The need to keep India strong and united after the trauma of partition reinforced the desire of the Congress leadership to continue to rule according to the imperial pattern.

No scope was left for empowering the people; nor any desire except for token gestures to Mahatma Gandhi. This was reflected in the Constitution. For different reasons, the leaders who left their impress on the document had more confidence in the power and authority of the State: Nehru because he thought it would direct the process of planning necessary for economic development; Sardar Patel because he was a manager rather than ideologue; Dr. Ambedkar because he believed that social reform could be more effectively imposed from above than below.

Yet popular empowerment – the right of every citizen to order his own life without imposition from above – is the most basic form of social justice in a country claiming to be a democracy. As noted earlier, it is also the bedrock of the Constitution in "We the People" that gives it legitimacy. It is not a gift handed down by superiors to inferiors, as suggested later in the document.

This was the essence of Gandhi's teaching, but the Congress leadership had already rejected him before the process of drafting the Constitution began. They justified their self-serving antipathy to the devolution of power to the grass-roots with the suggestion that village panchayats would be static and serve only the interests of local bosses. But the performance of the present system has not been much better. Face-to-face democracy has better prospects of changing their lives. But not if the real boss remains the district collector.

The nation deserves a new constitution, framed by representatives of the people elected by adult suffrage who do not see India as a British inheritance. Gandhi provided a model:

> Independence must begin at the bottom. Thus, every village will be a republic or panchayat having full powers. It follows, therefore, that every village has to be self-sustained and capable of managing its affairs even to the extent of defending itself against the whole world. . . . In this structure composed of innumerable villages, there will be every widening, never ascending circles. Life will not be a pyramid with the apex sustained by the bottom. But it will be an oceanic circle. . . . Therefore, the outermost circumference will not yield power to crush the inner circle but give strength to all within and derive its own from the centre.

Roots of Elitism

Y. RAFEEK AHMED

constitution and constitutionalism have become symbols of nationalism and modernism. Indeed, adoption of a constitution by a newly-emerged people is the most vocal expression of their freedom. There is always an effort to make the constitution an explicit declaration of the interests which the members of a political community would like to protect and promote. It is for this reason that constitutionalists tend to regard the framing of the constitution as the product of consensual politics. It articulates the ideals or intentions of the community it serves. A people in the course of a process of social thought reach consensus on the idea and ideal of justice and try and pursue its creation and sustenance with the help of the constitution. Therefore the constitution incorporates and embodies a people's approach to the whole concept of social justice. In other words, it espouses principles, values and ideals which the political community cherishes and strives for. It is for this reason that the constitution today is more than a legal document of a body of fundamental rules, written or unwritten, within whose framework the government is expected to function in order, not to be labelled 'unconstitutional' or 'autocratic'. Modern governments are expected to be at once popular, proper and effective and the constitution on whose direction the government functions becomes the guarantor of such an arrangement.

A country's constitution reflects the dominant beliefs and interests of the people at a particular period in its history. It is the resultant of a parallelogram of forces, political, economic and social as K.C. Wheare would put it. In other words, the constitution becomes a reflection of the dominant existing socio-economic forces and their relationships in society. Under such a situation, 'social justice' is what these dominant forces decide it to be. It is however, not suggested here that the dominant socio-economic forces cannot go beyond their framework and foresee a different scenario for the country in future or that they would be opposed to any radical change of their own perceptions of 'reality' although it is but human to expect them to protect and promote their own interests so long as they are dominant. It would not be wrong to perceive of the constitution itself not undermining its own philosophy by allowing any radical change. Unless there is a far-reaching and significant socio-economic transformation in society, it is futile to expect drastic and radical changes in the constitution and so long as the dominant socio-economic interests stay strong, the constitution would not allow any great transformation. It is indeed a vicious circle where the constitution becomes a very useful device in the hands of the ruling class to keep itself in power and prevent others from successfully challenging it. All constitutions in a way allow only small changes allowing mobility within the ruling class almost as a nominal recognition of the principle of rotation of leadership. But it would not be far from truth to say that no constitution in any positive way allows the non-ruling class to become the ruling class. This is not to say that the principle of change is rejected by modern constitutions. The concept of 'change' is indeed accepted but with the guarantee that it is controlled and calculated so as not to destroy the existing political arrangement and cause 'instability'.

Constitutions in general tend to be elitist, supporting and in turn being supported by the elites in society. In the name of the sanctity of the constitution, the ruling elites prevent any real challenge to the constitution thus overawing the masses and keeping them under perpetual control – very much on the same lines as suggested by Rousseau while discussing the origin of government and law. By clever manipulation, Rousseau suggests, the rich persuaded the poor to join them in setting up a commonwealth ostensibly to guard the poor and restrain the ambitious but actually to legitimize and perpetuate their own domination over the poor. This could well be the case even in the making of the constitution or its adoption.

In this paper an attempt is made to find if there was concern for social justice to start with at the time of writing of the constitution and to relate the concept of social justice with the composition of the Constituent Assembly and the socio-economic background of its members. The social justice content of the constitution assumes added significance in view of the discussions on complaints of the threat to part III and part IV of the constitution because of the fear of abandonment of social justice concerns in present years.

At the time of India's independence, Indian society had three very prominent and distinct groups of people operating. One group was very anglophile; it looked to British ways and British methods and pinned hopes on British constitutional tradition as found in the various Acts culminating in the Government of India Act of 1935. Another group was the one which led the national movement. Seeped in the English liberal traditions of freedom, justice and law, this group was supposed to represent the country. But it had its own limitations because of contradictions and complexities so very evident in Gandhi and Nehru. Yet this group managed to lead in the name of the people of India although it could not be identified with the masses – the ordinary people of India who constituted the third and the most numerous group. The representative of this third group was really on his own, oblivious of whatever was going on around him. His worry was his next meal and his hope was that all the developments, including the movement for national freedom, would bring much needed succour and save him from the degradation and humiliation of poverty and disease. Under these conditions, it was left to the leadership of the freedom movement to decide on the details of the polity they reckoned most appropriate for the country. The leadership, a very great part of it which dominated the Constituent Assembly was neither committed to a social revolution in depth nor it had a proper perception and understanding of the voiceless millions living in India. It indeed lived in a grandiose world of its own – very idealistic and rhetorical.

II

The framing of the constitution and its adoption were no doubt, the most stupendous and great events of independent India. It was perhaps easy and comparatively less controversial to adopt the constitution immediately after independence, because of the euphoria in the wake of freedom and also because of the fact that those involved in the drafting of the constitution were respected leaders of the national movement. Otherwise, the task of constitution-making is a very difficult one to all societies and in particular to heterogeneous societies with primordial loyalties. This is so because of the absence of consensus in societies where politics tend to be based largely on social and communal status and personal and group relations of various kinds with little integration among political participants.[1] In societies marked by the absence of homogeneity, the task of securing consensus on legitimate political ends and means becomes very difficult and proves an arduous exercise. Indeed there is always the danger of constitution-making proving itself more a nation-dividing exercise than a nation-making device in plural societies with fragmented political culture.

India was, in a way, lucky and fortunate that the Constitution came the easy way. Given the conditions existing in India, adoption of the constitution by the Constituent Assembly was almost a miracle. The wise and farsighted Indian leadership perhaps anticipating trouble later, went about the process of constitution-making rightly giving it top priority.

The Cabinet Mission had recommended on May 16, 1946 that a grand Constituent Assembly could be created by allowing each province and each Indian state or a group of states to have a total number of seats proportional to their respective population in the ratio of one to a million which in effect meant that 292 members would represent the provinces and the princely states would be represented by 92 members. It was also envisaged that Muslims and Sikhs would be represented in proportion to their respective population elected on the basis of proportional representation with single transferable vote by their own communities. Representation to princely states was to be decided through consultation. In the meanwhile the Indian National Congress displayed extraordinary confidence in the late 30s and 40s, to assert that India's destiny was to be decided by Indians themselves and that 'the constitution of free India must be framed without outside interference, by a Constituent Assembly elected on the basis of adult franchise".[2] Both Gandhi and Nehru, always made reference to the people of India as the sole arbiters of who should have the final power to decide the future constitutional framework of India. Ever since the Congress announced its official policy of the demand for a Constituent Assembly in 1934, it became evident that the masses in India would not accept anything short of it and indeed at all subsequent sessions, the Congress reiterated its demand for a constitution framed by the people of India. However, Congress acquiesced in the idea of the Cabinet Mission that the practicable course was to utilize the recently elected provincial Legislative Assemblies as the electing bodies thereby sacrificing the principle of election through adult franchise to constitute the Constituent Assembly. Delay was cited as the reason for going back on the demand for elections on the basis of adult franchise. It would not be far from truth to suggest that the Congress leadership was quite satisfied with its performance at the Assembly elections and was possibly apprehensive of elections involving the masses of India. The leadership was also in a hurry to adopt a constitution generally acceptable to it than allow it to be done later, when there was no guarantee of its predominant position. Accordingly, the Constituent Assembly adopted a resolution on April 30, 1947 for setting up a committee to report on the main principles of the Union constitution. The constitutional Adviser sent questionnaires to all the 12 members of the Committee of whom only one replied and another member, Mr. B.N. Rau prepared a draft constitution.

In the Objectives Resolution passed by the Assembly, it was stated that all power and authority of the Assembly had been derived from the people.[3] The Assembly was considered 'sovereign' although it was the British government's creation under the Act of 1935. It could however be dissolved only by 2/3 of the whole membership of the Assembly. But the major question which needs to be answered is the representative character of the Constituent Assembly. When one speaks of the 'people', who were these 'people'? Whom did the representatives of the Assembly represent? And would it be fair to talk of them as speaking for the whole country?

In the July 1946 elections to the Constituent Assembly, Congress victory was virtually assured because of the fact that out of 1585 seats in the Provincial Assemblies, the Congress had won 925 with 58% seats. And as a result Congress candidates swept the polls for the Constituent Assembly winning 203 of the 212 general seats and in the final count had 208 out of 292 seats of the Provincial Assemblies. And with the creation of Pakistan and the exit of the Muslim League, the Constituent Assembly was literally a Congress body with 82% of the seats. The 93 non-elected members from the princely states were representatives of the princes or princely interests. The electoral process was itself based on the restricted franchise established by the Sixth schedule of the 1935 Act which allowed voting for those who had property, educational qualification and paid tax. This meant that, in effect, economically and socially depressed sections of the population were virtually disenfranchised and only about 28.5% of the adult population (20 years and above) of the provinces could vote in the provincial Assembly elections. The same Assemblies were asked to elect members of the Constituent Assembly. To suggest that because the Congress covered a broad ideological spectrum it could be said to represent the diverse viewpoints of voters and non-voters alike is to over-simplify a very serious psephological problem and ignore the fact that the Congress which led India's freedom movement was under the bourgeois-landlord leadership – the upper classes, the capitalists and the enlightened section of the feudals. There was no representation of the communists, for example, in the Constituent Assembly, because it was difficult for them to find representation in the different Assemblies given the restricted nature of franchise used. Again to say that although the socialists and the R.S.S. were not represented but their ideologies found expression in the Assembly with the presence of a S.P. Mukerjee or a Tandon or a Nehru is to suggest that the breakaway of the socialists from the Congress was not really on ideological lines or that the extremist Hindu ideology of the R.S.S. had found accommodation in the Congress.[4]

The dominance of the Congress was seen as an assurance of both the liberal and secular character of the Constituent Assembly. Indeed the presence of such leaders as Azad and Ambedkar representing Muslims and Scheduled Castes respectively was projected as proof of the representative character of the Constituent Assembly. Nehru was, no doubt, very correct in asserting that the Congress was the 'mirror of the nation'.[5] But did it really represent the toiling millions? No doubt, National Congress leadership ensured that men of exceptional ability, minorities like Parsis, Anglo-Indians, Indian Christians, SCs, Tribes and women were represented in the Constituent Assembly but to suggest that all shades of opinion had representation was a myth and a superficial reality. The truth is that for most commentators on the Indian constitution representation of the different communities was the most vital aspect of proper representation and the end all of justice. This was quite reasonable in the context of the Indian political scenario at that time. But in retrospect, one is startled by the absence of attention being given to different classes and economically weaker sections of population.

G. Austin contends that the Constituent Assembly, though not responsible to the masses of Indians, was a "highly representative body".[6] But representative of whom? There is no doubt that it represented different communities but did it represent different sections of communities and castes? The Constituent Assembly was indeed an elitist body with elites from different castes and communities being represented. There is definitely truth in Bipin Chandra's conclusion that "an upper class Muslim had far more in common culturally with an upper caste Hindu than with a lower class Muslim".[7]

III

The Congress displayed a great sense of national unity and purpose to meet the needs and desires of the entire nation but it was always overshadowed and dominated by a very small oligarchy consisting of Nehru, Patel, Prasad and Azad. Hardly three dozen members were accommodated in the eight major committees viz., Rules Committee, Steering Committee, Advisory Committee, Drafting Committee, Union Subjects Committee, Union Constitution Committee, Provincial constitutional Committee and States Committee. And each of the top four leaders either chaired these committees or in many cases more than two of them were also on the same committees. By virtue of their enormous prestige and position, both in the Congress organization and in the government, these four leaders controlled the proceedings of the Assembly. They had a firm grip on the Congress Assembly Party and the Assembly's Committee system. This oligarchy, no doubt, displayed extraordinary accommodation and did try to respond to public opinion. There was general acceptance that the discussions on the draft constitution were free, frank and at times acrimonious and yet there were also allegations of party control and leadership's impatience with those who disagreed. This is clear from the criticisms voiced by such respected members as Dr. Ambedkar, Md. Saadulla, Tyagi, Kunzru etc.

Mahavir Tyagi in fact spoke of the constitution as "given by the majority party to the country".[8] There is no doubt whatsoever that it was the Congress fiat which reigned supreme in the deliberations of the Constituent Assembly and the control of the Congress leadership was complete.

It would be misleading to use the word 'mandate' or 'consent' to discuss the position of the Congress vis-a-vis constitution-making.[9] At the time when elections to the Provincial Assemblies on restricted franchise were held in 1945 under the Act of 1935, nobody had visualised the possibility of the same Assemblies being asked to send representatives to the Constituent Assembly which would later frame and adopt the constitution of India. Besides, the Congress which had all along pleaded for more power for the provinces and criticised the power and authority of the Centre, and had in fact made that an important issue in the election, now suddenly made a volte face and framed a constitution based on the Act of 1935 and what is more the same assemblies elected the members of the Constituent Assembly. In view of this, doubts regarding the use of the phrase "we the people" were reasonable and indeed was questioned in the Keshavanand Bharathi's case. Justice Hegde and Justice Mukerjee observed: ". . . from the Preamble we get that it is the people of this country who conferred this constitution on themselves. The statement in the Preamble that the people of this country conferred the constitution on themselves is not open to challenge before the courts. Its factual correctness cannot be gone into by this court. The facts set out in the Preamble have to be accepted by this court as correct. Any one who knows the composition of the Constituent Assembly can hardly dispute the claim of the members of that Assembly that their voice was the voice of the people. They were truly the representatives of the people, even though they had been elected under a narrow franchise. The constitution framed by them has been accepted and worked by the people for the last 23 years and it is too late in the day now to question . . . ".

The contention that questions regarding the framing of the constitution or the representative character of the constitution have indeed been asked earlier and that no purpose will be served by raising them now is rather puerile. There is need for continuous renewal of the democratic sanction of our polity to keep it democratic. Dadabhai Naoroji had spoken of the "Two Indias" - one the prosperous, the other poverty stricken, one of the British and other foreigners who were exploiting and the other of the poor and exploited. It could be said with justification that the two Indias continued to exist even after independence with the difference that in the place of the British and foreign exploiters, we had Indian capitalist, foreign educated landlords and upper class intellectuals who formed the representative India" as against the real India which remained silent and submissive.[10] There was definitely a great deal of truth in what one member of the Constituent Assembly spoke of as the 'visible we' and the 'invisible we'.[11]

Therefore, it is clear that high caste elitist leaders, western educated intellectuals and privileged men of competence and intelligence were sitting in judgement on the needs and problems of the rural masses, depressed castes, underprivileged and illiterate and exploited millions. It is not however, to suggest that the unfit should have assumed leadership but that they should have at least been considered for selecting and electing those among the elites who would represent their interest. At the time of independence, it was very obvious that Indians acquiesced in the political arrangement arrived at by the British and the Congress leadership with the hope that that arrangement would result in social justice. One could look at the constitution as a "solemn promise to the people of India that the legislature will do everything possible to renovate and rebuild society on new principles",[12] and yet it would not be wrong to suggest that the already privileged and entrenched sections of society might have manipulated to consolidate and legitimize their own power and position with the help of the constitution. The liberal-democratic values enshrined in the constitution had only cosmetic value and could be viewed as the facade with which the vested classes were trying to hide and protect their interests.

Political participation is especially significant for the deprived sections of population because it helps them to improve their conditions of life and equalize their opportunities through political activity. Karl Marx had himself advised that a right to vote means a significant share in power. A basic assumption of democracy is political participation. At a theoretical level participation alone may not be the criterion of political influence but it is definitely a fundamental requirement of democracy and it could be said with confidence that in actual practice the right to participate is an important source of political influence. Right to participate and voting, either actual or potential, does contribute in helping the underprivileged to exert influence on the elite and gain benefits. At the time of writing the constitution, the underprivileged and the deprived did suffer from a psychological feeling of deprivation, neglect and low-esteem which could have been removed if only they had been included as partners in the political arrangement. Indeed it could be said with remorse that a great opportunity was lost.

It is now clear that there was no doubt about the competence and intellectual capacity of the members of the Constituent Assembly but there could always be serious doubts about their representative character; and because of their socio-economic background, they could not have possibly reflected the ethos of the Indian society. Their first priority was to establish democratic order on firm foundations. Besides, for a people with colonial background and leadership soaked in the ideas of democracy as practised and theorized in England and U.S.A., it was difficult to go beyond the framework of their own experience. They were, in fact, restricted by their own limitations. It could be reasonably argued that the whole concept of social justice, its importance and the priority to be given were approached by the Constituent Assembly in a way quite different from what the common man had in mind.

IV

Constitution is a symbol of modernism and as such should allow and facilitate change and also become an instrument of change. There will always be a need for sweeping changes of major socio-economic consequence reflecting and in turn assisting socio-economic changes in society. There could be a need for redefining the concept of social justice and its incorporation in the Constitution with the emergence of political, economic and social forces of every new generation of Indians. An amendment here and an amendment there may not prove very helpful and reasonable when one is concerned with drastic changes in the philosophy of the constitution itself. The idea that the "basic structure" (the Keshavananda Bharathi case) of the constitution cannot be changed and that there is an "implied limitation" on the operation of Art. 368 of the constitution only goes to prove that 'change' of vital socio-economic significance is rather difficult. Under such circumstances, giving ourselves a new constitution may sound a very appropriate solution. But unfortunately writing a new constitution, much less its universal acceptance and adoption today, may be a difficult if not an impossible task. It is invariably an exercise fraught with serious dangers of providing excellent opportunities to hitherto low-lying traditional and primitive forces to assert and find a place for fragmented cultures in the new constitution if one could be framed and adopted.

Therefore, one may find fault with the making of the constitution, the procedure adopted and its relevance in the context of changing times. One is however, faced with the dilemma of the limitations of the present constitution and the difficulties of writing a new one. How could this dilemma be resolved? There is no need for summoning of a new Constituent Assembly or rejecting the present constitution. What we could do is to ensure the competence of Parliament to bring about far-reaching changes in the constitution from time to time, almost as periodic revision, to reflect the mood and approach of the people towards social justice.

It may not be difficult to conceive of every fifth election as a mandate to the new Parliament to propose and adopt fundamental changes. It might mean almost the power of writing a new constitution. This will necessitate all political parties to make changes in the constitution an important aspect of their manifestoes and election campaign. This way every fifth election will be a mandate for change in the constitution. In effect, people will have a chance of deciding whether there was any need for change and the direction in which that change should take place. There could be a provision that only political parties with a certain percentage of the vote in the previous four elections would be allowed to contest and only the political party or the coalition of parties which secured more than 50% of the votes and 51% of the seats would be eligible to propose and adopt changes in the constitution. This would eliminate the possibility of a transient majority toying with the constitution to suit its own political needs. However, it will not be a referendum pure and simple. It could be a way of repairing the damage done at the time of making of the constitution when people were not consulted and when the Constituent Assembly was elected on an electoral system which was not based on adult franchise. Those who are apprehensive of a role for the common man when he decides on issues of constitutional importance, only betray their lack of faith in democracy. No one should forget that people have a chance of rectifying their mistakes once every five elections. They could decide and define social justice and vote for the appropriate political arrangement for its attainment. If need be, voting could be made compulsory. The assumptions on which the whole exercise would be based, are that people will be both sensible and appreciative of the need for preserving India's plural and hetrogeneous cultural legacy and that the political parties would be responsive and responsible and display maturity and wisdom in keeping the country's interest above all other petty partisan interests.

In conclusion, it could be said that the doubt of the Indian Constitution being the product of 'Indian' mind, thereby representing India are reasonable. In the context of Indian society, 'social justice' cannot be a fixed concept. It is in fact a moving concept undergoing 'change' and also bringing about change in the society as a whole. What is desirable is that the changed contours of social justice should be properly reflected in the constitution itself. Unless some mechanism, as suggested above, is found, the constitution cannot be looked upon as reflective of a people's philosophy of social justice. A people's genuine respect for the constitution could be expected only when there is available conclusive proof of the constitution defining social justice in tune with existing reality and setting out means of achieving it.

NOTES AND REFERENCES

1. See, Lucian Pye, "The Non-Western Political Process", *Journal of Politics,* Aug. 1958 and also Spann, "Notes on Some Asian constitutions" in *Span* (Ed.), *Constitutionalise in Asia.*
2. Nehru at Tripuri Congress Session in 1938.
3. CADI, 5, 59.
4. Granville Austin, *The Indian Constitution: Cornerstone of a Nation,* Bombay: Oxford University Press, 1985, p. 1.
5. *Unity of India,* p. 139.
6. See Austin, *op. cit.,* p. 14.
7. *Communalism in Modern India,* Vikas Publishing House, 1992, p. 15.
8. See K.V. Rao, *Parliamentary Democracy in India: A Critical Commentary,* 2nd edn. p. 23.
9. "None but the Congress Party had obtained the mandate of the People". Johari *Indian Government and Politics,* Chapter 12, p. 10.
10. See, B.N. Ganguli, *Indian Economic Thought,* 1978.
11. C.A.D., 11, 1, p. 266. Dr. P.K. Sen (Bihar General).
12. K.M. Pannikkar, *Hindu Society at Crossroads,* pp. 63-64.

The Colonial Inheritance

AMAL RAY

In order to understand the nature of connection between social justice and the Constitution, it is desirable to treat the Constitution as an aspect of the wider political process. Since political power in post-independence India is not generally viewed as instrumental to human development, there is little one can expect from the rulers to bring about the necessary constitutional change to realise the ends of social justice. There is therefore a paramount need to look for suitable alternatives.

At the time of constitution-making there were two conflicting cultures, one representing the overall normative concerns for political liberty and social justice as derived from India's national movement, and the other was the tradition of colonial rule of which the principal structural frame was provided by the Government of India Act,1935.[1]

However, both require elucidation. First, the ideological foundation of the national movement had an element of looseness and did never acquire a stable meaning. Even during what is known as the Gandhi phase of the movement there was no single overriding framework of social change and development. There were two major constructs: the 'Gandhian' based on indigenous social insights, while the other struggling for supremacy was the popularly known as 'modern', essentially the Western view of development and nation-building. Jawaharlal Nehru, although siding with Gandhi on major issues of the struggle for freedom as he knew that without Gandhi's support he could not hope to acquire supreme power, was an ardent advocate of the latter view.

Gandhi's primary task was to lead a nation-wide movement against the semi-hegemonic colonial rule. Thus he tried to avoid any distinctive class bias in his ideological formulation, and to fulfil the primary task, favoured a multi-class collaboration. At the same time, he was a critic of the western model of development, and had a mature understanding of the needs of the people. So he formulated a basic needs approach which, he believed, could be accomplished within a decentralised polity. Thus Gandhi advocated a constitution with the village panchayat constituting the primary political unit.

However, the Gandhian blueprint was not accepted. Nehru argued that the Congress had "never considered" the Gandhian view of society, "much less adopted". So the Constituent Assembly opted for the so-called modern constitution in the Euro-American tradition which, the framers believed, could fulfil the task of a powerful nation-state building.[2]

In Euro-American constitutional tradition the state is essentially a civil state, and hence, civil rights are integral to constitutionalism. The concept of social justice is post-constitutional phenomenon, and the basic social rights are not generally acknowledged as an essential aspect of the fundamental law.

Hence, the basic social rights such as right to freedom from hunger, right to a living wage, right to education, right to health care, etc., received only peripheral importance in the Constitution, while the civil rights acquired substantive significance. In short, the demands for social justice are not adequately emphasised in the Constitution, notwithstanding the fact that the non-justiciable Directive Principles of State Policy embody these. The enforceable civil rights in which the toiling masses have little or no interest, dominate over the non-enforceable principles of social justice which are treated as moral precepts. Only in regard to certain categories of the population such as Scheduled Castes and Scheduled Tribes a system of preferential treatment to alleviate the conditions of these historically disadvantaged groups was provided by the Constitution.

It is also seen that the dominant groups were generally in sympathy with the aspirations of the propertied class, the sole exception being the zamindars who provided enormous support to the Raj. A perusal of the debate on the provision of the right to property will illustrate this. Pandit Pant proposed an amendment, as he would have left "the mode and manner of compensation entirely to discretion of the legislatures concerned". This had the effect of frightening many leading members of the Constituent Assembly. A.K. Ayyar was so disturbed that he immediately wrote to Sardar Patel. He said that if what he had heard of Pant's amendment was correct, it would have the effect of making capital shy and driving it in some measure out of industry. However, it was finally found that Pant's amendment was not directed at industry. It was actually meant for zamindars.

Thus Pandit Nehru's observation that the first task of the Assembly "is to free India through a new constitution, to feed the starving people and to clothe the naked masses . . ." had only cosmetic value. None of the dominant groups in the Constituent Assembly was committed to a social revolution in depth. The Socialists and the Communists were not represented in the Assembly, nor did the downtrodden have any voice in its deliberations. The elitist dominance was so pronounced that the masses did not figure in discussions except for some rhetorical purpose. Thus the Nehruvian view got diluted because of the elitist dominance of the political process. This contributed to the relegation of basic social rights aimed at justice and the focusing of civil rights in the Constitution.

This elite-dominated political process continued and eventually got manifested in the country's development planning. The Nehruvian path to development lacked concern for the basic needs of the people. In Nehru's heavy industry-oriented model of development the role of small and cottage industries in the country's economic development was neglected. The huge infrastructural facilities created at public cost had gone in the direction of helping the growth of large-scale rather then small industries. The prime status of agriculture too was neglected. Nor did he push decisively in the direction of restructuring agrarian relations, notwithstanding his earlier enthusiasm.[3]

Similarly, Nehru depended upon the elitist bureaucracy of an eminently colonial mould for implementing development programmes. The Indian bureaucracy had the necessary skill and experience only in handling rationing schemes in situations of shortage. It lacked the experience in managing a gigantic and complex programme of growth and development. More importantly, the huge gap in terms of both life style and overall outlook between the civil servants and the people, created an important barrier in the way of carrying the development benefits to the poorer sections of the population.

Thus for the early thinking on constitution-making, development planning and administration, the model is exogenous, and is not indigenous to the country and the people. I believe development has suffered because of this. There has never been any attempt at integrating political and economic structures with the basic needs of the people.

Since then the situation has grossly deteriorated. On the one hand, the linking of development with the electoral process, brought in a close connection between politics and business, and the consequent rise of an extensive corruption and the loss of public morality; and on the other, this has resulted in a fierce competition among various politically mobilised social groups for entitlement to development resources with an important erosion of the earlier united grassroots resistance and an enormous segmentation of the public.

The Indian State lacks the vital element of justice; this has intensified inter-group feuds and has further impoverished the poor. There is colossal poverty and increasing marginalisation of large sections of the population. Almost every major public policy has the effect of further marginalising the already marginalised sections. In regard to access to the minimum requirements of life such as food, shelter, medical care, education etc, there are vast disparities between castes and communities and between sections of such social groupings. As one of the world's largest concentrations of illiterates and persons suffering from malnutrition, India's status in human development touches almost the bottom line.

By and large India is governed by a coalition of upper-class power elites. And, the rise of a large mercenary class performing the crucial brokerage role in politics, provides the continued sustenance to this sort of rule.

The prime underlying idea of a democratic republic is one of intrinsic equality which in practical terms denotes fair play and justice in the public allocation of resources. This essential idea is generally absent both in the fundamental law of the land and its working structure. Actually social injustice has grown since this law was enacted. The legitimacy of the present politico-legal order emanates, not from its intrinsic human development focus which is not actually there, but from its capacity to sustain the elitist dominance.

The new economic policy recently formulated by the Government of India, is likely to enhance elitist dominance. With the opening-up of the economy in the wake of this policy, the dominant visible trend points to growing social injustice as manifested in rising disparities and employment deterioration in living conditions of the masses and loss of food security.[4] Their combined effect will eventually be on the already marginalised sections. The stage has abdicated its role as the final custodian of social justice.[5]

This has happened as in both political process and the Constitution: power is not viewed as instrumental to human development, especially at the level of the masses. So there is an imperative need to reform the political process as well as the Constitution in order to ensure that both are permeated with the vital element of justice. However, the current talk of reforms does not generally reflect the need for bringing the concept of constitutionalism to bear upon the problems confronting India's teeming millions.

Hence, to bring in the necessary constitutional reforms from people's point of view, it is necessary to articulate the needs of the masses and to mobilise them politically for their fulfillment. This is likely to create the required pressure at the decisional level, and the political elites will find it difficult to avoid this both in political and constitutional reforms.

REFERENCES

1. Amal Ray, 'From a Constitutional to an Authoritarian System of Government: Interactions between Politics and the Constitution in India', *The Journal of Commonwealth and Comparative Politics* (London: November 1987).
2. Granville Austin, *The Indian Constitution: Cornerstone of a Nation* (Bombay: Oxford University Press 1972), Ch. 2.
3. Sukhamoy Chakravarthy, 'Nehru's Legacy in Planning', Amal Ray (ed), *The Nehru Legacy* (New Delhi: Oxford and IBH 1990), p. 3.
4. Arun Kumar, 'New Economic Policy: An Assessment', *Economic and Political Weekly* (Bombay: December 11, 1993).
5. For the late-industrialisation countries there are two models. One is East Asian, and the other is Latin American. In the former countries a mix of market and state intervention approximately structured to secure social development and central private sector behaviour, lies at the root of their growth miracle, while in the latter countries in the absence of an adequate social and economic infrastructure the sole reliance on market has played havoc. It appears that India's economic reforms fall in the category of the latter rather than the former, and lack indigenous roots. Moreover, it is seen that in a country where there is a history of state intervention for human development, the sudden switch-over to market economy is apt to breed disasters.

The Impact of Electoral Politics

SANDEEP SHASTRI

> On the 26th day of January 1950, we are going to enter in a life of contradictions. In politics we will have equality and in social and economic life we will have inequality. . . . How long shall we continue to deny equality in our social and economic life? If we continue to deny it for long, we will do so only by putting our political democracy in peril. We must remove this contradiction at the earliest possible movement or else those who suffer from inequality will blow up the structure of political democracy which this Assembly has so laboriously built up.
>
> —B.R. AMBEDKAR
>
> (*Constituent Assembly Debates*, Vol. 11, p. 979)

APPROACHING THE THEME

A significant feature of political discourse, especially in recent years, has been the emphatic manner in which issues relating to social justice have been articulated. It is beyond a shadow of doubt that a fundamental factor that should govern the designing of political institutions and structures is the social dynamics in which it has to operate. Often a mismatch between the assumptions made while modelling the political institutions on the one hand and the socio-economic realities on the other, triggers off a situation wherein these institutions are unable to address and deal with the basic problems that confront the society. This paper attempts to focus attention on the impact of the dynamics of electoral process in India – as outlined in the Constitution – on the realisation of social justice. Have the lofty goals of justice – social economic and political, that the framers of the Indian Constitution so eloquently expressed in the constitutional document, been effectively addressed by the electoral process during the last four decades or does the Constitution need to be suitably amended/redrafted in the light of this experience? This paper – extremely tentative in its formulations and limited in its scope – attempts to specically address this question.

Ever since the Indian Government decided to celebrate the birth centenary of Baba Saheb Ambedkar with great fanfare and declared the centenary year as the 'Year of Social Justice', there has been a flurry of 'social justice' related activity throughout the country. The theme of social justice has been pushed to the centre-stage of politics and has become the most fashionable and common single point of political reference. The 'chameleon' chant of social justice (Iyer 1991:18) is seen by the political elite as the one best way of using a potentially powerful slogan to serve their short term political interests, in the process, hoping to deflect attention away from their abysmal failure – during the last four decades – to evolve effective strategies to usher in an era of genuine social transformation.

Social justice, in the context of the working of the electoral process is looked at from two different perspectives. If social justice were to imply one individual, one value, the electoral process becomes an important arena for its practice. Secondly, the Indian Constitution has made special provisions for reservation of seats in the Lok Sabha (Article 330) and State Legislative Assemblies (Article 331) for those belonging to the Scheduled Castes and Scheduled Tribes. It would be useful to examine as to whether these Constitutional provisions, specifically provided to ensure that the elected representatives from among Scheduled Castes and Tribes had the opportunity to participate in the decision-making process, have contributed to the achieving of social justice.

It is often asserted that the backdrop of a democratic polity – with all its attendent features – forms the ideal setting for the realisation of social justice. If social justice were to be viewed in terms of the emancipation and empowerment of the masses, the efforts towards the realisation of this ideal would be greatly encouraged in a political system which cherishes and respects the democratic values of liberty, equality and fraternity. A democratic polity is expected to create a 'neutral ground' that provides an opportunity for a negotiated and peaceful resolution of conflicts. Ideally, democracies are said to be concerned with:

> . . . setting up a government capable of ensuring social integration and therefore creating an awareness of citizenship and of respecting the multiplicity of interests and opinions.
>
> (Touraine 1991: 261)

The process of democratisation itself could be termed as an effort in the direction of providing 'more substantive forms of democratic rule' [Bangura 1992: 99]. In a democratic polity, the efforts initiated in the direction of equalisation and more meaningful citizen participation are part of the process of ensuring greater democratisation. The citizens are not mere silent spectators in the theatre of politics but should be encouraged to actively participate – through a wide range of channels – in the decision making process. The linkage between democracy, equalisation and legitimacy were most succinctly articulated by Rudebeck:

> People demand democracy, including political rights, most strongly when they think it is right and just and when they believe at the same time that such a system of rule will help them inprove their lives. (1992: 8)

In the context of Indian democracy, the quest for social justice could be seen in terms of the strategies adopted to ensure greater freedom and more meaningful equality. Partha Mukherji has viewed the pursuit of freedom and equality from the stand point of a 'set of counter concept: discrimination, exploitation and oppression (DEO)' (Mukherji 1992:26). Each of these represent 'sets of asymmetrical social relationship' (ibidem) and efforts in the direction of reducing DEO would, as a natural corollary, imply 'an overall gain in freedom and equality' (ibidem).

It needs to be stressed that in nascent democracies, it is the guaranteeing of the basic democratic norms and principles that facilitates the process of ushering in positive changes directed towards enriching the quality and content of democracy. This 'democratic space' has its own intrinsic value in the fight for social justice as it represents the take-off point in any strategy that aims at social change. Backman has rightly asserted that: "The democratic space has to be protected in order to be expanded, also to provide the bases from which further advances can be made." (1992: 148)

The equality that was guaranteed by the Indian Constitution in the political realm, could be termed as the 'democratic space' that was provided to initiate measures for achieving social equality and justice. It is in this context that the warning sounded by Ambedkar in his last speech in the Constituent Assembly, that the future of Indian democracy would be at stake unless sincere efforts were made to ensure that the equality guaranteed in the political domain spreads to the social sphere also, gains increasingly relevance. Thus, any meaningful review of the strategies adopted in India for achieving social justice, would have to be anchored in the analysis of the finer nuances of electoral politics. If electoral politics implies politics of 'power-sharing' and 'power-management', the impact of this process on realising the goals of social democracy are of added significance.

Indian Constitution And The Electoral Process

The provisions in the Indian Constitution with regard to elections deal with three specific issues.

In the first place, the Constitution categorically states that there shall be one electoral roll for every territorial constituency for election to either House of Parliament or to the State Legislature and no person shall be excluded from such roll on grounds of religion, race, caste, sex or any of them (Article 325). Further, elections shall be held on the basis of adult suffrage, – every person who is a citizen of India and who is not less than 18 years of age shall be entitled to vote at the election provided he is not disqualified by any provision of the Constitution or any law made by the appropriate Legislature on the grounds of non-residence, unsoundness of mind, crime, or corrupt or illegal practice (Article 326). While laying down the general principles with regard to the elections to the Legislatures of the Union and the States, the procedure for elections was to be decided by legislation framed by the competent authority.[1] The procedure that came to be prescribed for the elections to the Lok Sabha and the State Legislative Assemblies was the simple majority system – also referred to as the First-Past-The-Post System, with single member territorial constituencies and each voter enjoying a single non-transferable vote.

Secondly, the Constitution established an independent Election Commission for the superintendence, direction and control of the electoral roll and the conduct of elections (Article 324).

Finally, a specific provision was made to provide for reservation of seats in the Lok Sabha (Article 332) and the State Legislative Assemblies (Article 334), for the Scheduled Castes and Scheduled

Tribes for a period of ten years, which has now been extended upto the year 2000.[2]

The guaranteeing of universal adult franchise, the decision to adopt the simple majority system and the reservation of seats in the Lok Sabha and State Legislative Assemblies for those belonging to the Scheduled Castes and Scheduled Tribes, have all had a direct impact on the efforts to promote social justice and merit detailed scrutiny.

UNIVERSAL ADULT FRANCHISE AND SOCIAL JUSTICE

The decision of the Constituent Assembly to grant universal adult franchise can be considered as a bold and momentous decision which was reflective of the faith reposed by the members of the Constituent Assembly in the political wisdom of the Indian voters (Shastri and Vinod 1991:387). The manner in which the electorate has voted over the last four decades bears testimony to this fact. The voter turnout has increased from a mere 45.7% in the First General Elections (1952) to 64.1% in the Eighth General Elections (1984). In four of the ten General Elections to the Lok Sabha held so far – Fourth General Election (1967), Sixth General Election (1977), Eighth General Election (1984) and Ninth General Election (1989) – the voter turnout has crossed the 60% mark (Shastri 1994). While the formal process of exercise of vote could be termed as a reflection of the increasing involvement and participation of the voters, it needs to be stressed that studies have shown that the mere guaranteeing of universal suffrage has never resulted in the mobilisation of the masses. The 'user attitude' as against the 'participatory attitude' appears to be more common amongst the citizens (Hermet 1991: 456, also Tingsten 1936, Campbell et.al. 1976).

It must be noted that the guaranteeing of universal adult franchise provided an opportunity – which was earlier not available – to the Indian citizens to give expression to and mirror the multi-track diversities that were present in the society. Commenting on the scenario that emerged in India with the dawn of Independence, Oommen has very rightly stressed that:

> . . . once freedom was achieved the temporarily frozen identities (particularly the regional-linguistic; religious-caste; and tribal identities) gradually started assuming saliency. (1990: 95)

Inspite of the fact that successive General Elections have seen parties and individuals being voted out of power and have thus offered proof of the political sagacity of the voters, at the same time, the caste factor has came to play a critical role in shaping the electoral verdict. The recently concluded Assembly elections in Uttar Pradesh (November 1993) are indeed a case in point (Shastri 1993:16). Beteille has very rightly remarked that even though caste has ceased to be an important social institution it continues to be an important social fact and the 'morphological structure of caste . . . is still visible and prominent' (Beteille 1991). While M.N. Srinivas maintains that universal adult franchise has resulted in the re-assertion of caste based loyalties (1965), Rajni Kothari has opined that universal adult franchise has neither given caste a 'new solidarity' nor has it 'reestablished its legitimacy' (1989:72). Kothari goes on to add that:

> . . . both the quest for majority and the desire for stable support lead to a type of political organisation that on the one hand factionalises and on the other federalises castes . . . the politicisation of caste makes for outward moving and upward looking orientations and results in the phenomenon of multiple membership and identities among the participating strata among the public and the leadership.

The impact of the caste-factor on electoral behaviour, especially in the context of the Lok Sabha elections has been succinctly brought out by Kashyap in his analysis of the composition of the Ten Lok Sabha's (1992). In spite of universal adult franchise, the first Lok Sabha was, in Kashyap's view a 'highly elitist body' (*ibidem:* 13). While assessing the future prospects Kashyap believes that:

> The patience of the people seems to be on the verge of collapse. It has come to be widely believed that behind the disintegration and fragmentation of society and threats to national unity, the single-most potent force is our politics of vote merchants and power brokers busy building their vote banks. (*ibidem*: 251-52)

If the quest for social justice were to be seen as the assertion of individual autonomy in society, the guaranteeing of universal adult franchise could be viewed as being a positive measure in the direction of strengthening individual autonomy. However, caste based politics has resulted in the strengthening of group identities in society, at the cost of individual autonomy.

The First Past The Post System : A Stumbling Block In The Way of Social Justice?

For the elections to the Lok Sabha and State Legislative Assemblies the simple majority system (the term is infact a misnomer) or first-past-the-post system is followed. Under this system the electorate is divided into single member territorial constituencies and one representative is elected from each constituency. Every voter has a single non-transferable vote. A major trend that is noticed after four decades of electoral experience is that, under the present electoral system the electoral verdict is not effectively mirrored in the composition of the legislature and makes a mockery of the concept of social justice.

The first-past-the-post system permits a candidate to win an election from a constituency merely because he/she polls the highest number of votes. The fact that the winning candidate may have secured a very small percentage of the total votes polled in the constituency is of marginal electoral significance. As a result, the present electoral system has resulted in an alarming and disproportionate gap between the percentage of votes polled and the percentage of seats won by the various political parties. In all the ten General Elections to the Lok Sabha held so far, on no occasion has the party that assumed power after the elections polled more than 48% of the votes. The percentage of seats won by the ruling party has always been significantly higher than the percentage of votes polled.

The statistics contained in the Table 1 portrays this discrepancy between the percentage of votes polled and seats won by the ruling party which came to power after a General Election.

When viewed from the angle of individual candidates elected, a significant number of victors have secured less than 50% of the valid votes polled. The percentage of winners who secured less than 50% of the valid votes polled in successive General Elections to the Lok Sabha, is mentioned in Table 2.

TABLE 1

Percentage of votes polled and seats won by the party which formed the government after the elections to the Lok Sabha

Year of Election	Percentage of Seats Won	Percentage of votes polled
1991	46	37
1989	27	18
1984	80	48
1980	67	43
1977	55	41
1971	70	44
1967	54	41
1962	73	45
1957	75	48
1952	73	45

TABLE 2

Percentage of winning candidates in Lok Sabha Elections who secured less than fifty percent of the valid votes

Year of Election	Percentage	Year of Election	Percentage
1991	53	1989	45
1984	31	1980	46
1977	12	1971	31
1967	58	1962	56
1957	52	1952	61

This votes polled-seats won distortion and the fact that a large number of electoral victors secured less than 50% of the votes polled is primarily duc to the multi cornered contests witnessed in most constituencies. If in the 1952 general elections, there were 1874 contestants, in the 1991 General Elections there were 9107 candidates. Of these more than 5000 were independents (Shastri 1992:7).

In view of the glaring anomalies that have arisen as a result of the first-past-the-post system, there is a pressing need to replace the system with a more suitable one. Several suggestions have been made in this regard. Ways and means of discouraging the independents from contesting the elections have been put forward from time to time. The Election Commission had frequently drawn that attention of the government (in its Reports) to the fact that 'undue multiplicity of candidates' is both 'undesirable and confusing' (1957:231). In its Report on the Third General Elections held in 1962, the Commission emphatically stressed that:

> . . . (if) a clear verdict is to be obtained (in a constituency). . . it is essential that the contest be limited to a few worthy candidates, and light hearted participation by individuals who do not have any substantial electoral support must be checked. (1962: 123)

However, the desirability of discouraging independents from contesting the elections, needs to be viewed with caution as every citizen enjoys a fundamental right to offer himself/herself as a candidate in an election.

The Tarkunde Committee (Committee appointed by Jayaprakash Narayan on behalf of the Citizens for Democracy, for Electoral Reforms) in its report, spoke of the possibility of adopting the 'Partial List System'. As per this system, only candidates securing more than 50% of the valid votes polled are declared elected. For those seats where no candidate has secured 50% of the valid votes polled, a different method is followed. All seats not filled through direct election would be distributed among the various political parties in such a manner that the total seats the parties secure in the concerned legislature are in proportion to the valid votes polled by them. This would be done by declaring elected as many members from each party list (well before polling day each recognised party will be asked to submit a list of candidates in order of preference) as will result in the total strength of each party (directly elected + elected from the list) being roughly proportionate to the votes polled by the party. However, the committee also acknowledged the weaknesses of the system and called for a widespread public debate for a consensus to emerge (1991: 596).

Recently, the Governor of Andhra Pradesh, Krishna Kant, has suggested that a system of negative voting should be introduced. A negative vote provision, he asserts, would be a legal channel for the expression of dissent (1992: 31-32). The negative vote suggestion may at the most, serve as a negative solution to the problem and will in no way positively contribute to strengthening the electoral system.

In the context of social justice, a more meaningful and practical alternative appears to be the second ballot system. Under such a system, if no candidate secures more than 50% of the valid votes polled in the first round of elections in a constituency, a second run-off is held between the top two contestants within a week. As a result the candidate who wins the election from a constituency secures a majority of the votes polled. Adopting the second ballot system appears to be the most effective alternative for overcoming the defects of the first-past-the-post-system. Candidates would have to take their election campaigns more seriously and electoral victories would not be merely caused by dividing the opponents' votes on caste/religious lines or concentrating on securing the votes of one segment of the voters. Those elected could then be termed as being genuinely representatives of the constituency they have been elected from. While endorsing the utility of the second ballot system a caveat needs to be added. This reform cannot be considered in isolation and would have to from a part of a comprehensive package of electoral reforms that the system needs today.

POLITICAL RESERVATIONS AND SOCIAL JUSTICE

As mentioned earlier, Articles 330 and 332 of the Indian Constitution provide for reservation of seats in the Lok Sabha and the State Assemblies for the Scheduled Castes and Tribes. This provision was initially for a period of ten years and as a result of successive constitutional amendments, it has been extended upto the year 2000. Today, of the 543 elective seats in the Lok Sabha, 78 are reserved for the Scheduled Castes and 38 for the Scheduled Tribes.

The Advisory Committee on Minorities and Fundamental Rights of the Constituent Assembly, had made a recommendation in favour of this reservation. While participating in the discussion in the Constituent Assembly, on the Report of the Advisory Committee, the Chairman of the Committee, Vallabhai Patel stated that '... the general opinion in the Advisory Committee was, which was unanimous, that this reservation so far as the Scheduled Castes are concerned should be continued. . . ' (CAD: B: 270).

There was a lengthy debate in the Constituent Assembly on this important provision. A few members of the Constituent Assembly did attempt to oppose this provision on certain grounds. Thakurdas Bhargava expressed the view that the provision was anti-integration and expressed the hope that those hailing from the Scheduled Castes and Tribes would contest the elections from general constituencies and emerge victorious (CAD: 9: 648). Jaspat Roy Kapoor held the view that when the religious minorities have agreed to give up the political concessions that were conferred by the British, the Scheduled Castes and Tribes should also adopt a similar approach (*ibidem:* 641-43). Jaipal Singh while reacting to Kapoor's suggestion drew the attention of the House to the fact that those hailing from the depressed classes never enjoyed any political concessions so there was nothing to give up (*ibidem:* 649).

The Assembly also debated at length the question as to whether the concession should be limited to 10 years or given indefinitely. Jaipal Singh (*ibidem*), Khandekar (*ibidem*: 666) and Muniswamy Pillai (*ibidem*: 646) were convinced that 10 years was too short a period to hope for any change/major changes in the society. Ambedkar himself favoured a more open door policy. He felt that if at the end of the ten years, the Scheduled Castes find that their position has not improved or that they want further extension . . . it will not be beyond their capacity to invent new ways of getting the same protection which they are promised here (*ibidem:* 697).

It has often been argued that the constitutional provisions with regard to reservations of seats in the Legislatures for the Scheduled Casted and Tribes was the result of a compromise arrived at between Ambedkar and the Congress leaders (Baxi 1991: 12 and Rajasekaraih 1982: 231). While Ambedkar had himself earlier argued in favour of separate electorates for the Scheduled Castes, later as Chairman of the Drafting Committee he agreed to this transitional arrangement.

The provision for political reservation has often been viewed as a significant step taken by the framers of the Constitution to ensure social justice by providing for adequate representation to the depressed classes. The question is often raised as to whether those elected to represent the Scheduled Castes and Tribes have truly protected and mirrored the interests of the sections that they represent. Ambedkar himself appeared to be disillusioned on this score in 1951 itself. He gave vent to his anguish in a speech he delivered at Jullundhur on 27 October 1951:

It is a sorry tale of deception and betrayal . . . Congress (has). . .

> deprived the untouchables of their legitimate rights by employing all means fair and foul. People having no social standing in the Scheduled Castes are elected to the Legislature only because of the support of the Caste Hindus . . . we must have such representatives in the Legislature, who will voice our grievances fearlessly. But these Congress-appointed representatives of the Untouchables have faithfully sung the praise of their masters or kept their mouths shut inspite of the harrowing tales of denial of rights and even the basic amenities, of insults and humiliation, oppression and expolitation, persecution and numerous atrocities being committed daily in different parts of India.
>
> (Bhagwan Das 1962: 76-77)

The above statement gives clear expression to Ambedkar's disillusionment with the Congress party on the issue of safeguarding the interests of the depressed classes. Much earlier, the public statement that he issued on 10 October 1951, on the eve of his resignation from the Union Council of Ministers, stated in categorical terms that the government had neglected the Scheduled Castes and they (Scheduled Castes) were 'exposed to the same old tyranny, the same old oppression, the same old discrimination which existed before' (Bhagwan Das 1963: 71) but now in a worse form. It is interesting to note at this stage that even in the Constituent Assembly, during the debate on the political reservations provisions, one of the members thought it fit to state that it is through the grace of the Congress leaders, Nehru and Patel, that the Scheduled Castes and Tribes are getting these concessions (CAD: 9: 634).

What Ambedkar said at Jullundhur in October 1951, that only those individuals who have the support of caste Hindus are getting elected from the reserved constituencies is today being echoed by other leaders also. Several legislators[3] – hailing from different parties – who have been elected from reserved constituencies, have conceded that upper caste Hindus have come to play a critical role not merely in the choice of the candidates, to contest the elections but also in determining the electoral outcome. Even in the Constituent Assembly, one of the members, H.J. Khandekar, had forewarned that in the case of the reserved constituencies the caste Hindus would attempt to divide the scheduled castes and ensure the victory of only those who have their support (CAD: 9: 667). In this context the composition of the electorate in the reserved constituencies would have to be borne in mind. In these constituencies, even though those hailing from the depressed classes form a significant segment of the electorate, the majority of the voters are from the other sections of society. In the process the non-depressed classes voters have come to play a critical role in determining the electoral outcome even in the reserved constituencies. It is in this context that the statement made by the leader of the Bahujan Samaj Party, Kanshi Ram, gains relevance. He has asserted that those belonging to the depressed classes should not give too much attention to reservations as they are mere crutches. (Deccan Herald: 20: 12:1 993)

A survey of the electoral trends in the reserved constituencies (Lok Sabha) during the period 1952-1991, point to certain interesting trends. Table 3 clearly indicates the pattern with regard to the performance of the ruling party in the reserved constituencies.

TABLE 3

Percentage of reserved seats (Lok Sabha) secured by the party which formed the government after the elections are compared to the overall percentage of seats won by that party – 1952-1991

Year	Percentage of seates (overall) secured	Percentage of reserved seats secured
1991	46	52
1989	27	27
1984	80	79
1980	79	67
1977	55	54
1971	70	68
1967	56	65
1962	73	68
1957	75	76
1952	73	72

Table 3 clearly shows that there is not much of a variation between the percentage of seats secured overall and in reserved constituencies, with regard to the party that is voted to power. Variations can be seen only in the 1962, 1967 and 1991 elections.

In 1962, the percentage of seats the Congress[4] party won in reserved constituencies was much lower than its overall percentage of victories – 68% as compared to 73%. This discrepancy can be explained in terms of the fact that in the 1962 elections, the D.M.K. candidates emerged victorious in as many as six of the reserved constituencies in Tamil Nadu, leading to a reduction in the Congress tally. In 1967, the Congress party fared better in the reserved constituencies – 65% of reserved seats and 56% overall. In this case, a larger number of Congress candidates emerged victorious in the reserved constituencies – especially in Andhra Pradesh, Bihar and Uttar Pradesh. In 1991 too, the Congress performance was better in the case of reserved constituencies as compared to the general constituencies, especially in the states of Andhra Pradesh and Madhya Pradesh. However, the general trend that emerges is that the percentage of seats (overall) that a ruling party secures is more or less proportionate to the percentage of seats it secures in the reserved constituencies. This implies that the voting trend in the reserved constituencies is similar to the voting trend in the other constituencies.

Further, it is noticed that in nearly 10% of the reserved constituencies (11),[5] nominees belonging to a single party have emerged victorious in successive general elections. In all these cases the single party being referred to is the Congress party. In another 10% of the reserved constituencies (13),[6] Congress candidates have emerged victorious in all elections save one. The one exception invariably is that election when there was a clear anti-Congress wave (1977 and 1989). Further in another 16% of the reserved constituencies (19),[7] Congress nominees have been elected in all but two of the elections. Thus, there are as many as 43 reserved constituencies (close to 40%) which have in most cases returned Congress nominees.

If a distinction is made between the elections held before and after 1977, yet another clear trend emerges. In the pre-1977 period, in nearly 30% of the constituencies (33)[8] Congress party nominees were elected in successive elections. A study of the trend in the post-1977 period shows that in 20% of the constituencies (23)[9] nominees of only one party have won the seat. This party has not always been the Congress (in only 16 of the 23 cases). Viewed from a slightly different perspective, it is noticed that in nearly 40% of the constituencies (46)[10] one party has retained the seat in four or more successive elections.

It has often been said that political parties rarely change their nominees when it comes to reserved constituencies. It is noticed, especially, in the pre 1977 period – when the reserved constituencies were rotated – that the a candidate who had contested in an earlier election from a different reserved constituency, often filed his/her nominations from the new reserved constituency. No effort was made to find a candidate from the local area.

It would be interesting to note in this context that in nearly half the reserved constituencies, one indivdual has been elected from three or more consecutive terms. Further, it is noticed that in nearly 10% of the constituencies (10), on each occasion that a party won the seat, the same individual was sponsored by the party.[11] In more than 15% of the reserved constituencies (18), in the elections held between 1952 and 1991, whenever a party has won a seat it has been represented by only two individuals.[12]

An analysis of the individuals who represented a constituency in successive elections shows that there are three reserved constituencies which always returned the same candidate.[13] In four other reserved constituencies only two individuals have represented that constituency. In 17 other constituencies, save on one occasion, only two individuals have represented that constituency.[14]

It was earlier stated that the percentage of reserved seats secured by a ruling party in Lok Sabha election is more or less proportionate to the overall percentage of seats secured by the party. Inspite of this fact it is noticed that in the Union Council of Ministers the percentage of Ministers hailing from the Scheduled Castes and Tribes is extremely low. On only seven occasions has the representation accorded to those hailing from the Scheduled Castes and Tribes crossed 15%. At the Cabinet level, the highest representation has been 13%. It is interesting to note that it was only in 1970 that an individual hailing from the Scheduled Castes was made a Minister of State. Till then representation was confined to the Cabinet (one or two ministers) and Deputy Minister level. Before 1967, the representation to those hailing from the Scheduled Castes and Tribes was less than 10%. It was only after 1974 – except between 1989 and 1991 – that the representation increased to over 15%. In terms of numbers, prior to 1974, in the Council of Ministers, the number of ministers who hailed from the Scheduled Castes and Tribes was always less then 10 – in the 1952-57 period it was below five.

TABLE 4

Percentage of representation to Seheduled Castes and Scheduled Tribes in theUnion Council of Ministers: 1952 -1993 [total strength in brackets]

Year	Cabinet Ministers	Ministers of State		Deputy Ministers	Total
		Ind. charge	Others		
1952 12.8.52	1[15] 7%		-[16]	1[14] 7%	2[36] 5.5%
1956 1.5.56	1[16] 6%		-[16]	2[14] 14%	3[46]4.3%
1958 2.4.58	1[12] 8%		-[15]	2[19] 11%	3[46]4.3%
1959 6.3.59	1[14] 7%		-[14]	3[20] 15%	4[48] 8.3%
1962 10.4.62	1[17] 6%		-[12]	4[21] 19%	5[50]10%
1964 30.9.64	1(16) 6%		-[16]	4[21] 19%	5[53] 9.4%
1966 11.1.66	2(16) 13%		-[18]	3[19] 16%	5[53] 9.4%
1967 13.11.67	1[18] 6%		-[17]	6[20] 30%	7[55]12.7%
1970 30.6.70	2[16] 13%		1[23] 4%	4[19]21%	7[58]12%
1971 2.9.71	1[15]7%		-[23]	5[17] 29%	6[53]11%
1973 5.2.73	1[17] 6%		-[21]	8[23] 35%	9[61]14.8%
1974 10.10.74	1[18]6%		1[25]4%	8[22]36%	10[65]15.4%
1977 16.8.77	1[20]3%		9[24] 38%	–	10.44 23%
1979 4.8.79	2[22] 10%		5[17] 30%	–	7[38]18.4%
1980 19.10.80	2[19] 11%		7[22]32%	1[10]10%	10[51]19.6%
1985 31.1.85	2[15] 13%		2[6]3%	3[20]15%	7[41]17%
1989 Janata	1[18] 6%	-[3]	1[14] 7%	-[5]	2[40]5%
1990 Janata	(S) -[15]	-[3]	2[12]17%	1[4]25%	3[34]8.8%
1991 30.7.91	1[16] 6%	1[14] 7%	5[19]26%	2[17]29%	9[56]16%
1993 30.10.93	1[15] 7%	2[12]17%	5[26]19%	2[3]67%	10[56] 17.9%

THE QUEST FOR SOCIAL JUSTICE

The above analysis clearly indicates that the trend in electoral politics is essentially a trend of control by the ruling elite. Given the absence of intra-party democratic traditions in all 'mainstream' political parties, the electoral system has been manipulated and (ab)used by the ruling elite to strengthen their control over the political system and the levers of power. Commenting on the role of the power elite in a democratic polity, Ramashray Roy opines:

> The mass of voters, who are presumably politically disinterested, inactive and usually apathetic in the eyes of the specialists in the area of voting behaviour, have to be activated, presented with the choice of rulers as well as policies and programmes to be pursued by the contenders for people's support and give their consent. The active elements in a formal democracy are, thus, the political elites who activate the masses, present them with choices of policies and ask for their consent. (1991:288)

If as Poulantzas stresses, power refers to the capacity of a 'class to realise specific objective interests' (1968:107), the ruling elite in India, appears to have concentrated its attention on manipulating the political instrumentalities in such a manner that the summit level decision making that they desire to practice is further strengthened and if possible legitimized. In the context it would be relevant to quote Nandy who attempts to explain such developments from the perspective of the historicity of traditions and practices – the accumulated baggage that societies find difficult to discard:

> Continuous suffering inflicted by fellow human beings, centuries of inequity and deprivation of human dignity, generations of poverty, long experience of authoritarian political rule or imperialism, these distort the cultures and minds, especially the values and the self-concepts, of the sufferers and those involved in the manufacturing of suffering. Long term suffering also generally means the establishment of powerful justifications for the sufferings in the minds of both the oppressors and the oppressed. . . It is thus that institutionalized suffering acquires its self-perpetuating quality. (1987: 26)

The political structures that were painstakingly modelled by the framers of the Indian Constitution appear to have today become the instruments of manipulative politics controlled by a chosen few. In the process, the goals that these structures were required to realise appear to be respected more in their breach. The politics of double speak – which has become the accepted style of political activity – requires the formal display of commitment to these goals even as considerations of *realpolitik* steer the instrumentalities of power in the direction of ruling elite interests. Social justice is a case in point. Even as all the instruments of state power express their unequivocal commitment to the cause of social justice, in practice they are geared towards realising the interests of the political elite.

In such circumstances, a second look at the Constitution would be a mere exercise in futility as we may in the process, unwittingly, permit the legitimisation of the abuse of authority. For, if a new constitution were to be drafted at this stage, the political elite would once again play a decisive role in determining its features.

The solution lies in making an attempt to wrest the levers of power from the political elite and return to genuine mass base politics. Strengthening democracy and the fight for social justice would imply strengthening mass movements that are in a position to challenge the domination of the political elite. Merely initiating constitutional reforms cannot set the system back on the right track. A structural remedy can never be an answer for problems triggered off by operational incompetence.

NOTES

1. Parliament has enacted the Representation of Peoples Act, 1950, 1951 and the Delimitation Commission Acts, 1962 and 1972.
2. This provision which was initially for a period of ten years, was extended to twenty years by the Constitution (8th Amendment) Act, 1959, to thirty years by the Constitution (23rd Amendment) Act, 1969, to forty years by the Constitution (45th Amendment) Act, 1980 and till the year 2000 by the Constitution (62nd Amendment) Act, 1989.
3. The names of the legislators who were interviewed are not being quoted as they agreed to speak on this issue on the condition that they were not quoted by name.
4. The term 'Congress party' is used for the Congress(R) in the post 1969 period, Congress(1) in the post 1978 period.

5. Mandvi (Gujarat); Chamarajanagar and Chikkodi (Karnataka); Mandla (Madhya Pradesh); Dhulia, Nandurbar and Osmanabad (Maharashtra); Koraput and Nowrangpur (Orissa); Rasipuram and Tenakasi (Tamil Nadu).
6. Bhadrachalam, Nellore, Parvathipuram and Tirupathi (Andhra Pradesh); Shimla (Himachal Pradesh): Bidar and Kolar (Karnataka), Bilaspur, Sidhi and Sarangarh (Madhya Pradesh); Jalore (Rajasthan); Chail (Uttar Pradesh) and Lakshadweep (UT).
7. Siddipet (Andhra Pradesh); Karimganj (Assam), Chotta Udaipur and Dhohad (Gujarat); Sirsa (Haryana); Jhabua, Kanker, Raigarh and Surguja (Madhya Pradesh); Buldhana, Dahanu, Malegoan and Pandharpur (Maharashtra); Outer Manipur (Manipur); Philaur and Ropar (Punjab); Banswara and Ganganagar (Rajasthan); Dadra and Nagar Haveli (UT).
8. Bhadrachalam, Nellore and Tirupathi (Andhra Pradesh); Karimganj, Kokrajhar and Autonomous Dist (Assam); Sasaram, Bahagaha and Palamu (Bihar); Mandvi (Gujarat); Shimla (Himachal Pradesh); Bidar, Chamarajnagar, Chikkodi and Kolar (Karnataka); Mandla (Madhya Pradesh); Nandurbar (Maharashtra); Koraput and Norwangpur (Orissa); Philaur and Ropar (Punjab); Banswara and Ganganagar (Rajasthan); Rasipuram and Tenakasi (Tamil Nadu); Chail, Ghatanpur, Jalaun and Mohanlalganj (UP); Alipurduars and Birbhum (West Bengal), Karol Bagh (New Delhi); Lakshadweep (UT).
9. *Congress:* Mandvi and Dhohad (Gujarat); Chamrajnagar and Chikkodi (Karnataka); Mandla and Surguja (Madhya Pradesh); Dhulia, Nandrubar, Osmanabad and Pandharpur (Maharashtra); Outer Manipur (Manipur); Koraput and Nowrangpur (Orissa); Rasipuram and Tenakasi (Tamil Nadu); Robertsgunj (Uttar Pradesh); *CPM*: Durgapur, Jhargham, Nabadwip and Vishnupur (West Bengal); *RSP:* Alipurduars and Balurghat (West Bengal); *Forward Bloc:* Cooch Bihar (West Bengal).
10. *Congress:* Amalapuram, Bhadrachalam, Nellore and Tirupathi (Andhra Pradesh); Karimganj and Kokrajhar (Assam); Mandvi and Dohad (Gujarat); Shimla (Himachal Pradesh); Bidar, Chikkodi, Chamrajnagar and Kolar (Karnataka); Bastar, Jhabua, Kanker, Mandla, Dhar and Sarangarh (Madhya Pradesh); Dahanu, Dhulia, Nandurbar, Osmanabad and Pandharpur (Maharashtra); Outer Manipur (Manipur); Koraput and Nowrangpur (Orissa); Phillaur and Ropar (Punjab); Ganganagar (Rajasthan); Rasipuram and Tenakasi (Tamil Nadu); Ghatanpur, Mohanlalganj and Robertsganj (Uttar Pradesh); Birbhum (West Bengal); Dadra and Nagar Haveli (UT); *CPM:* Durgapur, Jhargham, Nabadwip and Vishnupur (West Bengal); *Forward Bloc*: Cooch Behar (West Bengal); *RSP*: Alipurduars and Joynagar (West Bengal); *Janata*

Party/Dal: Sasaram (Bihar).

11. Only when a party has won the seat on atleast three occasions has it been considered for analysis. *Congress:* Bagaha and Sasaram (Bihar); Jhabua (Madhya Pradesh); Chikkodi (Karnataka); Nowrangpur (Orissa); Lakshadweep (UT); *RSP*: Alipurduars, Balurghat and Joynagar (West Bengal); *Forward Block*: Cooch Bihar (West Bengal).
12. Only when a party has won the seat on atleast five occasions has it been considered for analysis.

    Amalapuram and Sidipet (Andhra Pradesh); Karimganj (Assam); Palamau and Rajmahal (Bihar); Bulsar and Dhohad (Gujarat); Ambala and Sirsa (Haryana); Sarangarh (Madhya Pradesh); Pandharpur (Maharashtra); Bhadrak (Orissa); Ganganagar (Rajasthan); Ghatanpur and Robertsgunj (Uttar Pradesh) Durgapur, Nabadwip and Vishnupur (West Bengal).
13. Chikkodi (Karnataka); Nowrangpur (Orissa); Lakshadweep (UT).
14. Siddipet (Andhra Pradesh); Autonomous Districts (Assam); Bagaha (Bihar); Bulsar, Mandvi and Dhohad (Gujarat); Bidar (Karnataka); Kanker and Sarangarh (Madhya Pradesh); Malegaon and Osmanabad (Maharashtra); Ambala (Punjab); Rasipuram and Tenakasi (Tamil Nadu); Cooch Bihar, Nabadwip and Vishnupur (West Bengal).

REFERENCES

Bangura, Yusuf. 1992. 'Authoritarian Rule and Democracy in Africa: A Theoretical Discourse', in *Rudebeck:* 69-104.

Baxi, Upendra. 1991. 'Emancipation as Justice: Babasaheb Legacy and Vision'. *The Life, Mission, Contributions and Relevance of Babasaheb Dr. B.R. Ambedkar.* New Delhi: Ministry of Social Welfare: 1-17.

Beckman, Bjorn. 1992. 'Whose Democracy; Bourgeois Versus Popular Democracy', in *Rudebeck*: 131-150.

Beteille, Andre. 1991. 'Caste and Intellectuals: An Uneasy Relationship'. *Times of India* (Bangalore), 30 December 1991.

Campbell, A., et.al. 1976. *The Quality of American Life.* New York: Russel Sage.

Das, Bhagwan. 1962. *Thus Spoke Ambedkar.* Jullundur: Bheem Patrika Publications.

—— 1963. *Selected Speeches of Dr Babsaheb B.R. Ambedkar.* Jullundur: Bheem Patrika Publications.

Hermet, Guy. 1991. 'The Disechantment of the Old Democracies'. *International Social Science Journal.* 43(129):451-462.

Iyer, V.R. Krishna. 1991. 'Social Justice to Dalit and Soshits', in *The Life, Mission, Contributions and Relevance of Babasaheb Dr. B.R. Ambedkar. New* Delhi: Ministry of Social Welfare: 18-22.

Kant, Krishna. 1992. 'Consensual Nationalism'. *Mainstream,* Annual 1992:27-36.

Kashyap, Subhash. 1992. *The Ten Lok Sabhas.* New Delhi: Shipra.

Kothari, Rajni. 1991. *Politics and the People.* vol 1. New Delhi: Ajanta.

Mukharji, Partha N. 1992. 'Class and Ethnic Movements in India', in *Rudebeck:* 13:30.

Nandy, Ashis. 1989. *Traditions, Tyranny and Utopias.* New Delhi: Oxford.

Poulantzas, Nicos. 1968. *Political Power and Socialcl Classes.* London: Verso.

Oommen, T.K. 1990. *State and Society in India.* New Delhi: Sage.

Rajashekaraiah, A.M. 1982. *Constitutional Philosophy of Dr B.R. Ambedkar.* Aurangabad: Marathwada University.

Report of the Committee Appointed by Jayaprakash Narayan on behalf of Citizens for Democracy for Electoral Reforms. *Indian Journal of Public Administration.* New Delhi. 37:3(1991): 588-602).

Report of the Second General Elections in India, 1957. vol.1. Election Commission. New Delhi.

Report of the Third General Elections in India, 1962. vol.1. Election Commission. New Delhi.

Roy, Ramashray. 1991. 'What Ails our Electoral System'. *Indian Journal of Public Administration,* 37:3(July-September); 288-293.

Rudebeck, Lars. 1992. Editor *When Democracy Makes Sense.* Stockholm: Akut, Working Group for the Study of Development Strategies.

Shastri, Sandeep and M.J. Vinod. 1991. 'The Dynamics of Electoral Politics : A Case Study of the Karnataka Assembly Elections, 1989'. *Indian Journal of Social Science,* 4:3:387-406.

Shastri, Sandeep. 1992. 'Electoral Reforms: Need to Replace the First Past the Post System'. *Mainstream,* 30:47 (September): 7-8, 19.

——. 1993. 'Winter of Political Discontent'. *Mainstream.* 32:6 (December): 15-16.

——. 1994. 'Elections to the Lok Sabha from Karnataka (1952-1991): An Analysis of the Voting Pattern and Electoral Trends'. *Indian Journal of Parliamentary Information.* 60: 3: 378-401.

Srinivas, M.N. 1965. *Caste in India and Other Essays.* Bombay: Asia Publishing House.

Tingsten, Herbert. 1936. *Political Behaviour.* New York: Arno Press.

Touraine, Alan. 1991. 'What Democracy Means Today'. *International Social Science Journal.* 43(128): 259-268.

Wright, J.D. 1976. *The Dissent of the Governed.* New York: Academic Press.

A Tragic Experiment

G. HARAGOPAL

The Indian Constitution is not merely a mechanical arrangement of power and institutions for governance. Unlike several constitutions of the world, it has attempted to set a goal, provide a vision and direction in building a new social order which is not only democratic but equal and just. While it may not be a socialist vision, it is a vision which is humane, democratic and therefore egalitarian. More than that it envisages a very positive role to the Indian state in reconstruction of the social order, protecting the political freedom and contributing to the "gradual" transformation of the economic order. In other words it was expected to strive to build a democratic society which includes political, social and economic democracy. The concrete experience and evidence suggests that during the last four and half decades of development experience the nation drifted, drifted so violently that the social justice vision got completely blurred. The recent moves under the pressure of structural adjustment lay the last straw on the back of Indian model of development for social justice. This paper proposes to examine the forces that account for this tragic experiment.

The historic resolution of Pandit Nehru adopted by the Constituent Assembly on January 22; 1947 reads "wherein all powers and authority of the Sovereign Independent India, its constituent parts and organs of Government are derived from the people; and wherein shall be guaranteed and secured to all the people of India justice, social economic and political; equality of status, of opportunity, of freedom of thought, expression, belief, faith, worship, vocation, association and action". It was added "wherein adequate safeguards shall be provided for minorities, backward and tribal areas and depressed and other backward classes." Keeping in tune with this aim, Nehru maintained that "a vote by itself does not represent very much to a person who is down and out, to a person who is starving or hungry". He added "political democracy by itself is not enough except that it may be used to obtain a gradually increasing measure of economic democracy, equality and the spread of good things of life to others and removal of gross inequalities". Dr. S. Radhakrishnan held "poor people who wander about, find no work, no wages and starve, whose lives are a continual round of sore affliction and pinching poverty, cannot be proud of the Constitution or its law". (D.D. Basu, *Constitution of India,* 1992)

The economic justice, it is obvious, was given a place of importance. The Directive Principles not only envisaged banishment of poverty by the multiplication of the national wealth and resources and an equitable distribution thereof amongst all who contribute towards its production, but under the Directive Principles Article 38, requires the state to provide work for all, improve the living conditions of the common man, provide sufficient food and clothing to all, provide relief for the ailing and pension for the old and infirm and educate all the children.

Article 38 (2) states that the State shall strive to minimise the inequalities in income and endeavour to eliminate inequalities in status, facilities and opportunities not only amongst individuals but also amongst groups of people residing in different areas or in vocations.

Article 39 categorically states that the state shall direct its policy towards securing:

(a) that the citizens, men and women equally have the right to an adequate means of livelihood;

(b) that the ownership and control of the material resources of the community are so distributed as best to subserve the common good;

(c) that the operation of economic system does not result in the concentration of wealth and means of production to the common detriment.

Articles 38 and 39, read with the various other articles concerned with welfare and justice, raised hopes high; the promise was that there would be greater equality among the people and all monopolising tendencies would be discouraged, if not halted. If we consider dignified and decent life with greater equality in society is a part of the constitutional vision of justice, the nation has certainly moved in a direction that is different from this vision. In fact, recent trends forcefully indicate that it is moving exactly in the opposite direction. The structural adjustment is literally culmination of this change.

The structural adjustment programme would come into conflict with the entire Part IV of the Constitution. It would affect certain provisions to such a serious extent that retaining these provisions even in the so called non-justiciable category of rights would be totally hypocritical. For Article 13 does say that the principles laid down are "fundamental in the governance of the country. It shall be the duty of the state to apply these principles in making laws". It is not only that this directive is hurt beyond recognition, but several provisions will have no meaning in the changed context.

II

The Constitution in general and Part IV of the Constitution in particular were products of the freedom movement and also the global context of the late forties which was infused with liberalism, socialism and democracy. In the late forties of this century, there was no option except incorporating ideology of social justice as a part of the constitutional scheme. But when the actual process started after the transfer of power, the drift began in the very early stage and there was not enough popular or democratic pressure to prevent the drift.

In the very first stage of development while there was some emphasis on certain agrarian changes; soon there was a compromise. While there was abolition of Zamindari and intermediary institutions, there was no attempt to radicalise the land reforms. A radical land reform programme ought to have been thc first step to realise the goals of Part IV of the Constitution. Instead the changes were incremental, if not ornamental. The ownership structure underwent some changes more on account of market intervention and not the State. Innumerable rural studies indicate the skewed distribution of land in the rural structure. The studies also indicate that the number of the landless agricultural labourers has been swelling. There are also studies which indicate that the situation continues to be the same and the overall income of agriculture has further declined. These are the trends one has to take note of.

The tensions intrinsic to the uneven, unequal and unjust rural structure were evident in their symptomatic form by the mid-sixties. Instead of attempting structural changes, the managers of the economy and power opted for technological substitutes. Thus the notorious Green Revolution became a substitute for structural changes. The Green Revolution, being a biased technology towards capital and water, reinforced uneven development across the regions and widened the disparities between classes. This led to considerable tensions resulting in political crisis between 1967-1971. This was the period which witnessed disequilibrium of a higher order – regional and sub-regional agitations, secessionist trends, food riots, collapse of one party dominance, rise of united fronts so on. Above all this period gave birth to the Naxalite movement.

The sixties crisis produced a political and also an economic response. At the level of economy the response was the anti-poverty programmes and at the level of politics it was rise of Mrs. Indira Gandhi. The anti-poverty rhetoric and charisma of Mrs. Gandhi legitimised one another. As she took up the anti-poverty rhetoric and initiated some symbolic programmes, they generated a different type of political economy consciousness. For the impact that these programmes made was marginal on the living conditions of the people, but people grew conscious of their own living conditions. Politically speaking this has had more far-reaching implications than the anti-poverty programmes per se. The rural poor became restless and therefore "unmanageable". The agrarian crisis was not only unable to sustain industrial development, particularly in terms of demand genration, but entered into a more serious conflict with the urban, industrial, market development syndrome. In the process of managing this conflict, dependency on foreign technology and assistance further increased.

As the rural poor started becoming increasingly restless, the power managers shifted their emphasis to industrial modernisation by updating technologies. This was what came to be described as the 21st century vision of development. The dead end in agrarian structure and over emphasis on modernisation of industry eliminated the poor even from the political rhetoric. This strategy of development involved politics which had to de- emphasize social justice. As social justice concerns got margina-lised, the poor particularly the restless and conscious, had to be managed through greater coercion. In the process the State in the eighties started becoming more and more brutal at the grass roots level and assumed greater sophistication and modern postures at the technological level. In this process they resorted to massive doses of imports of technology. This gave a jerk to the economy. The pace of rate of growth increased from its 2.5 per cent – the Hindu rate of Growth – to 5 to 5.5 per cent – the Silicon rate of growth.

III

The deep economic crisis confronting India in the decade of the 90s is a fall-out of what happened in the Indian economy from the 1950s in general and the decade of eighties in particular. The economy showed some vibrancy but the illusion was due to the induction of foreign technology in the name of modernisation, catching up, twenty-first century so on. While technology pushed up production, the products had neither the quality nor the innovative touch to generate international demand. Once the products lacked demand in the international market, the exchange became totally lopsided creating a tremendous trade deficit. The trade balance in the year 1950-51 was only – 2 crores. This rose continuously and by 60-61, it was 479 crores. Interestingly by 1970-71 it fell to 99 crores, and touched 1229 crores in the emergency years 1975-76 and 2725 crores by 1979-80. Between 79-80 and 80-81, this deficit got more than doubled and touched 5838 crores, which by the mid-80s stood at 8763 crores. This figure slightly declined in 86-87 but went on rising and touched its highest 10644 crores – in the crisis year 1990-91. (see Table-II). This led to massive borrowings from the IMF and World Bank to pay for the import of technology. Thus India was pushed into a logic of global economic order.

The trade deficit and helpless borrowings – the major causes of the deep economic crisis – are traced not to the structure of the overall economy, not to the inefficiency of the private sector, not to the over-all inability to produce indigenous technologies and R and D. They are traced to the public sector, Government regulations, subsidies, protection and other controls. It is this consciously directed and publicised "diagnosis" that led to the announcement of a series of policy measures which have very serious and far-reaching implications for the Indian Constitution and more so for the social justice concerns of the Constitution. The liberalisation, privatisation, marketisation and globalisation processes have been thrust on the economy as a part of the effort to overcome the crisis. They, however, are not policy measures emanating from either the Indian economic elite and much less the political elite. They emerged as a part of the structural adjustment. This is true not only of India but several other so-called developing countries. The power-holders in India have given in to the whole strategy without much resistance as it served their temporary purpose as much as it serves the long-range purpose of the imperialistic or the neocolonial objectives. This process did not stop there. The culmination point came with India becoming a part of the Dunkel Regime.

The entire structural adjustment policy has very serious implications for the people and more so to the working class and the rural and urban poor. That quite a number of industries may have to be closed down under the criterion of efficiency and competitive ethic. The fact that India had created a National Renewal Fund to meet the contingency of closure of industry, that the IMF and World Bank pledged to assist India's safety-net measures, that the Bank promised $500 million for the fund (10th Jan, 1992 *Times of India*), are indications of the consequences of the New Economic Policy. Dr. Manmohan Singh has committed to the IMF that he would pursue a restrictive monetary policy and slash the fiscal deficit partly by freezing dearness allowance. (*Indian Express,* 17th Dec. 1991). The new policy also involves severe cuts on development expenditure. The implications are that there will be no restructuring but only unemployment, and what Arun Ghosh fears is merely a repeat of the Latin American situation of 1980s. (*Frontline,* Jan. 3, 1992)

On the welfare front, there are going to be serious effects. The World Bank instructed the Government of India to lower buffer stocks of food. The Bank wanted India to reduce its buffer stocks of foodgrains and review its management systems, reconsider FCI's role in market operations and trim the public distribution system. The Bank felt that the high levels of buffer and working stocks for wheat and rice, currently over 19 million tons, are both expensive and unnecessary. (*Financial Express,* 23 Oct., 1992). The Bank recommended discontinuation of government monopoly on cotton procurement and export and diversion of Government investment on oilseeds to other crops and suggested liberal import of oil seeds and edible oils. (Naresh Minocha, *Indian Express,* 2 December 1991).

They have also suggested massive cuts on subsidies which cuts into the welfare programmes. The effect can be seen on the two most vital sectors of welfare – Health and Education. The difference in allocation of the resources for the social service sector between 91-92 and 92-93 indicates a decline in allocation of resources in real terms; this is – 10 per cent in respect of health and – 13 per cent in the case of education. As it is India is one country which has one of the least allocations for health and education – 1.6 and 2.5 per cent – among most of the developing countries of the world. This decline was seen for all the social sectors; it was – 2 per cent for women and child development, – 22 per cent for rural development, – 24 per cent for small and agro industries, – 10 per cent for labour. These trends are alarming and have serious implications to the future of social justice.

IV

Given the above trends what would be the long range implications to part IV and also part III of the Indian Constitution? Let us examine the impact of structural adjustment on certain very important directive principles. For instance while the Article 38 requires the State to provide work for all, improve the living conditions of common men and provide the basic needs, the structural adjustment requires the State to undertake such activities which would result in loss of work to several workers. The thrust seems to be more to provide relief through the National Renewal Fund than work. People work not only for livelihood, they also work to express themselves. This whole spirit is abandoned. In the case of basic necessities there is insistence that food subsidies are dropped. In that event what happens to the large sections of the people who have no purchasing power or have low purchasing power. This de-emphasis on food procurement and reduction in the role of Food Corporation of India would aggravate the living conditions of the people. This would be exactly opposite to what Article 38 stands for.

Article 38 requires the State to strive for a better distribution of the ownership of the means of production while the structural adjustment requires the policy of privatisation. Privatisation is essentially a process of creating dualism in the economy giving rise to the skewed distribution of the resources and ownership of the means of production. Further, the process of globalisation gives ownership to foreign or multi-national companies. Such type of liberalisation would give them grip over certain vital means of production. These trends are bound to go against the entire spirit of yet another aspect of this article which says that operation of the economic system should not result in concentration of wealth. For in the structural adjustment there is no mechanism whatsoever for checking the centralizing and monopolising trends in the economy of the society.

Article 45 requires the State to provide for universal literacy within 10 years after the adoption of Indian constitution. The Indian State was not able to realize this goal. The retreat of the State and reduction in the budgetary provisions for education and health would further remove the State and society from the set goal. The structural adjustment would not only abandon the universal literacy programme but require child labour in the economy.

The structural adjustment, thus, goes against the very spirit of Part IV of the Constitution. It is not that the situation earlier was qualitatively better. But there were some checks in the economy and certain policy measures which were aimed in this direction. The structural adjustment requires the State to alter the very direction. In the earlier scheme of things there were some positive signs, in the recent policy the entire direction is in the reverse order. Now the emphasis is on export-led growth, competition, efficiency, modernisation, technological transformation and so on. The goal is at best 'material growth' without the large millions forming a reference point. The constitutional vision of social justice is substituted, if not replaced, by the Bank/Fund vision of growth subserving imperial needs.

As social justice concerns are abandoned, there is danger not only to the Part IV but equally great danger to Part III of the constitution. Danger to justice always poses danger to freedoms. For the dichotomisation of justice and freedom is a consciously contrived political device intended to misdirect the debate and also the direction of development.

Chapter Three has been abridged ever since it came into force. It started with preventive detention in the very early fifties and culminated into TADA – one of the most oppressive weapons against freedom and the overall spirit of Part III of the Constitution. This trend was very sharply reflected in the 42nd and 59th Amendments which touched the core of the Constitution. This continuous tampering with the Constitution is very closely linked with the neglect of Part IV. For the neglect of Part IV leads to tremendous restlessness in the society. The restless masses start using the freedoms permitted in Part III to articulate and assert their deprivation. The State, under these circumstances, is left with two options; one, tackling the basic problems through policy measures and structural changes, or use repressive measures to contain, if not silence, the restless masses. The Indian State seem to be opting for the second alternative. Hence an imminent danger to both the vital parts of the Constitution.

The structural adjustment programme, as has been argued above, requires abandoning of Part-IV of the Constitution. For the changes severely affect this part of the Constitution directly and indirectly. This will lead to a major upsurge both in the industrial and agrarian front. The structural adjustment has no space whatsoever for a democratic handling of the situation. With the result the State has to inevitably become brutal. This inverse relation between democracy and development would lead to marginalisation of the Constitution itself. The crisis is far deeper as the sovereign decision-making power is fast shifting from the national boundaries to international financial agencies. Thus, the structural adjustment is setting formidable tasks – defending democracy, protecting national sovereignty, ensuring social justice – before the Indian people. In fact, the struggle for restoration of constitutional governance is one of the immediate tasks of Indian society. This is not going to be an easy task !

Confusion of Concepts

V.K. NATRAJ

The background paper of this Seminar quotes, with considerable approval, the view of Subhash Kashyap, that the composition of the Constituent Assembly was largely responsible for the 'elitist bias' of the Indian Constitution. The argument is that the Constituent Assembly was in no meaningful sense a representative body and that this led to certain rights gaining precedence over others. For instance basic right such as the right to work, right to a living wage etc. were not made justiciable while those dealing with freedom of speech and personal liberty were. The former are of utmost conern to the poor and the downtrodden while the latter appeal to a wholly different segment of society.

This argument, admittedly an important one, provides the framework for some of the questions which this paper attempts to raise. The central concerns of this paper can be summarised as follows:

- how far can the biases in the Constitution be attributed to the composition of the Assembly which formulated it?
- following from the preceding question, are there inbuilt conflicts in the Constitution between 'basic' and 'elitist' rights? And if there are, how far are they caused by the dominant interest groups in society and their influence over ideology and policy?
- finally, to what extent can the Constitution actually promote social justice, and do we have unrealistic expectations of the Constitution?

It is a fact that some of the most essential requisites of the majority in a poor country are not incorporated as rights in our Constitution. Most of them find a place in Part IV under Directive Principles. Article 39 (a) to (f) enjoins the State to direct its policy towards securing an adequate means of livelihood for all citizens "ensuring that the ownership and control of the material resources of the community are so distributed as best to subserve the common good" and that concentration of wealth and income is prevented, that there is equal pay for men and women, and, that children in particular are not abused. Similarly the "right to work, to education and to public assistance in cases of unemployment, old age, sickness and disablement, and in due cases of underserved want" is enshrined in Art. 41. It is interesting that though this Article is hedged in with caveat to the effect that the "State shall, within the limits of its economic capacity and development" make provision for the rights described above. Similarly Art. 43 speaks of a living wage while Art. 45 provides for free and compulsory education for children. Every one of these Directive Principles represents the core areas of concern in development but none are justiciable. In contrast Part III, essentially Art. 19, contains fundamental rights which, it is arguable, have an appeal only to those whose basic survival needs are already taken care of.

It is not proposed to enter here into the comparative merits of basic economic rights and the personal rights which part III confers upon us. Suffice it to state that in a poor country collective economic rights ought to occupy a place of centrality while the importance of personal rights can never he denied. The question sought to be raised here is why attempts have not been made to shift the ideals so succinctly expressed in Part IV to the sphere of rights fundamental or otherwise. If the Constituent Assembly was truly not representative, the successive Lok Sabhas have been insofar as they can be given the forces which exercise dominant influence over our electoral processes. It should not have been impossible to sanctify a few at least of the Directive Principles as rights. The explanation obviously lies elsewhere. In large part the lack of motivation must have resulted from the fact that the Lower House has been dominated by different interest groups which have battled with each other (and continue to do so) for control over resources. One can readily think of agrarian and industrial interests vying for a greater share of resources. Neither has been interested in transforming society or imbued with a compelling desire to establish a more just socio-economic order. The disconcerting truth is that ballot-box democracy – its virtues are not meant to be denied – is no guarantee that the voice of the oppressed is effectively heard.

It is interesting that the Constitution in its original form did not contain an enabling provision for reservation in education. It was the First Amendment which brought it in the wake of the judgment of the Madras High Court in Champakam Dorairajan's case, a judgment affirmed by the Supreme Court. While reservation in service under the State was always contemplated under Art. 16(4), the enabling provision in Art. 15(4) was a later addition. Further, the power which these two provisions have acquired over the years is mainly because of pressure exercised by potential beneficiaries who have been able to utilise these clauses and influence public policy. No matter how much controversy surrounds positive discrimination they cannot be removed from the agenda. The inference, therefore, is clear that even the most eloquent of constitutional safeguards become meaningful and effective only when there is a strong pressure group urging its implementation. In passing it is prudent to note that the benefit of protective/positive discrimination has not yet percolated to those who need it the most. This results partly from the uncomfortable reality that there is a visible element of 'class' among all section of the population. An extreme position on this would be to argue that unless the most oppressed have awareness enough to feel discontented they are unlikely to reach out and claim what is their due. In this sense the Constitution, indeed any law, can only provide us with a legal sanction with which to legitimise our claims. This is important, even essential but it would be a folly to assume that this is all that is required.

Viewing the Constitution as an expression of our most cherished ideals there are other questions which need to be confronted. The Preamble (as amended) declares that India shall be a sovereign, socialist, secular, democratic republic. It is no easy matter to define what a socialist society should possess to qualify as one. Particularly this is true of India where our conception of a socialist society has always had considerable ambiguity. In spite of the Preamble being specific that ours is a socialist republic we are now engaged in a series of policies aimed at making our economy market-friendly and at slowly divesting the State of some of its major responsibilities. Assuming a continuation of the present trends it might become fanciful to call ourselves and socialist republic. Yet it would be equally fanciful to imagine that 'socialist' will be deleted from the Preamble.

Another example of the dichotomous relationship between the Constitution and reality was recently mentioned by a former Chief Justice of India, E.S. Venkataramaiah. Art. 47 says inner alia, that the 'State shall endeavour to bring about prohibition of the consumption except for medicinal purposes of intoxicating drinks and of drugs which are injurious to health'. This explicit statement has not prevented state governments from taking over the responsibility of liquor trade.

A cynical conclusion could be that the more idealistic parts of the Constitution such as the Preamble and the Directive Principles are no more than expressions of pious intent which, having been articulated, can be quietly forgotten. It is more realistic to argue that this visible lack of consonance between word and deed is basically the result of our own ambiguous positions on basic issues. Discerning students of India's economic development and planning have for long noticed our unsettled stance on basic issues. It is not irrelevant to point out that India's present drive towards liberalisation is not as sudden and dramatic as it is made out to be. Some ambivalence regarding how planned the economy should be was always inherent in our approach.

It is these examples of ambivalence and the disjunction between constitutional precept and policy prescription which raise doubts about the role which the Constitution can play in furthering justice. This is best explained with reference to the three kinds of instruments which the Constitution makes available in the sphere of policy. These are prohibitionary, permissive and promotional. Article 17, which abolishes untouchability and makes its practice in any form an offence, is an example of a prohibitionary instrument. So are Article 23 and 24 which prohibit respectively traffic in human beings and forced labour and employment of children in factories. No right (especially Art. 19) is conceivable as an untrammelled right. Everyone of them can be scaled or read down through reasonable restrictions. The right to property is no longer a fundamental right but it is still a right. In this broad sense most of the rights are permissive in nature. For instance Art. 19(1) (g) confers upon citizens the right "to practise any profession or to carry on any occupation, trade or business". Not only is this subject to 'reasonable restrictions' it does not give the state unrestricted power to prevent wholesale trades/professions unless the test of reasonableness is satisfied. It does, however, give the State the power of regulation. Then there are the promotional parts of the Constitution which are, in the main, contained in Part IV under the Directive Principles. These ought to be read along with the Preamble.

It would appear that the prohibitory parts are least open to dispute. The language is specific and unequivocal. Any vidation is declared by the Constitution to be an offence. Hence the vidation attracts punishment. Arts. 17 and 23 are excellent examples. The same rigour and clarity are absent, by comparison, when was read Art. 24. This Article prohibits employment of children below fourteen "in any factory or mine or engaged in any other hazardous employment". But it does not declare violation an offence. One is entitled to wonder why Arts. 23 and 24 both of which deal with degrading phenomena are couched in perceptibly different language. Did the Constitution-makers envisage the horrendous difficulty of enforcing the ban on child labour in an economy where the existing order compels children to add to family income? If so, their gloom has been vindicated by events.

Despite the lack of equivocation the prohibitory parts – and these include Arts. 14, 15 and 16, the later two toned down by clause (4) in both cases – have a mixed record in terms of implementation. Untouchability is still alive on the social agenda. Child labour is rampant. Where does one locate the lacuna? It is surely not in the language or the intent of the Constitution. If this is the fate of explicitly worded prohibitory Articles what can we expect of those which are susceptible of plural or multiple interpretations.

The promotional aspect suffers from fundamental problems. By their very nature they cannot but be expressed in language which is hesitant and tentative, Arts. 41 and 42 provide ample proof. The former start with an apologetic qualifying clause "the state, shall, within the limits of its economic capacity and development make effective provision for securing the right to work". Who is to determine these 'limits' and how? Obviously the ruling classes can and do. There are collective rights which must appeal to the vast majority in our society. Not only are they not enforceable but they are founded in circumstantial logic. A polity and a ruling group different from what we might have construed these 'limits' in distinctly diverse ways.

In other words while the prohibitory portions deal with absolutes the permissive and promotional aspects cannot. Much if not everything depends upon who is to arbitrate on the ripeness of the time or the circumstances to implement, even to take the first steps towards attainment of the promotional aspects. Basically what a society regards as desirable varies with time. Few of our preferences are immutable and, therefore, the degree to which a document like the Constitution which embodies the basic values of a society can remain fixed is a moot point. Nowhere is this more true than in that highly complex sphere called social justice. What we are witnessing today is an expression of the discontent and frustration of huge sections who feel, often rightly, deprivation stretching back almost endlessly in time. Of course the issue is politicised by those whose survival in power is contingent on the availability of incendiary material. But that apart there is still the conundrum: how does a society expect the present to make amends for the past? Expiation for social or group sins while being admirable ethically and morally, is not easy to practise when the individual perceives a threat to his/her personal welfare. Add to this the fact that the positions of the different class/caste groups are not fixed but are changing in a kaleidoscopic fashion, and we have a veritable cauldron in front of us. How reasonable is it to expect any Constitution to be able to have the resilience to adapt to these changes?

Social justice, the focal point of this seminar, hinges on collective rights. It has to do with those attainments which are central to development. Put briefly development should result in the continuous absorption of the marginalised peoples into the mainstream. Those currently without a stake ought to acquire one if development is to have any meaning. Development deals with the erosion of deprivation and want. It can be achieved only when there is broad agreement on its central focus. So long as that eludes us so too will a consensus on social justice. And so too will a meaningful agreement on ideas as to how to reach that goal. Ultimately it is the prevailing and changing social, political and economic order that determine the answers. And let us not forget that in today's world we are influenced by global developments much more than we dare admit.

Social Activism and State Process

B.K. ROY BURMAN

The concept of social justice is not sui generis; it is contextual. Similarly the implication of social activism and the pattern of State process are historical-ecology specific.

In the 19th century in the context of colonialism, the issues of social justice in India were a complex mix. First was the demand of the social elite for social justice in elite level social relations and also in the realms of political, administrative and economic powers from which they were being dispossessed. Second was the rising but hesitant expectation of social justice of the suppressed masses of the centuries who found a chance for themselves in the context of weakening of grip of the indigenous elites as a sequel to the advent of the colonial rule.

The first type of claim to social justice drew mainly upon the postulates of Western liberalism. The second type of low-key assertion of social justice took two forms in the 19th century – one was espoused by persons like Phule. It was related to the symbols of dignity in the traditional socio-cultural setting. The other aimed at access to levers of power in the colonial administrative setting. Recruitment of lowly castes in the army, along with other factors facilitated the second process. Besides, with the emergence of the indigenous elites as competitors to colonial rulers, there was a natural tendency among a section of the latter to support the rising claims and action for justice of the unprivileged of the Indian society.

In the first two decades of the 20th century the contradiction of the two types of claims to social justice: one oriented primarily against colonial rule, the other oriented primarily against the caste-class combined elites of the Indian society became accentuated.

Gandhi, with his basically anarchist-syndicalist political approach to the State apparatus and a synthesis of Western liberalism and Indian communitarianism in the state process tried to resolve the contradiction, but did not succeed much. Nehru could catch the imagination of a forward-looking Indian elite by trying to bring about a synthesis of Western liberalism and Indian pluralism in the State apparatus and Western liberalism and pragmatic egalitarianism in the State process.

The assertion of the endogenously suppressed and deprived sections of Indian society also took several twists and turns. One was the rejection of the ideology of inequality, while many of the practices particularly in the realm of rituals continued (though divested of the inegalitarian ideology and the symbols that go with the same). Sri Narayan Dharma Paripalan Yogana of the Ezhavas represented this trend. A variant of the same with a primarily political focus was the self-respect movement nurtured by Periyar Ramaswamy Naicker in Tamil Nadu. The other was adoption of the idiom of Western liberalism and struggle to orient the State apparatus accordingly, and at the same time insisting on the incorporation of tenets of egalitarianism in the social process. By and large Ambedkar represented this stand.

Not only the elite leadership who were at the helm of the struggle for political freedom from the clutches of the British, but even those who were seriously committed to Gandhi's communitarian synthesis, with an egalitarian holistic ethos, failed to touch the right chord in the minds of the dalits of both the strands. The dalits wanted the colonial rulers not to transfer power to the elite section of the Indian society without setting the issues of social justice. This provided an opportunity to their detractors to project them as collaborators of colonialism. As a result they could not broaden their operational base, though the spectrum of social interest represented by them was much wider than that represented by the elite leadership.

The colonial rulers undoubtedly tried to take advantage of the contradictions within Indian society, but after the second world war when they found that the cost of retaining colonial domination was becoming much higher than the gain out of it, they had to move for transfer of power. The class character of the colonial state made it a logical imperative to transfer power to the section of Indian leadership which could protect the same class interest in the global framework; at the same time the pattern of mobilisation of social forces within the country made it necessary to have a special mention of protection of the interests of the Scheduled Castes as an inherent condition in the new dispensation. The Transfer of Power Act adopted by the British Parliament incorporated this concern.

An examination of the debates in the Constituent Assembly

shows that a powerful section of the elites of the society interpreted social justice in terms of the parameters embedded in Western liberalism; there were others who were pragmatic enough to realise that unless social justice in terms of satisfaction of the expectations and aspirations of the dalits and other disadvantaged sections of the Indian society was projected in the politico-social horizon of the new State, the State process would have to constantly pass through hazardous shoals. Though this section of the leadership concealed its pragmatism in idealistic rhetoric, it is difficult to say that it could transcend its social roots. The alternative was the anarcho-syndicalist frame of Gandhi, which envisaged minimal state and maximal communitarian management. Obviously the anarcho-syndicalist frame of Gandhi could not be expected to be custodian of the class interest of the colonial rulers who were ready to give up political control but not economic privileges. More importantly the communitarian process envisaged by Gandhi did not inspire the confidence of the dalits and many other disadvantaged section of the population as the dimensions and strategy of transvaluation of the inegalitarian values informing the communitarian process was not adequately spelt out publicly by Gandhi and those close to him. It now transpires that in the mid-40s Gandhi himself recognised the need of sharply focussing on transvaluation of values and of the strategy of spelling out the same, but he was prevented by his "Gandhian" followers from doing so.

The compromise between pragmatism and idealism is reflected in the fundamental Rights and Directive Principles of the State Policy respectively as enshrined in the Constitution. Nehru made it clear during the debate in the Lok Sabha on the first amendment of the Constitution. Here it is important to note that the amendment had to be brought about to overcome the conservative stance taken by the judiciary to protect the elite interest by invoking the principle of social justice as envisaged in Western liberalism.

Judicial pronouncements along with legislative enactments and functions of the bureaucracy constitute three crucial dimensions of the state process. Though political pragmatism tried to overcome judicial conservatism through legislation, the grass-root mobilisation in favour of long range political pragmatism was not strong enough. In this context two processes gradually crystallised along the axis of long range political pragmatism and two other processes as counter-force of the above two processes got entrenched along the axis of functioning of bureaucratic apparatus and short range political manipulators. Along the axis of long range political pragmatism one was the attempt of Sri Jayaprakash Narayan to impart some amount of non-violent militancy in the anarcho-syndicalist platform with greater emphasis on egalitarianism. The other was the advocacy of Rammanohar Lohia in favour of non-violent militancy of the disadvantaged sections in every sphere of social injustice to capture the State apparatus. But both failed to educate the people at large about the implication of their respective strategies. The ruling party tried to meet the challenge through ideological rhetoric and symbolic action without serious attempt to change the State process, which would have required wholesale restructuring the Constitution. The stalemate thus created, helped the bureaucracy to covertly convert the State process to serve its own interest. So long as its own interest was served the bureaucracy would allow short-range political manipulators to settle score among themselves through a criminal nexus.

A situation has been reached today when restructuring of the Constitution of India, will not by itself ensure social justice. The world-system, marked by global hegemonic control of economic and even political processes, has rendered isolated state action considerably ineffective even to meet the internal social-political processes of the States. To break the grip of hegemonies in the world system, informed social activism in every sphere of life has become indispensable. But in such social activism, one must differentiate between actions of sponsored N.G.Os and of community-rooted voluntarism. One may entrench dependency even on world hegemonic forces; the other may trigger a chain action leading to liberation. It is only in the context of informed social activism that constitutional changes may ensure social justice. But such complimentary role of State will challenge not only the character, but also the Western paradigm of the State as an institution. Perhaps then, through quirks of history Gandhi will be resurrected inspite of the obscurantist projection of him by the 'priests' of Gandhism.

The Bulwark of Social Justice

R.C. VYAS

The quest for justice has been as challenging as illusory. The mastermind analysis of Aristotle (384-322 B.C.) still serves as a model into which the most modern analysts attempt to find solution of the modern problems of the current times in the hope that an acceptable brew will emerge. He provides an excellent starting point to comprehend such concepts as "particular justice" and "universal justice" and their species "distributive" and "corrective" justice. The concept of distributive justice is that among equals, there has to be equal justice whereas the latter seeks to restore equality when this has been disturbed by wrong doing. All attempts to provide a comprehensive definition of justice have been futile since the concept of justice has meant different things to different persons at different times. It cannot be conceived of in isolation. Politico-legal, socio-cultural, economic and religious ethos of a particular period provides different contents and approaches to the study of law and social justice. Ancient Hindu Law prescribed norms of social conduct as revealed in Vedic texts and Shastras. Its observance was mandatory and equated with Dharma, on the part of king as well as the subject to follow these edicts, regulating their conduct. In our Shastras justice is equated with Dharma. Dharma of a person is to exhibit respect for life, love, compassion in dealing with fellow beings.[1]

In the ordinary usage "justice" is in fact connected to "law" in a double way. In some contexts "justice" is a synonym of "law" or the legal process: "penal justice", for example, may mean "penal law". In such cases the word "justice" is homonymic, covering both law and justice. The two terms do occur in legal contexts, and even in privileged propositions of the law field. Statutes and Constitutions contain the expression "just" in some field or senses and such usages, and judicial exegesis upon them may be illuminating.[2] It may be a psychological truth, that men best recognise justice by the absence of it, justice can still only be conceived as a value which men affirmatively seek. Justice is an ethical value, a value by which men judge the conduct of reasonable beings that is, behaviour directed by will of the actor. The adjunctive "just" may be found to characterise either the actor or the conduct or both. The main Aristotelian position is that justice is a social value; that is it pertains to a conduct which takes place in the context of inter-personal relations.[3]

The role of law in a modern industrial society is "social solidarity". The sine qua non of such an industrial society and economic organisation is the unbroken carrying on of all the functions involved by human beings to whom they are respectively assigned. Leon Dugit demolished the entire system of private law, substituting for individual rights, the protection of social functions. He declared that acts done in violation of "social solidarity" cause social disorder and a spontaneous, almost a reflex, movement towards readjustment. Under this law the individual had, not rights, but only functions dictated by social solidarity to which he is held, and in which he is protected. Dugit's philosophical and juristic ideas reflect ancient Indian socio-political philosophy in which emphasis was on "duties" rather than "rights". It also corresponds to Gandhian political philosophy of ownership of property as "trustees".[4]

In the ancient Indian political tradition there was no conceptual formation of rights against some body or the rights versus duties. First, the concept of right could not develop because of the formidable institution of the joint family, the caste and the village community. Secondly, the absence of a concept of rights at that time was due to the non-interference of the State in matters personal, including religion. In such a politico-social organisation the individual could scarcely find enough avenues for the development of his personality. The greatest stumbling block in his way to progress was the rigid caste system. It was considered as divinely ordained, hence there was no alternative for the individual but to submit to its bans and taboos and accept the status and functions assigned to him by the divine created caste system. The status of a man born into a particular caste was determined by the rank of that caste in the social hierarchy. Once born in that caste his status was fixed and unalterable. The vocation of a person was determined by the caste into which he was born. The untouchables who occupied the lowest position in the caste ridden Hindu society were debarred from the right of using the public wells and tanks. They were denied the right to temple entry and were prohibited from indulging in any intellectual or spiritual pursuits. The caste system amounted to negation of equality. It was an organisation of inequality based on inheritance, and therefore, it prevented the emergence of such concepts as social justice and individual rights.

With the authority of the village community and the joint family represented by the rigours of the caste system demanding complete allegiance from the members the individual, initiative was completely stultified. In these circumstances the concept of individual rights was practically absent. However, the most decisive factor was the latitude given by the State to the individual in matters of religion. There being no State- controlled church, the individual was free to found or follow any religion or sect he liked. In the west this sort of religious freedom did not exist; heretics were not tolerated and were ruthlessly stamped out; and the individual was made to conform to the tenets of the organised church. The spirit of religious intolerance being unknown in ancient India the people did not suffer any disability on account of their religious beliefs. The rules of caste were likewise never enforced by the State. In these circumstances people did not think in terms of rights and social justice.[5]

In this period of millennium in ancient India, more thought was applied to the conceptual formulation of duties than that of rights. It implies respect for the rights of others both in positive and negative forms. In Mahabharata this concept has been expressed by Bhishma Pitamah in these words, "This is the sum of duty; do naught to others which if done to thee, would cause thee pain". He further says, "What one loves for himself, one must love for others also."[6] This principle receives further elucidation and extention in Upanishadic maxim applied to the possesion and enjoyment of wordly goods which says that the real ownership of the estate of the world inheres in the Divine Being. We are allowed to use the world and its goods but we should never forget that we hold whatever we have in trust for others. Bhishma-Pitamah further elaborated the principle thus, "with the surplus wealth which one may happen to own, one must relieve the want of the indigent." It was thought that if everybody is discharging his duties, the rights of all the members of the community would be safe and there would be no need for the state to make use of its coercive authority to safeguard the rights of its citizens. Thus the rights of individual living in ancient India are to be deduced from the list of duties that they were required to perform. These duties were all pervasive. They covered every sphere of life, family clan, caste, village and religion and their observance was regarded obligatory for all the members of the society including the king. It is a welcome augury that "Fundamental Duties" are constitutionalised obligations. However, those need to be more vigorous and activist implementation.

In medieval India, the advent of Islam did not introduce any fundamental change in the socio-economic structure of the country. The only change which it initiated was the creation of antagonism between the rulers and the ruled on the ground of religion. This resulted in second class citizenship for non-Muslims and consequent curtailment of many of their traditional customs, rights and privileges. Every class of citizen was required to make compulsory contributions to the coffers of the rulers. In this period there was no such thing as property right and in its absence a general concept of rights could not develop.

Inspite of the democratic professions of Islam, Muslim kings in medieval India had a tendency towards arbitrariness. The only limitation upon the absolute power of the king was that he should conform his actions to "some verse of Koran" and always keep the "real benefit" of the people before him. However, the gulf between theory and practice is so wide that any attempt to trace the roots of the medieval Indian Muslim kingship in Islamic theory would be a futile adventure. The tenets of Islamic kingship were violated even by an orthodox and devout Muslim king like Aurangzeb. It is evident that during this period as well essential conditions which give rise to the consciousness of rights and social justice were lacking.

The concept of rights developed as a direct result of the impact of the Western political thought on Indian leaders. Among the Western thinkers Laski occupies an important place because in his political philosophy there is an effort to bring about a reconciliation between liberalism and socialism. Laski has given a concept of rights which is functional rather than individualistic. He says, "My rights are built always upon the relation my function has to the well-being of society". Therefore, we do not possess rights "as avenues of personal enjoyment". Further, "By a functional theory of rights is meant that we are given powers that we may so act as to add to the richness of our social heritage. We have rights, not that we may receive, but we may do". Thus rights are correlative with function, and though their content varies with changes in time and place, the general test of rights is their utility to all the members of the State.[7]

Laski strikes a balance between the mutual claims of the State and the individual. According to him in the long run, "the welfare of the community is built upon the happiness of the individual".[8] As such, nobody can have a right against public welfare, for that is tantamount to having rights against one's own good. Laski also regarded harmonization of "liberty" and "equality" the indespensible condition for maintaining a system of rights within the State. On these premises, Laski has given the first place to the "right to work" in a rationally organised system in which an individual should have the right to live only by the sweat on his toil. Besides the "right to work" the citizen should also be guaranteed "the right to an adequate wage for his labour."[9] In order to prevent the "ownership of capital from degenerating into dictatorship",[10] it is essential that the citizens should have the right to participate in the management of industry. The other important right is the right to education, necessary to enable a person to perform consciously the duties of a citizen.

The socialist concept of rights is based on two major premises. First, surrender of individual liberty to permit any individual to exploit anybody. In a socialist society, the people belonging to the dispossesed class are not exploited and therefore they cannot have any real grievance against the State. They are offered the same chance of working for and profiting by the common good as anybody else. The socialist State uses its coercive authority only when they undermine the foundations of the established order. It is pointed out that "the exercise of political freedom cannot be tolerated up to a point where it menaces the foundations of society."[11] Second is the right to equality. The equality of citizens "lies in their equal relation to public property."[12] The socialists hold that equality can be meaningful only if people enjoy equal status in society. It implies that means of production should be equally accessible to all and everybody should have "an equal right to payment for their work in accordance with its quantity and quality".[13]

Thus in a liberal state the individual enjoys certain negative freedoms which imply his protection from certain encroachments on his rights. Socialism, on the other hand goes a step further and enlarges the area of freedom by adding positive rights. These rights are the right to work, right to education, right to living wage, right to human conditions of work, workers participation in the management of industries, and the promotion of education and economic interests of Scheduled Castes, Scheduled Tribes and other weaker sections of society. These rights constitute what Aristotle called "the good life" whose "extent" is limited only to such goods as can be shared, i.e. which all can enjoy without excluding others; its guarantee is the final removal of social privilege based on private ownership the means of life."[14]

The concept of rights hitherto in ancient and medieval India was that these were gifts of the ruler. In the liberal extremist tradition, leaders like Tilak and Pal did not subscribe to this view. They believed in the equal rights of all, irrespective of fact that one was a "prince or a peasant, Brahman or Pariah, man or woman, Hindu or Mohammedan, Buddhist or Christian, rich or poor, ignorant or learned."[15] Tilak said, "Freedom is the very life of individual soul which vedanta declares to be not separate from God, but identical with him. This freedom was a principle that could never perish." It follows that all men were essentially equal. In a speech at the First Depressed Classes Conference at Bombay, Tilak said, "If a God were to tolerate untouchability, I would not recognise God at all."[16]

The national movement for freedom and emancipation of downtrodden and toiling millions gathered momentum after 1918. Gandhian political philosophy believed that ". . . the right to perform one's duties is the only right that is worth living for and dying for. It covers all legitimate rights." He held the view that the rights were created by the individual himself as he developed the fitness for the rights in his pursuit of truth and non-violence. Individual had rights for the well-being of society. Gandhi was not in favour of dispossessing the rich because he thought that by doing so, "society will be poorer, for it will lose the gifts of a man who knows how to accumulate wealth". He suggested that owners of property should work as "trustees" of the people for the wealth they possess. He was a great champion of the principle of equality and fought for the eradication of untouchability, evil of caste system and the uplift of the women folk.

In the beginning of the twentieth century the socialist ideology dominated the political scene. It was mainly due to the success of socialist revolution in Russia, Nehru saw in socialism the only panacea for the ills of suffering humanity. Nehru stated, "I am convinced that the only key to the solution of the world's problems lies in socialism, and when I use this word I do it not in a vague humanitarian way but in the scientific economic sense. Socialism is, however, something even more than an economic doctrine; it is a philosophy of life. . . I see no way of ending the poverty, the vast unemployment, the degradation and the subjection of the Indian people except through socialism. This involves . . . ending of vested interests in land and industry as well as the feudal and autocratic Indian states system." Socialism as a concept found place in the manifestos of various political parties declaring that the "party stands for social justice viz., the elimination of all vested interests which are instruments of exploitation in lands, factories and mines and aim at reconstruction of India's national life on socialist basis, making the toilers in fields and factories the masters of the means of production."[17]

The demand for inclusion of fundamental rights in the constitutional setup for India was first made by nationalist leaders after the Montford Declaration, 1918, that the progressive realisation of the self-government was the ultimate objective of the His Majesty's Government. In pursuance the Nehru Committee in its Report demanded a Declaration of Rights in the future Constitution of India. The Indian National Congress at its Karachi Session in 1931 for the first time in its resolution drew up a comprehensive scheme not only of the fundamental rights and duties, but also of economic re-organisation which could ensure "social justice" to workers and peasants. The Preamble of the charter declared: "In order to end the exploitation of the masses, political freedom must include real economic freedom of the starving millions."[18]

In terms of Cabinet Mission Plan, 1946, the Constituent Assembly was elected to frame a Constitution for independent India. A cross section of Indian intellectuals were enabled by the Indian National Congress to be elected to the Assembly. The Congress was never ideologically a homogenous party and hence it was natural that persons elected on the Congress ticket had different visions on fundamental issues. However, no country in the world could boast of having so many intellectuals at a time, on a common platform for a common cause. There were distinguished lawyers like Sir Alladi Krishnaswamy Ayer, "a distinguished jurist whose complete mastery of the constitutions of the world was a great asset to the members," retired judges like Bakshi Tek Chand and P.K. Sen, retired civil servants like Sir N. Gopalswami Ayyangar, and H.V. Kamath, retired teachers like Dr. H.C. Mukherjee, Dr. S. Radhakrishnan and Professor K.T. Shah, and moderates like H.N. Kunzru. In the Congress Party, persons like Sardar Patel, K.M. Munshi, Pandit Nehru made significant contribution in framing the Constitution. Dr. B.R. Ambedkar, as Chairman of the Drafting Committee, proved his genius as an eminent constitutionalist and modern law giver. In the words of Pandit Nehru, Dr. Ambedkar was, "a champion of the oppressed and the suppressed".

A sub-committee under the chairmanship of Sardar Patel was appointed to advise the Constituent Assembly about the rights which ought to be included in the constitution. The sub-committee decided that a difference should be made in the list of fundamental rights, between justiciable rights and non-justiciable rights. Sir Alladi Krishnaswami Ayer submitted a note on the nature of these two rights. Moderate leaders like Hriday Nath Kunzru held the view that it was difficult to make a fine distinction between justiciable and non-justiciable rights.[19] Promotha Ranjan Thakur lamented that due place was not given to economic rights in the list of fundamental rights. He pleaded for the nationalisation of mines, key industries and basic industries.[20] Som Nath Lahari, the lone communist member, expressed the view that it was arbitrary to make distinction between what are justiciable rights and what are economic and social rights.[21] R.K. Sidhwa stated that the "non-justiciable rights are merely to adorn the pages of the constitution and to give just a little consolation, but I would prefer them to be a part and parcel of the constitution so that every citizen may be proud to state, now my time has come to enjoy equality and wealth so that I may not remain poor for all time."[22] Similarly Bishwanath Das expressed dissatisfaction with the interpretation of the function of the government as justiciable and nonjusticiable. In his opinion it was "the primary duty of the government to remove hunger and to secure social security."[23] The absence of economic rights led V.D. Tripathi to declare that "except for the right to vote, the poor man has not yet got any other right under the Constitution."[24] The other important point related to the existing evil of caste system. Pramotha Ranjan Thakur stated, "I do not understand how you can abolish untouchability without abolishing the caste system."[25]

Sardar Patel thus stated in the Constituent Assembly:

> There are two schools of thought in the committee and there was a large number of very eminent lawyers who could scrutinise every words of every sentence . . . These two schools viewed the matter from two angles. One school considered as advisable to include as many rights as possible in the Report – rights which could straightway be enforced in a court of law. . . The other schools of thought considered it advisable to restrict fundamental rights to a few very essential things that may be considered fundamental.

Thus, rights relating to social justice such as citizen's right to work and employment, education, maintenance in old age, sickness or loss of capacity to work, living wage for workers, their participation in management, uniform civil code for the citizens were made non-justiciable while the rights related to equality, life and personal liberty and property were declared justiciable.

From the general tone of the discussion it seems that the Founding Fathers of the Constitution were overwhelmed with the abnormal conditions created by communal elements in the wake of partition and independence of the country and hence they thought it desirable that the rights of the citizens should be subject to reasonable and adequate restrictions. They could not be expected to draw a scheme of rights on the basis of the theory of natural rights. The framers were also conscious of the fact that the individualistic setting which had given birth to American Bill of Rights had gone for ever and that it had given place to a new era of the welfare state. They at the same time thought that the State in India was not yet in a position to assume the responsibilities of guaranteeing employment or education to all its citizens. They, therefore, divided the rights into two categories viz., justiciable and non-justiciable. They were also anxious to provide some safeguards against the rapacious greed of the people occupying a higher position in the social hierarchy, hence the inclusion of "Right against Exploitation" as a Fundamental Right. They were in fact not guided by any political philosophy or idealism – rather by pragmatic and down to earth considerations. Professor Jennings has rightly observed that "possibly the draftsmen had no clear theory in mind".

The Preamble to the Indian Constitution crystalise the concept of "social justice". It enumerates the objectives and the socio-economic goals for the achievement of which the Constitution has been established. The people of India have given unto themselves a Sovereign, Socialist, Secular, Democratic Constitution and to secure to all its citizens, justice, social, economic and political; Liberty of thought, expression, belief, faith and worship; Equality of status and opportunity; and to promote among them all; Fraternity assuring the dignity of the individual and the unity and integrity of the Nation. The ethos of "social justice" found its expression from the slogans of "Liberty, Equality and Fratenity" in the French Revolution into Dicey's Rule of Law and the American War of Independence. The echo of these words finds a place of pride, passion and power in Articles 38 and 39 of the Indian Constitution. "Social justice" provides a balancing force in the dilemma presented in the two conflicting view points relating to "social interest" and "individual interest". It represents the former as against the later. The dilemma, however, is not laid to rest, it has presented itself before the Supreme Court in one form or the other ever since the Constitution came into force.

Article 38 provides: "(1) The State shall strive to promote the welfare of the people by securing and protecting as effectively as it may a social order in which justice, social, economic and political, shall inform all the institutions of the national life."[26]

Article 39 provides for certain principles of policy as set out in clauses (a) to (f), to be followed by the State in order to secure "social justice" in specific situations.[27]

Article 39A provides for Equal and free legal aid. Article 40 provides for villages panchayats and Article 41 provides for Right to work and education.[28]

Professor C.K. Allan is of the view that the term "social justice" is not capable of precision. It connotes several meanings such as "equal opportunity" or "distribution or redistriction of wealth".[29] According to Julius Stone, the implications of "social justice" remain dubious. To talk about "justice" at all implies a community context or a community frame of criteria, or what we ourselves have termed a "justice constituency".[30] Friedrich thinks "that justice and injustice cannot be related to any one value, be it equality or any other, but only to the complex value system of a man, a community, or mankind".[31]

In view of Gajendragadkar, former Chief Justice of the

Supreme Court, the concept of "social justice" has dual objectives of "removing all inequalities and affording equal opportunities and "economic activities" to all the citizens. He thus combines both "social justice" and "economic justice". He accords primacy to social justice over individual freedom. A harmonious blending of justice and liberty is the corollary of social justice. The objective of a social welfare state can only be attained through "social justice."[32] In a social justice order every member is a "useful, participating, sensitive, discrete being".[33] Directives, states Dr. Gajendragadkar, "lay down a policy of action for the different State Governments, and in a sense, they embody and recognize the validity of the charter of demands which the weaker sections of the citizens suffering from socio-economic justice would present of the respective Governments for immediate relief."[34]

Justice Krishna Iyer's constitutional philosophy of socialism agrees with Karl Marx, Leon Dugit, H.J. Laski, Mahatma Gandhi and Jawaharlal Nehru. His unflinching faith that entire resources of the community, be those natural or human and their distribution, each getting according to his need, is social justice in its productive and distributive facets. He has expressed the concept of "Social Justice" in these words:

> Social justice is a generous concept which assures to every member of the society a fair deal. Any remedial injury, injustice, inadequacy or disability suffered by a member, for which he is not directly responsible falls within the liberal connotation of social injustice.

Social justice covers "right to life" and begins with a child in the mother's womb and spreads to all the basic, material, cultural and spiritual requirements of a human being. Justice Iyer visualises in social justice a divine flame which has a potential to bloom into a creative genius. His concept of justice is based not only on the noble sentiments expressed in the Preamble but certain other provisions of the Constitution such as Article 39.[35] In his view, "the socio-economic emancipation of India truely comes through a joint enterprise of law and politics endeavouring to equalise, homogenise and integrate the Dalit proletariat, animated by social mission".

Gandhiji was also of the view that in a country where starvation and unemployment was a common sight, freedom could have no real meaning.[36]

Prembular dictates and provisions of Directive Principles of State Policy clearly ordain and prescribe social justice as the ultimate constitutional commitment.

The Constitution sets out two categories of rights. These are justiciable and non-justiciable. The former are Fundamental Rights whereas the later are named Directive Principles of State Policy. The ideas in the Directives are borrowed from the Irish Constitution of 1937 which contains similar provisions. The Directives are fundamental to the governance of the country and spells out a social order in which justice, social, political and economic, shall inform all the institutions of national life. As stated by Justice Krishna Iyer, "Our national mind should not be split on this goal. If there is broad consensus of this, the demanding tasks of the day are dynamic legislative action, purposeful judicial reform and sensitive administrative streamlining so as to transform our conditions of socio-economic life and other values."[37] To Dr. Ambedkar, Directives were like the "Instruments of Instructions".[38] In Constituent Assembly Debates Directives were also hailed as the essence of the Constitution and also as most cardinal, important and creative provision.[39]

In the view of Pandit Nehru:

> The Directive Principles of State Policy represented a dynamic move towards a certain objective . The Fundamental Rights represented rights which exist. Both are right. But somehow and some time it might so happen that the dynamic movement and that a static standstill do not quite fit into each other. A dynamic movement towards a certain objective necessarily means certain changes taking place that is the essence of movement.[40]

Granville Austin considers these directives as aimed at furthering the goals of social revolution, "by establishing these positive obligations of the State, the members of the Constituent Assembly made it the responsibility of future Indian Governments to find a middle way between individual liberty and the public good . . . between preserving the privileges of the few and bestowing benefits on the many in order to liberate the powers of all men equally, for constructions to the common good."[41]

It is, however, a "judicial penury" that our Supreme Court in the initial stages interpreted the Chapter of Fundamental Rights provided in Part III, as sacrosanct and not liable to be abridged by any legislative act or order and that the Directive Principles of State Policy have to conform to and run as subsidiary to Fundamental Rights.[42] But nowhere in the Constitution it is provided that the Directives are subsidiary and that the courts could give more weight to Fundamental Rights than the Directives. It is tragic and unfortunate that the Court should have given this opinion.[43] The Supreme Court had retrieved its position in subsequent cases by taking cognizance of the Directive Principles. Thus, relying on Art. 39(b), held that certain zamindari abolition laws had been passed for "public purpose" and that the State control or ownership over land was a necessary preliminary step towards the implementation of the Directive Principles,"[44] under Article 47, the State Government was under a duty, to take steps for raising the level of nutrition and standard of living of the people, prohibit the slaughter of cows etc.;[45] Orissa High Court held that, "Any piece of legislation which implements Directive Principles . . . would prima facie be reasonable unless it could further be shown that there was arbitrary or excessive invasion of the Fundamental Right to Property;[46] The Allahabad High Court held that fixation of minimum rates of wages was a reasonable restriction and that the Directive Principles embodied in Article 43, justified restrictions upon freedom of contract by fixation of minimum rates of wages.[47] The Supreme Court seems to have taken a somewhat inverse view in the Hanif Qureshi case[48] and in the Kerala Education Bill Case.[49] In the later case clause 20 of the Kerala Education Bill prohibited collection of any tution fee from students in primary classes. It was contended that the said clause violates the right of minorities to establish and administer educational institutions of their choice guaranteed by Article 30. The State on the other hand maintained that the Bill sought to implement the Directive Principles embodied in Article 45 which enjoined on the State to provide free and compulsory education for all children below the age of fourteen years, S.R. Das, CJ. applied the doctrine of harmonious construction in permitting the State to implement directive principles in such a way that its laws do not take away or abridge the Fundamental Rights.[50]

A subtle but positive change is evinced in the attitude of the Supreme Court in Sajjan Singh Vs. State of Rajasthan.[51]

Mudholkar J. stated that Directive Principles "are also fundamental in the governance of the country and provisions of Part III must be interpreted harmoniously with these principles".[52] In Golaknath V. State of Punjab, Subba Rao CJ. observed, "The Fundamental Rights and Directive Principles of State Policy enshrined in the Constitution formed an "integrated scheme" and was elastic enough to respond to the changing needs of the society."[53] The doctrine of integrated scheme propounded in Golaknath rejected the theory of subordination enunciated by the Supreme Court in Champakan Dorairajan and M.H. Qureshi situations. In C.B. Boarding and Lodging V. State of Mysore, Hedge J. dealing with position of Fundamental Rights versus Directive Principles stated that, "Provisions contained in Part III and Part IV . . . are complementary and supplementary to each other. The provisions of Part IV enable legislatures and the government to impose various duties on the citizens. . . . The mandate of the Constitution is to build a welfare society in which justice, social, economic and political shall inform all the institutions of our national life. The hopes and aspirations aroused by the Constitution will be belied if the minimum needs of the lowest of our citizens are not met."[54]

The Parliament being aware that Directive Principles though made complimentary and supplementary to Fundamental Rights are never accorded supremacy over them. In order to rectify this situation Parliament accorded supremacy to Directive Principles. The First Amendment gave primacy in respect of agrarian reforms by inserting article 31A and 31B nullifying Champkam's case by amending Article 15. The Fourth Amendment gave primacy to the laws relating to management of any property by the State or amalgamation of corporations for better management and in the public interest specified in the Article 31A(b) to (e) and to three specified laws relating to land acquisition included in Schedule 9. Article 31 gave supremacy to laws whatever their subject matter, so long as they implemented Directive Principles relating to ownership and distribution of the material resources to subserve the common good and operation of the economic system in a manner which does not result in the concentration of wealth and means of production to the common detriment as prescribed in the Directive Principles contained in Article 39(b) and (c).

Again, the 25th Amendment inserted Article 31C providing that in case of conflict between law enacted in implementing

Directive Principles in Article 39(b) and (c), which provide for management and acquisition of estates and the Fundamental Rights relating to equality before law, rights regarding freedom and right to property, conferred by Articles 14, 19 and 31, the former shall prevail over the latter. (Significantly, the right to property is replaced by the Constitution 44th Amendment Act, 1978 from the list of Fundamental Rights and made an ordinary constitutional right). Article 31C is the beacon light of "social justice". Upholding the greater power to implement the socio-economic programmes, Mathew J. observed, "in building up a just and social order, it is sometimes imperative that the Fundamental Rights should be subordinated to Directive Principles – Economic goals have an uncontestable claim for priority over ideological ones on the ground that excellence comes only after exercise. It is only if men exist that there can be fundamental rights."[55] In view of the learned judge a constitutional amendment giving priority to Directive Principles of State Policy over Fundamental Rights cannot be adjudged as unconstitutional on the ground that the framers of the Constitution intended them to be subsidiary.

Justice Krishna Iyer reminded us of the solemn preambular promise of "social justice," that "under our constitutional system courts are havens of refuge for the toiler, not the exploiter, for the weaker claimant of social justice, not the stronger pretender who seeks to sustain the status quo ante. . . . in the name of Fundamental Rights."[56] He applauded the role of the executive branch of the government in finding a solution to alleviate the miserable lot of rickshaw-pullers and exclaimed in the words of Blaise Pascal, "Justice without power is inefficient; power without justice is tyranny. Justice and power must, therefore, be brought together, so that whatever is just may be powerful, and whatever is powerful may be just".[57] He thus pleaded for blending of "justice and power" in the cause of social justice. Similar sentiments found expression in Nehru's historic tryst with destiny speech wherein he stressed the objective of the new constitution as "ending of poverty and ignorance and disease and inequality of opportunity".[58] Everything that comes in the way will have to be removed, gently if possible, forcibly if necessary.[59] In Bhim Singhji's case, he reiterated his views that part IV which seeks to build a social justice society is basic to our constitutional order and any law in transgression to Article 39(b) and (c), by any statute would not be valid.[60] He exclaims: "The imperatives of equality and development are impatient for implementation and judicial scapegoats must never be offered so that those responsible for stalling economic transformation with a social justice slant may be identified and exposed of. Part IV is a basic goal of the nation and now that the court upholds the urban ceiling law, a social audit of the Executive's implementation a year or two later will bring to light the gaping gap between verbal valour of the statute-book and the executive slumber of law-in-action."[61] Again Chief Justice Chandrachud, in Waman Rao's case confirmed the view that clauses (b) and (c) of Article 39 contain Directive Principles which are vital to the well-being of the country and welfare of its people and it is impossible to conceive that any law passed for the purpose of giving effect to it can at all violate Article 14, 19 or 31.

In a recent judgment the apex court[62] held that a stipulation in Rule 9 of the Corporation to the effect that "the employment of a permanent employee shall be subject to termination on three months notice on either side", with payment of three months basic pay in lieu of notice, is violative of Article 39 (a) and Article 41. The former provides that State shall in particular direct its policy towards "securing that the citizens, men and women, equally have the right to adequate means of livelihood" and the latter requires that the State, within the limits of its economic capacity, and development, is to "make effective provisions for securing the right to work. The court held the view that an adequate means to livelihood cannot be secured to the citizens by taking away without any reason the means of livelihood. The judgment thus lays down that any action of the State which is violative of Directive Principles is unconstitutional.

The Fundamental Rights and Directives Principles have to be balanced and harmonised so that as much possible effect may be given to both the Directives and the Fundamental Rights.[63] In the Olga Tellis Case, "right to livelihood", a Directive Principle is treated as part of the constitutional "right to life". Deprive a person of his right to livelihood and you shall have deprived him of his life.[64] "If there is an obligation upon the State to secure to citizens an adequate means of livelihood and the right to work, it would be sheer pedantry to exclude the right to livelihood from the content of the right to life. The State may not, by affirmative action be compellable to provide adequate means of livelihood or work to the citizens" since the Directive Principle under Article 41 provides that the State shall within the limits of its economic capacity make provision for securing right to work.[65] In Bandhua Mukti Morcha Case, Bhagwati, J. while affirming the proposition that Fundamental Rights must be construed in the light of Directive Principles of State Policy stated: "This right to live with human dignity in Article 21 derives its life breath from the Directives Principles of the State Policy (Articles 39, 41 and 42) and at least, therefore, it must include protection of the strength and health of the workers, men and women, and of the tender age of children against abuse, opportunities and facilities of children to develop in a healthy manner and in conditions of freedom and dignity, educational facilities, just and human conditions of work and maternity relief . . . are the minimum requirements which must exist in order to enable a person to live with human dignity . . .".[66] On the same analogy in the Unnikrishnan Case, the right to education, though a Directive Principle under Art. 41, is held implicit in the right to life and personal liberty secured under Art. 21. Thus in both, the situation of Bandhua Mukti Morcha and Unnikrishnan, the apex court interpreted Fundamental Rights in the light of Directive Principles. It is rightly stated that, "The Directive Principles in Part IV constitute the stairs to climb the high edifice of a socialistic State and the Fundamental Rights are the means through which one could reach the top of the edifice."[67] They are complementary and supplementary to each other.

The Directive Principles of State Policy in Chapter IV of the Constitution are as important as the Fundamental Rights. The directives are the ultimate goals of our "social revolution". Some of them are even more important than the Fundamental Rights. Legislation relating to Panchayati Raj, land ceilings, urban property ceiling, compulsory education for children up to the age of fourteen, free legal aid, living wage for workers have been passed by the legislatures of all the States of our federal polity. In all fairness it sounds like paradoxical perversity to say that the destiny of our Constitution has been determined by our colonial heritage. The fact that the Constitution of India is framed on the structure of Government of India Act, 1935 is perhaps the greatest monument to their drafting skill and constitutional insight. We have while framing our Constitution borrowed ideas from several countries of the world.

It has been amply proved, that Part III (Fundamental Rights) and Part IV (Directive Principles) of our Constitution have been an effective instrument of "social change", through legislative, judicial and political activism. Both embody all the necessary elements of "Social Justice".

There are certain provisions in the Directives Principles of State Policy like adequate means of livelihood, right to work, right to free education up to a certain age, maintenance in old age and sickness may be made part of the Fundamental Rights after making necessary amendment in the Constitution. It is a welcome augury that the Parliament has recently passed the Constitution Seventy Third Amendment Act, making it obligatory for all the States to implement provisions relating to Panchayati Raj. Legislation relating to "free legal aid" has been implemented by all the states of the Union.

The amending process in the Constitution is expedious, simple and at the same time unique. Whenever amendment to the Constitution is deemed necessary by the elected representatives of the people to achieve the goals of "social justice", the Parliament assumes the character of Constituent Assembly and with the required majority, amendment to the Constitution may be effected by elected representatives of the people. Our Parliament has been picturesquely described as a "Constituent Assembly in perpetual session."

The Constitution has provided the country with social, political and economic stability, which may be a matter of pride to any civilized, democratic and freedom loving nation in the world.

According to Justice Krishna Iyer, "The Directive Principles jurisprudence and Fundamental Rights constitutionalism spring from the same spiritual source and finer values and it is false dilemma of exotic legalism to pit one against the other. The confrontational culture must, if we are to survive, reincarnate as a consensus democratic order where the legislature, the judicature and the executive will not enter a boxing ring, punching and bleeding and gnashing but will start an orchestra of harmonious human notes".[68]

Otherwise, he warns: "The imperatives of equality and development are impatient for implementation . . ." and in a rapidly changing society running on the rails of rule of law and operated according to constitutional paradigms, the proprietariate is bound to suffer but the country cannot defer the transformation, because, then, hunger will know no law".[69]

REFERENCES

1. Gobind Das, *Justice in India,* 1967, p. 14.
2. Julius Stone, *Human Law and Human Justice,* 1965.
3. Ibid. p. 30.
4. Ibid. p. 161.
5. D.C. Chaturvedi, Indian Fundamental Rights, 1991, pp. 10-12 .
6. Ibid. pp. 13-22.
7. Ibid.
8. Dugit, *Droit Public,* pp. 278-80
9. Ibid.
10. Ibid.
11. Ibid.
12. Laski, H.J., Theories of Law , 1993.
13. Ibid.
14. Ibid.
15. Ibid.
16. Ibid.
17. Ibid.
18. D.C. Chaturvedi. pp. 5-6 (Ibid.).
19. Ibid. p. 52.
20. Ibid. p. 52.
21. Ibid. p. 52.
22. Ibid. p. 52.
23. Ibid. p. 52.
24. Ibid. p. 52.
25. Ibid. p. 52.
26. Article 38. State to secure social for the promotion of the welfare of the people. Clauses (1) and (2)
27. Article 39. Certain principles of policy to be followed by the State, Clauses (a) to (f).
28. Article 39A. Equal Justice and Free Legal Aid: Article 40. Organisation of Village Panchayat. Article 41. Right to work, education and to public assistance in certain cases.
29. C.K. Allen, *Aspects of Justice,* 1958, p. 31.
30. Julius Stone, *Human Law and Human Justice,* 1968, p. 6.
31. Friedrich, *Philosophy of Law,* p.199
32. G.B. Gajendragadkar, *Law, and Social Justice,* p. 47.
33. Ibid.
34. Ibid.
35. Ambedkar Memorial Lectures, 1976, delivered by Justice Krishna Iyer. 16,18,39.
36. Ibid.
37. D.C. Chaturvedi, *Indian Fundamental Rights,* 1992.
38. Ibid.

39. Ibid.
40. *Parliamentary Debates*, Part II, XII, 1951.
41. Granville Austin, *The Indian Constitution: Cornerstone of Nation*, pp. 50-52.
42. A.I.R. 1951 S.C.226 and A.I.R. S.C. 1951, 229.
43. P.K. Tripathi, *Spotlight on Constitutional Interpretation*, 1972, p. 293.
44. Golak Nath V. State of Punjab, A.I.R. 1967 S.C. 1643 and Keshwanand Bharti V. State of Kerala, A.I.R. 1963 S.C. 1461.
45. Mohammad Hanif Qureshi V. State of Bihar, A.I.R. 1958 S.C. 731.
46. A.I.R. 1953 Orissa 171.
47. A.I.R. 1954 All.144.
48. (1959) SCR. 955 and A.I.R. 1958 S.C. 731.
49. Ibid.
50. (1959) SCR. 629 at p.648.
51. A.I.R. 1967 S.C. 845.
52. Ibid., at p. 846.
53. A.I.R. 1967 S.C. 1643. at p. 2050.
54. CIWTC Ltd. V. Brojo Nath. A.I.R. 1986 S.C. 1571.
55. A.I.R. 1973. S.C. 1461 at p. 1466.
56. A.I.R. 1981 S.C. 14.
57. Ibid. at p.17.
58. Quoted in A.I.R. 1981 S.C. at p. 239. *Parliamentary Debates*, Part II. Vols. XII & XII.
59. Ibid. A.I.R. 1981 S.C. 235 at p. 239.60.
60. Ibid. at p. 243.
61. Ibid.
62. A.I.R. 1986 S.C., 1571.
63. A.I.R. 1993 S.C. 2178 at p. 2229.
64. A.I.R. 1986 S.C. 180 at pp. 193-94.
65. A.I.R. 1993 S.C. 2178 at p. 2192.
66. A.I.R. 1984 S.C. 802 at pp. 811-12.
67. A.I.R. 1993 S.C. 2178 at p. 2794.
68. V.R. Krishan Iyer, *Law Versus Justice*, 1981, p. 64,
69. A.I.R. 1982 S.C. 234 at p. 243.

The Limits of Textual Meddling

K. RAGHAVENDRA RAO

The thrust of this brief theoretical intervention is not to reject constitutionalism or to dismiss the utility of a constitution, but to suggest that the Indian Constitution, like any constitution, functions within a framework of constraints. This will be done in order to caution against an over investment of energy, enthusiasm and optimism in constitution-meddling on the ground that it may be non-productive or even counter-productive. Once a realistic appreciation of the limits of constitutionalism is made, one can, in fact, engage more effectively and successfully in the game of constitutionalism. The theoretical strategy deployed here revolves round (a) a historical deflation of the constitutionalism mystique, and (b) a theoretical demystification/deconstruction of an idea of a constitution as a "text". Such a theoretical clearing of the ground is a necessary prelude to any meaningful discussion of the constitutional possibilities of realising the goal or goals of social justice in India.

I

Against a backdrop of the global history of the theory and practice of constitutionalism, we need to draw a distinction between ancient constitutionalism and modern constitutionalism, noting the fact that modern constitutionalism began with the American constitutional experiment. But first we should recognise that, in theory, a constitutional tradition may be embodied in a written "text" or in an unwritten non-textual form. In the latter case, there will be no privileged master "text" which controls the political process. However, despite this theoretical situation, there is no doubt that constitutionalism can be best practised under a textual tradition. In any case, the two traditions entail different qualities of political life and culture. Primarily, the distinction is between a fundamental law that governs the structuring and operation of the political system and a non-fundamental law which operates within the framework of the former.

The pre-modern constitutional paradigm, even in the case of a written "text" such as a charter or a law promulgated by a law-giver, did not advance any claims of textual privilege. Further, it also did not attempt to mark off a fundamental law of the State from a whole set of supportive elements such as customs, conventions and ethnic norms. In his last major work, *The Laws,* Plato offers a detailed blue-print for an ideal State, including its physical, socio-cultural and economic ecology. What he offers is an ideal state, not just a constitution in a narrow sense. Its force is that of normative prescription rather than that of legal enactment. In the surviving fragment of his account of the Athenian constitution, Aristotle exemplifies the constitutional culture of ancient Greeks.[1] While the Greeks did not recognise any strong sense of legalism, they did make a distinction between what was "natural" and what was man-made or conventional, as may be noted in the seminal physis-nomos controversy among ancient Greek philosophers.[2] Thus, the Greeks initiated a recurrent and central *leit motif* of Western civilization, the complex tradition of natural law. This tradition proved resilient and elastic enough to accommodate medieval Christian theology and modern liberal individualism. Aristotle himself talks about an omnibus and complex "laws of a country" rather than of any fundamental or constitutional law in a narrow legal sense. When he writes that Solon gave to Athens a constitution as well as other laws, this seems to be the implication.[3] In countering the criticism that Solon had given a deliberately obscure constitution so that its obscurity would give the people more freedom, Aristotle attributes the obscurity not to any deliberate motive but simply to Solon's inability to gain a clear idea of "the best principles in general terms".[4] This suggests that he meant by a constitution an ideal state rather than any institutionally enforceable legal prescription. In his discussion of the best Athenian statesmen, he understands them as persons committed to the "the (fundamental) laws" but by that what he seems to mean are moral-religious-cultural-ethnic customs and norms rather than constitutional law in the modern sense.[5] In his account of the Athenian law-courts, he lists among their functions, the indictment of motions contrary to the laws and the indictment of legislative proposals contrary to the interests of the State.[6] But these functions should not be confused with the modern functions of judicial review.

The Romans did inaugurate a strong legalistic and juridical

tradition and culture in the West but their essential focus was more on a general rule of law than on any privileged, textually enshrined fundamental law. It was much later, as late as in the eighteenth century constitution-making, that one finds a crystallised emergence of constitutional law as a privileged fundamental law, generally embodied in written texts. Even then the concept was not without its ambiguities and self-contradictions.

When we take a quick look at the admittedly scantily documented record of pre-colonial and pre-Muslim India, we do not find any legalistic constitutional culture. What we do encounter is a systematic interpenetration of three kinds of rules – the omnibus transcendental-moral "Dharma", the proclamations of specific rulers and an intricate mosaic of highly parochial customary traditions associated with such local groups such as castes or guilds. The modern notion of constitutionalism was absent.

The modern notion of constitutionalism proper makes its first historical appearance as the political-legal foundation of modern European, constitutional monarchies, resulting from the eighteenth century bourgeois democratic revolutions. The new bourgeois democratic States drew their legal legitimacy from the older tradition of natural law and natural rights as may be seen in the theoretical discourses centering on them in the works of social contract ideologues like Hobbes and Locke. The new constitutionalism arose as a challenge to the feudal-monarchic absolutism of early modern European States. This new tradition of constitutionalism presupposed the existence of a constitution embodying a fundamental law which defined and regulated the structures and functions of the State as well as its relationship to the citizenry. Though a written textuality did not form part of this tradition, the general tendency was to produce written texts in order to make a strict adherence to constitutional provisions more easy and effective. It was also necessary to define precisely the limits to monarchical absolutism. Above all it involved unwriteable assumptions of a particular political culture which combined the ideas of popular sovereignty and individual rights.[7]

The *locus classicus* of any discussion of modern constitutionalism must be American constitutionalism. Therefore, we need to pay considerable attention to this phenomenon. In maintaining its commitment to the values and principles enshrined in the constitution, the American political system has to commit itself to principles not written into the constitution but nonetheless central to its operation, such as the principle of separation of powers or federalism or judicial review. Moreover, constitutional theory and practice remained within the ideological bounds of a free market economy. One of the founding fathers of American constitutionalism, Thomas Jefferson, defined the constitution in terms of two contradictory propositions. On the one hand, he held that the constitution derived its legitimacy from the authority of the people themselves, thus upholding the doctrine of popular sovereignty. On the other hand, he held that the people should not choose to change it, thus suspending the principle of popular sovereignty. Jefferson wrestled with this issue in an important letter to Joseph Priestly of Washington, dated 19 June 1802. He wrote, ". . . It is still certain that though written constitutions may be violated in moments of passion or delusion, yet they furnish a *text* in which those who are watchful may again rally and recall the people; they fix, too, for the people the principles of their political creed. . ."[8] It is significant that Jefferson links the notion of a "text" to the notion of a political creed transcendental to history.

The seminal text in the making the of the American constitutionalism is *The Federalist Papers.* One of the recurring themes in this rich mine of constitutional discourse is a conflict between democratic rights of historically changing generations and an allegedly trans-historical fundamental principle. Constitutionalism in its specifically American version is haunted by an explicit fear of democracy as a source of threat to property. The Federalist Paper 55 authored by Madison, draws sharp attention to this question in its concluding remark,"... Were the pictures which have been drawn by the political jealousy of some among us, faithful likenesses of the human character, the inference would be that there is not sufficient virtue among men for self-government; and that nothing less than the chains of despotism can restrain them from destroying and devouring one another."[9] Though the issue is formulated in terms of human nature as anarchically prone in the absence of an overriding sovereign power, one can see that it articulates at bottom a basic fear of democracy.

The preceding capsule history of global constitutionalism should dispel the impression that the concepts of constitution and constitutionalism are transparent and unproblematic products of history. It points to the possibility, even the necessity, of decomposing the notion of constitutionalism into its three constituent assumptions: (1) the notion of a trans-historical and universally valid principles, (2) the assumption that though trans-historical, there exist certain principles and ideals, rooted in a collective historical consciousness, and (3) the need to legitimise these principles by popular sovereignty. The fusion of these presuppositions in the eighteenth century European ethos of bourgeois democracy and capitalism created the pre-conditions for the emergence of modern constitutionalism. But its bourgeois democratic origin need not scar it beyond redemption! We can speak with historical hind-sight and say that constitutionalism is no less necessary for socialistic societies. This is because, in a sense, the rule of law transcends ideological divides, though there is also a sense in which it has specific historical ties with one particular ideology, that of liberal, capitalistic democracy. However, neither Marx nor Lenin nor Mao were able to see the socialistic potentialities of constitutionalism.

II

If, as suggested, the notions of constitution and constitutionalism are textual notions, then it follows that they attract all the problems recently raised by the post-structural assaults on the very idea of textuality in the West, especially by Foucault and Derrida. Foucault's seminal idea of discursive practice involves an analysis of the formation of intellectual disciplines (sciences) through which such practices are theoretically grasped, an analysis of the systems of power that regulate and manage such practice, and finally an analysis of the process by which individuals become subjects of such practice.[10] This framework tends to dissolve the written text into a field of interactive forces and factors, generating meaning through a dynamic mediation by institutionalised power and politics.[11] Thus a text is always located on a politically contested terrain where two fundamental human games intersect – the games of truth and the games of power.[12] Clearly this is a position which challenges the idea of the text as a privileged category, transcendentally self-sufficient, containing within itself the totality of meaning, with no epistemological necessity to refer to anything outside it. Derrida is even more radical in de-mystifying the text by inserting it in the flux of human action and history, divesting it of all epistemological stability and referentiality. For instance, he refers to the turbulent disruption of the text by its margins both in terms of its materiality and meaning. As he puts it, a written text "overflows and cracks its meaning".[13] Or he opens up the text to its "other" so that it can deconstruct itself and yield the secrets hidden in its silences, in-between spaces, when he asks, "... where has the body of the text gone when the margin is no longer a secondary virginity but an inexhaustible reserve, the streographic activity of an entirely other ear?. . ."[14] He rejects the traditional notion of the text which implies "the supposed end and beginning of a work, the unity of a corpus, the title, the margins, the signatures, the referential realm outside the frame, and so forth . . ."[15] He claims that this conventional text has, under the post-structural revolution, suffered "a sort of overrun (debordemont) that spoils all these boundaries and divisions . . ."[16] Now the text is "no longer a finished corpus of writing, some content enclosed in a book or its margins, but a differential network, a fabric of traces referring endlessly to something other than itself, to other differential traces. . ."[17] Derrida's attack on the written text through his deconstructive operations leads to a reversal, a return of the written text, now defrozen, to the original speech text, historically more contingent and laden with immediacy. In Derrida's own words, ". . . Henceforth, a text, if it is living and animated, full and authentic, will be of value only by virtue of the speech it will have as its mission to transport . . ."[18] This brief detour through the self-destructive epistemology of post-structuralism has been made to underscore the fact that non-Western epistemologies during their pre-colonial history did not need any post-structural operations because they were never victims of transcendental textuality and textual reification. But to the extent that they have been historically mixed up with the Western fate, post-structural perspective may be relevant and even unavoidable. The Indian tradition of textuality, prior to the Islamic and European incursions, was not characterised by any marked inclination towards textual reification or authorial obsession. It tended to disconnect the text both from its immediate author and its immediate history so that it became a transhistorical resource for the community. The textual culture of classical India fused fruitfully the traditions of written and oral modes of communication and transmission in its sophisticated dialectic of *Smrithi* and *Shruthi*.

The ambiguities that surrounded the notions of constitution and constitutionalism in their historical journey, the difficulties surrounding any understanding of the very idea of a text pinpointed by the post-structuralists in the West, and our own classical tradition of textuality, combine to warn us against placing too much faith in the ability of a written constitution to deliver individual and social goods smoothly and unmediated by politics. In short, the naive approach to a written constitution as a reified text, as an event frozen against the perils of history and politics, must be abandoned. But this does not mean that we have to give up wholly the ideas of constitution and constitutionalism. They do matter, though not as much as a simple-minded textualism claims. What a constitution can really accomplish is to provide the broad boundaries within which the political and judicial processes can occur. These boundaries are necessarily flexible, permitting the possibility of a variety of historical options. Even a meticulously detailed constitutional text cannot fully articulate its own possibilities.

III

Once the framework of textual reification is abandoned, one can see the text of a constitution as a wide open opportunity for the full play of political contextualisation. A whole range of historically constituted forces and factors – socio-economic groups, classes, primordial groups such as castes or families or kin networks, institutional forces, ideological propulsions and international or multinational interventions – come into play when the constitution is politically contextualised and mobilised. The issue of political contextualisation is especially crucial to the cause of social justice. It is common knowledge that many provisions of the Indian Constitution aiming to promote social justice have never been implemented simply because there has been no significant political mobilisation generated over them. A constitution is not a vending machine which can automatically deliver social justice at the pressing of a button! Whatever the textual rhetoric, it is clear that the deprived and the dispossessed in India – whether Dalits, the Backward classes, the women and the poor – have benefitted from the operation of the constitution only marginally. It is significant in this connection that Ambedkar lost faith in the "text" in whose production he had played an important role and showed greater commitment to his own draft constitution more decisively oriented towards the goal of social justice than the official Constitution.[19]

Where do we go from here? Certainly we can indulge in the formal textual game of either amending the Constitution, which is more easy and likely, or the designing of a new constitution which is more explicitly biased towards social justice. The latter course can hardly be said to be on active political agenda at the present historical juncture. But in either case, a simple meddling with the constitution textually will not do, though it may be helpful. Therefore, all textual meddling must be translated into political praxis, political contextualisation and political mobilisation. The "text" will really speak only to those who act to make it speak. Perhaps a seminar such as this, enmeshed heavily in a theoretical-textual culture, is hardly the place for political praxis. Nonetheless, it can help if it attempts seriously to link its theoretical concerns to practical concerns by showing, *even if only theoretically,* what are the best courses of action that may politically contextualise the text of the constitution in the cause of social justice. The non-textual writing on the wall, if we can read it, tells us that social justice will come, with the help of the "text" of the constitution, if it is politically contextualised, but it will certainly come in spite of or even against, the "text" of the constitution. One need not be a Marxist to be sensitive to the illusory nature of textual promises.[20] But one can certainly learn from Marxism that formal structures derive their meaning from their real social content. We may also remind ourselves that Gandhiji practised a fine balance between constitutionalism and extra-constitutional politics of contextualisation and mobilisation. The goal of social justice can be realised only by a constant politicisation and political mobilization of the constitution as a back-up to textual amendments and revisions.

REFERENCES

1. *Aristotle's Constitution of Athens and Related Texts,* translated with an Introduction by Kurt von Fritz and Ernst Kapp, Hafner Library of Classics, Hafner Publishing Company, New York, 1966.
2. Ibid, Introduction, p. 30.
3. Ibid, p. 74.

4. Ibid, p. 77.
5. Ibid, p. 99.
6. Ibid, p. 136.
7. Avgust Mishin and Vasili Vlasikhin, *200 Years of U.S. Constitutionalism,* Progress Publishers, Moscow, 1988, Introduction.
8. *The Political Writings of Thomas Jefferson,* Ed., Edward Dumbauld, Forum Books, Liberal Arts Press, New York, 1955, p. 128.
9. *The Federalist Papers by Alexander Hamilton, James Madison and John Jay,* Ed., Gerrry Willis, Bantam Books, New York, 1988, p. 234.
10. Michel Foucault, *The Use of Pleasure,* Vol. 2, Penguin Books, London, 1987, p. 4.
11. Ibid, pp. 6, 7.
12. Ibid, pp. 6, 7.
13. *A Derrida Reader - Between the Blinds,* Ed., Peggy Kamuf, Harvester Wheatsheaf, New York, 1991, p. 163.
14. Ibid, p. 163.
15. Ibid, p. 256.
16. Ibid, p. 256.
17. Ibid, p. 257
18. Ibid, p. 479.
19. See his "States and Minorities" in *Dr. Babasaheb Ambedkar, Writings and Speeches,* Vol. I, compiled by Vasant Moon, Education Department, Government of Maharashtra, Bombay, 1989, pp. 383-449. Also K. Raghavendra Rao, *Babasaheb Ambedkar,* Makers of Indian Literature Series, Sahitya Akademi, New Delhi, 1993, especially the Chapter on Political and Legal Theory.
20. In this connection, Lenin wrote, "... A constitution is fictitious when law and reality diverge; it is not fictitous when they coincide..." cited in op.cit., Mishin-Vlasikhin volume, p. 15. Marx himself held different positions on this issue at different times.

Justice For Minorities

A.S. NARANG

In the present-day social situation most political concepts have become intrinsically controversial, "essentially contested", open to interpretation and appreciation by competing doctrines and strategies of inquiry. This is conspicuously true of the term "justice" which is commonly used in a great variety of ways and to make a variety to political and moral points. Whatever may be the use of the word justice today, it is definitely taken in a rather wider sense. In that justice is taken as a condition in a well functioning society. Accordingly, the ideal of providing or attaining justice is not considered to be limited in economic terms. It is also related to social and ethno-cultural issues.

While forging of unity through political organization subsumes the autonomy of the individual and the sanctity of his choice in owing allegiance to whatever structures he prefers, there pre exist certain socio-cultural structures which the individual is born into and shapes his beliefs, orientations and behaviour patterns. These structures not only constitute resources essential for the development of the individual but also signify certain boundaries circumscribing his freedom in developing a project and adopting means in implementing it. As Ramashray Roy points out:

> Given the differentiation of functions – in political as well as social structures – the completely atomised individual remains a myth, even perhaps in the state of nature. He forms a part, either in aggregative or in organic sense, of an aggregate, and his relations with the nation is usually mediated through the aggregates.[1]

Here it is also useful to keep in mind the suggestion of T.K. Oommen; that is the human need not only has impersonal ties with entities, such as political parties and the bureaucratic State, on the one hand, and privatized ties provided by primary groups such as family and kin groups, on the other, but also for intermediate structures and processes which blend and balance the two. In a country like India such ties are often provided by caste, religion, language and region which are often labelled communal, parochial and anti-national. But these loyalties and ties cannot be dismissed.[2] Now we know from the world experience that even after a socialist revolution or utter modernisation attachment to such groups remains.

It is against this background that in today's world democratic consciousness has been seeping down to millions who were so long oblivious or deprived of their right to identity in the complete sense of the term. Minorities have become cautious about loss of their ethnic identity from two causes. The first is the dominant majority, generally politically powerful also, questioning the so-called privileges or rights of a minority and attempting to impose its own religious or cultural values as that of the whole society. It means making the political ideology of the core group also the basis of nationalism in the State. The second is the ideology of the modern State to equate the State with the nation. This modern centralised nation-state, even in formal democracies, thinks of regions and local units as its subordinates and agents. Any challenge from them is considered anti-national and subversive of national unity. It is this apprehension that has raised the issue of justice for minorities.

In the contemporary world one of the most important issues is how polyethnic or multinational states deal with the minorities. The problem in many States is that while pluralism is accepted as an ideal the actual practice moves close to the statist approach. It is particularly so in post-colonial States where in the idiom of "nation-building" minority issues are conveniently swept under the carpet. India presents one such example of ambivalence which starts from the Constitution itself.

II

The ethnic-minority situation in India presents a most complex and confusing picture. She has geo-political and historical characteristics which have few parallels. Minorities in India are a fact, not fiction. History has, in many ways, provided a definite sense of identity to various minority groups. During the British colonial rule, there was both fission and fusion. The British created a national market and unified the various nationalities by building a centralised state structure. The historical, civilisational and administrative unity under colonialism also generated sentiments of all-India nationalism among the masses, especially in the wake of the national movement. The very existence of foreign rule that oppressed all the Indian people, irrespective of their social class, caste, region, religion or language, acted as a unifying factor.

However, in the absence of full-fledged development of the different regions and their economies, cultures and languages, nationalities (along regional, cultural and linguistic lines) also started emerging particularly during and after the second half of the nineteenth century. A sense of distinct identity and an urge for a separate compact territorial unit had begun to take root and grow among several linguistic groups, more so if they also shared a common culture. The factors that contributed to this trend included: adoption, under British rule, of local languages as a medium of instruction in schools so that people instructed in common medium began to look upon themselves as a single entity, distinct from people using a different medium; the availability of newspapers, literature and other reading materials and rise of regional intelligentsia in Indian languages; concepts and modes of thought imported from Western Europe where the nation-state had become the predominant form of state organisation.

The freedom movement played a dual role in relation to the emergence of such regional consciousness. Inasmuch as it relied upon mass support, it could not but give great impetus to the politicization of the content of literatures in regional languages, and thus laid the foundations of nationality, consciousness. On the other hand, by invoking the greater loyalty to the Indian motherhood in a united struggle against British rule, it subjugated the urge of the people of the various regions for developing into separate nationalities.

In general, behind the apparent struggle between the nationalists with their slogan of "India – a United Nation" and the British rulers who highlighted the multiplicity of castes, communities, tribes and linguistic groups was the reality that India was developing its national unity against the British but along with it the various linguistic cultural groups were being consolidated into distinct ethnic and communal groups.

III

Because of vastness of territory and population, the integration of the princely states with their historic and institutional differences, on the eve of independence there was little disagreement about the need for pluralism and provision of justice for minorities. In the Constituent Assembly Dr. B.R. Ambedkar made the point clear saying:

> To diehards who have developed a kind of fanaticism against minority protection I would like to say two things. One is that minorities are an explosive force which, if it erupts, can blow up the whole fabric of the state. The history of Europe bears ample and appalling testimony to this fact.
>
> The other is that the minorities in India have agreed to place their existence in the hands of the majority. In the history of negotiations for preventing the partition of the Ireland, Redmond said to Carson "ask for any safeguard you like for the protestant minority but let us have a United Ireland". Carson's reply was "Damn your safeguards, we don't want to be ruled by you."
>
> No minority in India has taken this stand. They have loyally accepted the rule of the majority which is basically a communal majority and not a political majority. It is for the majority to realize its duty not to discriminate against minorities. Whether the minorities will continue or will vanish must depend upon this habit of the majority. The moment the majority loses the habit of discriminating against the minority, the minorities can have no ground to exist. They will vanish.

With this in view the Constituent Assembly set up an Advisory Committee under the chairmanship of Sardar Patel on the subject of Fundamental Rights including rights of minorities, with the twin objective of eliminating the chance of religion exploiting the State and vice-versa. Moving the resolution for the setting up the Advisory Committee, Govind Ballabh Pant emphasized:

> A satisfactory solution of the question pertaining to minorities will ensure the health, vitality and strength of the free state of India. . . . So far the minorities have been incited and have been influenced in a manner which has hampered the growth of cohesion and unity. But now it is necessary that a new chapter should start and we should all realise our

responsibility. Unless the minorities are fully satisfied, we cannot make progress; we cannot even make peace in an undisturbed manner.[3]

The Advisory Committee appointed five sub-committees. One was the minorities sub-committee headed by H.C. Mukerjee, a Christian leader from Bengal. To facilitate the task of the sub-committee, K.M. Munshi formulated a questionnaire as under:

(i) What should be the nature and scope for the safeguards for a minority in the new Constitution?
(ii) What should be the political safeguards of a minority (a) in the Centre, and (b) in the Provinces?
(iii) What whould be the economic safeguards of a minority (a) in the Centre, and (b) in the Provinces?
(iv) What should be the religious, educational and cultural safeguards for a minority?
(v) What machinery should be set up to ensure that the safeguards are effective.
(vi) How is it proposed that the safeguards should be eliminated, in what time and under what circumstances.[4]

Memoranda were submitted on behalf of the Scheduled Castes, Scheduled Tribes, Sikhs and Anglo-Indians, demanding constitutional safeguards. No specific communal safeguards were asked for on behalf of the Indian Christians and Parsis. No memorandum was presented on behalf of the Muslim League as it was still not participating in the proceedings of the Assembly.

On the basis of memoranda received and other suggestions made by members the issues for the consideration of the sub-committee were:

(i) Representation in legislatures; joint versus separate electorates and weightage;
(ii) Reservation of seats for minorities in Cabinets;
(iii) Reservation for minorities in the public services; and
(iv) Administrative machinery to ensure protection of minority rights.[5]

After a long discussion on these issues, the following decisions were taken:

1. The demand for separate electorates and weightage should be rejected and the principle of joint electorates with seats reserved for the minorities on a population basis should be accepted.
2. The demand for reservation of seats in the Cabinet should be rejected.
3. The demand for reservation of posts in the public services on a population basis should be accepted; and
4. Special officers should be appointed to look after the safeguards and interests of minorities.[6]

The Advisory Committee rejected separate electorates of any kind, as in the past they had sharpened communal differences and proved to be a stumbling block to the development of a healthy national life. All elections to Central and Provincial 'legislatures were to be held on the basis of joint electorates, with reservation of seats for certain specified minorities according to their population ratio. This reservation, to start with, was to be for a period of ten years, at the end of which the position was to be reconsidered. There would be no weightage, but members of the minority communities for whom seats were reserved would have the right to contest general seats.

The Advisory Committee recommended, as a general rule, that seats for the different recognized minorities (Muslims, Scheduled Castes, Sikhs, Anglo Indians, Indian Christians, Parsis and tribals living in the plains of Assam) should be reserved in different legislatures on the basis of their population.

The Draft Constitution prepared by the Constitutional Advisor in October 1947, incorporated these decisions. The drafting Committee which met on February 5 and 6, 1948 formulated the various provisions into ten Articles and placed them in Part XIV under the title "Special Provisions Relating to Minorities.

Article 292 reserved seats in the House of the People for Muslims, Scheduled Castes, Scheduled Tribes and in the states of Madras and Bombay for Indian Christians. Article 294 made a similar provision for these communities in the Legislative Assemblies of Part I states. Article 283 authorized the President to nominate not more than two members of the Anglo-Indian community to the House of the People. Article 295 contained a similar provision in relation to State legislatures. Article 296 required that, consistently with the maintenance of efficiency of administration, the claim of the minority communities should be taken into consideration in the making of appointments to public services. Article 297 continued the reservation of posts for Anglo-Indians in the Railways, Customs and the Posts and Telegraph Services on the same basis as immediately before 15 August 1947; the reservation was to last for ten years. Article 298 made provisions for educational grants for minorities. The special provision was to last for ten years. Article 299 made provisions for appointment of a Special Officer for Minorities to look after their safeguards. Article 300 empowered the President to appoint a commission to report on the administration of the Scheduled Areas and the welfare of the Scheduled Tribes. A similar provision was made under Article 301 for appointment of a commission to investigate the conditions of all socially backward classes. As the position of East Punjab and West Bengal was uncertain on account of large-scale shifting of population following partition, the Draft Constitution did not incorporate any provisions with regard to these provinces.

However by 1949 the Advisory Committee changed its views. At its meeting on 11 May 1949, the Committee felt that since 1947 when it had made the recommendation on reservation of seats, conditions in the country had changed after the partition and it was no longer appropriate in the context of free India to reserve seats for Muslims, Christians, Sikhs or any other religious minority. Jawaharlal Nehru explained the position:

> A safeguard of this kind would have some point where there was autocratic or foreign rule which would enable the monarch to play one community off against the others. But where you are up against a full-blooded democracy, if you seek to give safeguards to a minority, and a relatively small minority, you isolate it. May be you protect it to a slight extent, but at what cost? At the cost of isolating it and keeping it away from the main current in which the majority is going – I am talking on the political plane of course – at the cost of forfeiting that inner sympathy and fellow feeling with the majority.[7]

The Sub-committee on Minorities had also prepared an interim report which dealt with the question of Fundamental Rights from the point of view of minorities. The report recommended:

(i) All citizens are entitled to use their mother tongue and the script thereof, and to adopt, study or use any other language and script of their choice.

(ii) Minorities in every unit shall be adequately protected in respect of their language and culture, and no government may enact any laws or regulations that may act oppressively or prejudicially in this regard.

(iii) No minority, whether of religion, community or language shall be deprived of its rights or discriminated against in regard to the admission into state educational institutions, nor shall any religious instruction be compulsorily imposed upon them.

(iv) Notwithstanding any custom, law, decree or usage, presumption or terms of dedication, no Hindu on grounds of caste, birth or denomination shall be precluded from entering in educational institutions dedicated or intended for the use of the Hindu community or any action thereof; and

(v) No disqualification shall arise on account of sex in respect of public services or professions or admission to educational institutions save and except that this shall not prevent the establishment of separate educational institutions for boys and girls.

The Advisory Committee accepted the recommendations partially and recommended the following clause to the Constituent Assembly:

1. Minorities in every unit shall be protected in respect of their language, script and culture, and no laws or regulations may be enacted that may operate oppressively or prejudicially in this respect.

2. No minority whether based on religion, community or language shall be discriminated against with regard to admission into state educational institutions, nor shall any religious instruction be compulsorily imposed on such minority.

3. All minorities whether based on religion, community or language shall be free in any unit to establish and administer educational institutions of their choice.

3.b. The State shall not, while providing state aid to schools, discriminate against schools under the management of minorities whether based on religion, community or language.[8]

The clause was incorporated as clause 24 with some drafting changes in the Draft Constitution prepared by the Constitutional Advisor. The Drafting Committee revised the text of clause 24 twice, the most significant change being the re-drafting of sub-clause (1). The clause finally took the shape as Article 23 of the Draft Constitution:

The Drafting Committee, at the revision stage divided Article 23 into two separate Articles – Article 29 and 30.

> 29(a) Any section of citizens residing in the territory of India or any part thereof having a distinct language, script or culture of its own shall have the right to conserve the same.
>
> (b) No citizen shall be denied admission into any educational institution maintained by the state or receiving aid out of state funds on grounds only of religion, race, caste, language or any of them.
>
> 30(a) All minorities whether based on religion or language shall have the right to establish and administer educational institutions of their choice.
>
> (b) The State shall not, in granting aid to educational institutions, discriminate against any educational institution on the ground that it is under the management of a minority, whether based on religion or language.

Thus in spite of the fact that the problem of minorities in India figured prominently in the Constituent Assembly and the founding fathers bestowed much thought and attention to it in all its facets, except for a few concessions which the Assembly admitted for the Anglo-Indian community, no other religious minority could secure any political rights. In fact no attempt was made on any occasion even to define the term "minority" in the precise words. So much so that on the suggestion of T.T. Krishnamachari the word "certain classes" were substituted for the word "minorities" wherever it occurred in the text of the Constitution. Not only is the use of the term minority in the Constitution very rare but also no group is mentioned explicitly as a minority therein. The term 'minority' is mentioned in only two Articles, 29 and 30. Here too the use of the term is not for definitional purposes. In one of the Articles it is used only in the sub-heading of the Article and not in the text of the Article. More so Article 366 of the Constitution, which is exclusively utilised to give the meaning of words and terms used in the text of the Constitution, gives meaning to 30 such expressions. But here too the term "minority is not covered. This attitude of the founding fathers vis-a-vis the term shows that they had grown allergic to the use of the term in the Constitution."[9]

The concession to Anglo-Indians, as finally incorporated in the Constitution, comprised of provisions authorizing the President to nominate not more than two members of the Anglo-Indian community to the House of the People if in his opinion that community happened to be inadequately represented, (Art. 331). A similar provision was made for nomination in the State Legislative Assemblies (Art. 333). Both the provisions were to remain in force for a period of 30 years only (Art. 334); a provision for reservation in railways, customs and postal and telegraph services for ten years, the reservations being on the same basis on which they were made before 1947 (Art. 336). A special provision for continuance of special educational grants for a period of ten years, which were available to that community in 1948. (Art. 337)

The Constituent Assembly did not concede any political rights to any minority except those of equality in Arts. 14, 15, 46, 330, 332, 335, 338 and 341, 347, 350, 350A & B. What it ultimately conceded turned out to be certain rights relating to education, language and culture, incorporated as Articles 29 & 30.

Thus the attitude of the leadership as reflected in the Constitution was that by providing equal rights and opportunities to all of India's citizens they were respectful of the cultural specificities of particular ethnic groups. Minority demands for group rights and provisions for assured share in political power were conveniently swept under the carpet in the name of "national unity", "integration" and "development". The same attitude was reflected with regard to its ambivalent stand on question of federalism.

IV

From its inception the Indian National Congress was made up of an English-educated elite. This composition plus the fact that the main purpose of the Congress was to provide an Indian alternative to the centralized British power, meant that the Congress early in its history had developed a strongly centralist thrust.

But the Muslims, being a minority community, had their apprehensions about this concept of centralisation. They thought that this would inevitably mean a Hindu-dominated India. Since they were in majority in some provinces and princely states, they thought that they could minimise this danger by demanding a federal structure with a large measure of autonomy to the provinces. The Congress leaders in their anxiety to draw the Muslims into the struggle against the British, conceded the federal concept. The Lucknow Pact (1916) between the Congress and the League and all subsequent negotiations between the two over next three decades, were based on this concept. At Nagpur Session (1920) the Congress also resolved that the federal setup of India would be based on the principle of language.

In 1928, the Motilal Nehru report, keeping the 1920 Resolution in view, recommended the necessity of restructuring the provinces on a linguistic basis. In the policy adopted at the Karachi Session (1929) of the Congress, the approach was to give substantial powers to the states or provinces as they were then called. Within Congress, Gandhi was particularly a champion of decentralisation of power and an advocate of a close tie between cultural values and political life.

During 1946, as a result of negotiations between the British Government on the one hand, and the Congress Party and the Muslim League on the other, the Cabinet Mission Plan emerged. This plan envisaged a very weak Centre and a two-tier governmental system below the Central government. The jurisdiction of the Union was to be limited to Foreign Affairs, Defence, and Communications and the power to raise finances for the discharge of these functions. All subjects other than Union subjects were to be within the jurisdiction of provinces. They were also to be vested with residuary powers. The princely states were to retain all subjects and powers other than those ceded to the Union.

As such, on the eve of Independence there was little disagreement about the need for a federal rather than a unitary form of Constitution. In December 1946, Jawaharlal Nehru introduced in the Constituent Assembly a resolution which envisaged "a Republic of India wherein the various territories would possess and retain the status of autonomous units together with residuary powers, and exercise all powers and functions of government and administration save and except such powers and functions as were vested in or assigned to the Union or as were inherent or implied in the Union or resulted therefrom". Debates in the Constituent Assembly suggested that it clearly intended the proposed political system to be basically federal in character.

However, once independence was attained, the Indian National Congress, which had spearheaded this movement and was now dominating the Constituent Assembly, took an ambivalent attitude. It seems that there was a failure of nerve on the part of the leadership in 1946-47. With the exception of Gandhi, they were unable to rely on their own capacity to compose the outburst of communal rioting accompanying partition, the early hostilities over Kashmir, and the administrative problems associated with the initial period of independence. For them, "the circumstances following the partition of India made stability more important than autonomy, efficiency more important than initiative and expediency more important than federalism or any ism".[10] While Gandhi put his faith in the reformed, ethically refined individual, in creating a better if not ideal society, Nehru and his associates considered the shaping of suitable institutions as the best means to achieve the same goal. And of the modern institutions it was the centralised nation-state which they believed would be the principal engine of social change. Thus, the leaders of the independence movement and the largely middle class intellectuals who supported and gave strength to these leaders were all imbued with resurgent nationalism. The prospects for linguistic and other minorities within the ethnolingual states looked worrisome to them. They were thus induced to move towards a Constitution with strong unitary features because (a) they felt that once the Muslim majority areas had opted out of the Indian republic, the major reason for having a loose federal structure had vanished; and (b) they feared that fissiparous tendencies might be fostered by outsiders or generated within some of the constituent units which had to be safeguarded against. This attitude is expressed best of all in a letter written by Jawaharlal Nehru, on 5 July 1947, to the President of the Constituent Assembly. Interalia it reads:

> Now that the partition is a settled fact, we are unanimously of the view that it would be injurious to the interests of the country to provide for a weak Central authority which would be incapable of ensuring peace, of coordinating vital matters of common concern and of speaking effectively for the whole country in the international sphere.

When in power in a free India, the Congress was notably less happy about the prospect of reconstructing the country on a linguistic basis than when it sought mass support for the overthrow of the British. Nehru tried every technique of diversion available to a politician to avert the redrawing of state boundaries on linguistic lines. Under pressure from those advocating the creation of linguistic states – Andhra, Karnatka, Kerala and Maharashtra – the Committee of the Constituent Assembly responsible for the drafting of the Constitution appointed a special committee to look into the question of linguistic provinces (known as Dhar Commission). The Committee in its report, submitted in 1978, argued against the immediate formation of linguistic states. The Jaipur meeting of the Congress (December 1948) appointed a committee consisting of Jawaharlal Nehru, Vallabhai Patel and Pattabhi Sitaramaya (known as JVP Committee) to look into the report of the Dhar Commission and put forward final recommendations. This committee also rejected the principle of linguistic states on the ground that the consolidation of language communities after the recent partition of the country would give rise to new separatist trends.

Thus, at the time of framing of Constitution the great diversity of the nation was almost ignored. India's new rulers, as D.L. Sheth puts it, viewed creation of a national society, the necessary concomitant of a modern state, as the task of devising an overarching political arrangment for a people divided along the lines of religion, language and other ethnic attributes, lines which had become sharper during the colonial regime. Nehru and his colleagues would rather pin their hopes on the possibility (in their view inevitability) that with the development of communication and industrialisation India would increasingly become a polyglot nation.[12]

In this context Nehru insisted that these ideals were not speculative but based on practical experience. At one place he wrote that once the national state came into being economic problems would acquire salience; there might be 'class conflicts' but not religious conflicts, except insofar as religion itself expressed some vested interest.[13] Related to this was the belief that the greatest safeguard for the religious minorities lies in a secular polity.

V

There in no doubt that a genuine secularism that embodies the clear separation of religion from public affairs could have given minorities a sense and feeling of being equal. But here too the leadership faltered on two important grounds. First by twisting secularism to mean not the confinement of religious faith to private life but the conferment of equal patronage on all faiths, the State has itself been mainly instrumental in creating a dangerously potent counterweight to the concept of secularism.

In the name of defining an Indian form of secularism, basic universal ingredients like separation of State from religion, of religion from education, and adherence to rationalism and scientific temper are overlooked. In the name of equal respect for all religions and toleration of all communites and their eventual harmonisation, what is finally achieved is a reconciliation of multiple communalism. P.N. Haksar points out:

> If the words secular, secularism and secularisation are to be understood as part and parcel of a universal process of secularisation of the human mind, then we have inflicted enormous damage on the nation-building process in India, by a totally unacceptable and false translation of the word secular and secularism by equating them to the doctrine of religious tolerance expressed in the words like *Dharmanirpekshta* and *Sarva Dharma Sambhava.* These translations have produced great schizophrenia in our politics which, in time has produced the situation with which we are now actually confronted.[14]

When secularism means giving equal treatment to all religions and not separation of State and religion or using of public funds for religious purposes, if some religions are more equal than others they may get more funds and more State patronage. In this content S. Gopal points out that to contend that all religions are equal and leave it at that is to give secularism a Hindu bias and doom it from birth.[15]

The second point with regard to secularism is that the dominant leadership had expected that the propagation of science and modernism would suffice to erode the hold of religious orthodoxy and dogma on people's minds. They ignored the fact that beliefs have material roots. For popularisation of rights. On the contrary it allowed market forces to play and further deepen the inequalities that our society had inherited.

In a situation of scarcity and no guarantees for economic and social emanicipation, the conviction that minorities are vulnerable to discrimination, exploitation and suppression by those who control the State and its resources takes hold easily. This danger exists particularly when it is government by majority. The minorities usually fear oppression from the majority who are in power by virtue of numerical strength. As democracy provides for majority rule, the numerically strong group can gain political power by mobilizing itself on communal lines. And in a situation where the constitution in the name of equal respect to all religions allows state patronage, a communally minded party in power can use that power against a minority community without constitutional provisions.

VI

Thus while the makers of the Indian Constitution were faced with the problem of achieving a consensus on a constitutional arrangement that could accommodate diverse interests, allay real and imaginary fears, and, at the same time, instill a sense of security among the minorities out of their orientation of a strong nation-state, they did not give due significance to ethnic and linguistic plurality and down played ethnic and minority issues. The principles of equality and non-discrimination were held to be sufficient guarantees for the protection of minorities. They felt that no special attention need be given to minorities as such. Therefore the essential basis of the Constitution is that all citizens are equal, and this basic equality (guaranteed by Article 14) obviously proclaims that the religion or language of a citizen is entirely irrelevant in the matter of his fundamental rights. It also means rejecting privileges for any particular ethnic group. Of course, the Constitution does make provisions for maintenance of linguistic, religious, cultural or religious identities by minorities themselves. The State does not owe loyalty to any particular religion. While it is not irreligious or anti-religious, it gives equal freedom to all religions and respects them equally. While no language has been declared India's national language, it recognizes Hindi to be the ultimate official state-language of the Union.

language has been declared India's national language, it recognizes Hindi to be the ultimate official state-language of the Union.

The national leadership's excessive concern for national integration as the criterion of a nation state giving primacy to modernisation as the means of erosion of traditional loyalties, could reduce various minority groups. To begin with, linguistic minorities felt dissatified and resorted to agitation. Consequently within five years of the adoption of the Constitution, the States had to be reorganised on the basis of language to accommodate the growing ethnic aspirations of major linguistic groups living by and large within identifiable territories. As the ethnic apprehensions coincided with major failures of the system in delivering the goods in socio-economic terms and consequent rise in discontent and unrest, the ethnic movements began to grow. Around the same time the elite strata began to show a tendency to close options for others and corner resources and privileges for themselves.[17] This process of exclusiveness and centralisation continues.

This increasing centralisation and intervention of the Central government is making ethnic/cultural minorities apprehensive. The Central government does express its concern for protection of minorities and even provides separate institutions and policies for different religious/cultural groups. But the problem today is not that minorities seek protection for their cultural values against deliberately hostile actions by the majority in the field of schools and languages, so much as the desire for protection against the effects on their culture of natural economic and social developments. The cultural minorities are only too aware that failure to maintain themselves politically, economically and socially leads to erosion of cultural identity. This means that a cultural minority must be able to develop so as to keep pace and compete with the host state majority at the economic and social level. This in turn means that when one talks of 'protection of minorities' it is not merely a question of introducing measures that would preserve minorities like flies in amber, but that their ability to develop themselves will be an inherent part of the process of protection. But upon what does the ability to do this – the source of cultural power – depend? The short answer is that cultural power depends on political and economic power.[18]

Thus, re-sacralization of primordial ties, T.K. Oommen points out, is partly an indication of the 'quest for community' and partly a response to the processes of marginalization, actual or imaginary, the peripheral communities are threatened with. The quest for community is likely to crystallize more easily among the deprived, and deprivation is perceived not only in economic and political terms but also in terms of denial of one's cultural identity.[19] Therefore centralisation, along with other factors has been proving counter productive particularly since the beginning of 70s. One of the consequence of centralisation of politics is that it has led to the creation of dichotomies of majority-minority communities.

It can thus be said that the ethnic movements in post-independence India may be characterised as a response to the imposition of alien process of nation-building in the framework of a single political community. As Sajal Basu points out, most surprisingly, economic regionalism, or movements based mainly on economic issues, remain less explosive than campaigns based on socio-cultural issues.[20] N.T. Rama Rao created the Telugu Desham Party and swept the 1983 polls with a single point programme of restoring Telugu honour. Similarly no one can buy the theory of Punjab being economically backward or deprived. The agitation here had been primarily on the issue of psyche. If an objective analysis of the Gorkhaland agitation is made, it becomes quite clear that the agitation was mainly because of neglect of the sentiments of the ethnos. At the same time, the experience in Nagaland, Mizoram, Assam, Punjab and Kashmir are indicative enough of the very limited reach and effectiveness of coercive ways in suppressing in modern times the urges and aspirations of aroused and alienated people.

In this background, as D.L. Sheth suggests, the project of the Indian State, to build a modern centralised nation-state, has gone awry. Yet the State, in response to growing ethnic and other pressures, has become more and more centralised and coercive, its federal character has been considerably diluted and democratic institutions have been emasculated. The project of transforming ethnic identities into a national identity of citizens is now subject to centrifugal ethnic pulls in society. In the process, majority ethnicism is beginning increasingly to be seen by the State and some sections of the elite as providing a new, and in their view a stable basis for nationalism. As a result, ethnic minorities feel ever more insecure. Some of them are now demanding an autonomous political arrangement for themselves.

A few demand total independence.[21]

Therefore there is an urgent need to think afresh over minority and ethnic issues. The starting point in terms of rejuvenating Indian pluralism has to be the recognition of the plural character of our society and growing reality of ethno nationalism/sub-nationalism. In this, the federal centre will have to be viewed as the focal point at which the various sub-nationalities converge rather than a source from which power is imposed upon them. Devolutionary measure would, as a consequence, need to be worked out in a spirit of partnership between the central and regional levels rather than unilaterally by a dominant centre.[22] What is needed is a functioning federal system composed of autonomous governments and institutions, an approach which permits and facilitates the dignified existence of various ethnic groups under the same "political roof" and that does not take refuge under the misconceived doctrine of supra nationalism. And for this is required drastic decentralization, establishment of grassroots participatory system and respect for human rights through Constitution itself.

NOTES

1. Ramashray Roy, *Social Diversity, Modernization, and National Integration: A Theoretical Perspective.* Delhi: Centre for the Study of Developing Societies: n.d. (mimeo).
2. T.K. Oommen. *State and Society in India: Studies in Nation Building.* New Delhi: Sage, 1990, p. 65.
3. *Constituent Assembly Debates,* Vol II , pp. 310-11.
4. B. Shiva Rao, *The Framing of India's Constitution: Select Documents,* Vol. II.
5. *Constituent Assembly Debates,* Vol.V, p. 248.
6. Ibid. p. 248
7. Ibid. Vol VIII, p. 330.
8. B. Shiva Rao, *The Framing of India's Constitution: A Study.*
9. K.K. Wadhwa "Problem of Defining Minorities", *Hindustan Times,* September 21, 1986.
10. Pradeep Kumar, "Why is our Constitution Centre-oriented? *Journal of Constitutional and Parliamentary Studies,* 1983, p. 265.
11. D.L. Sheth, "State, Nation and Ethnicity: Experience of Third World Countries", *Economic and Political Weekly,* March 15, 1989, p. 624
12. Ashis Banerjee, "The Politics of Indian Federalism: Some observations" (mimeo) n.d.

13. Quoted by T.N. Madan, "Secularism in its Place" in T.N. Madan (ed), *Religion in India.* Delhi: Oxford University Press, 1991.
14. P.N. Haksar, "Fundamentalism and Secularism", *Mainstream,* March 21, 1992.
15. S. Gopal, "The Problem", *Seminar* 363, November 1989, p. 13.
16. Krishna Kumar, "Why Secularism has not worked", *Times of India,* January 9, 1991.
17. Rajni Koothari, "Integration and Exclusion in Indian Politics", *Economic and Political Weekly* , October 22, 1988.
18. Antony E. Eloock, et.al. (eds.), *The Future of Cultural Minorities.* London: Macmillian 1979, pp. 109-10.
19. Oommen, n 2. p. 45.
20. Sajal Basu, *Regional Movements: Politics of Language, Ethnicity, Identity,* Shimla: Indian Institute of Advanced Study, 1992, p. 116.
21. Sheth n.11, p. 624.
22. Nirmal Mukharji, "A More Federal India", *Mainstream,* April 18, 1992.

Enumerating For Social Justice

PAPIYA GHOSH

During the colonial period the earlier "fuzzy", many-layered sense of community gave way to a more determinate, "enumerated" and hierarchized sense of community.[1] To elaborate briefly, the colonial enumeration of Indian society on the basis of caste and religion shaped mobilization seeking representation in the state domain, i.e. representation by caste or religion.[2]

Post-colonial Indian politics, it has been remarked, continues to run along these channels of colonial discourse. The most obvious example is the notion of majority and minority communities on the basis of religion, language and tribe being applied over a wide variety of territorial units. The other is the continued preoccupation with precise calculations of proportionality in demands both for and against reservations for Scheduled Castes, Tribes and Backward Classes. Despite the fact that caste enumerations have been dropped from census schedules, the political discourse clings to the idea of representation by enumerable communities.[3]

It has been suggested that an important entry point in situating transformations in the terms of political discourse is the changing interface of the twin constituents of political discourse in the modern domain. These are the categories of the liberal democratic state produced theoretically in the West and the categories that made up the Orientalist construction of India, i.e. religion and caste.[4]

This preliminary exploration of three Bihari Muslim *biradaris* (broadly caste/occupational brotherhoods), the Momins, Rayeens and Kulahias, mobilizing for access to social justice, is an attempt in that direction.

Though a non-monolithic entity, the Indian Muslims comprise the largest minority segment in India (12%). As many as 53% of the Muslim population lives below the poverty line and 50.5% are illiterate.[5] In a recent study of the broad trends of politics among Muslims it has been implied that in north India, unlike the Kurmis, Yadavs and Gujars, Muslims have not mobilized for access to compensatory programmes of social justice.[6] This paper corrects this picture and underlines the enumerative mobilizations of *biradaris,* which are different from the discourse and politics of homogenization, more often in focus.

I

The Indian Constitution [articles 15 (4) and 16 (4)] authorizes preferential treatment not only for Scheduled Castes and Scheduled Tribes, but for "other socially and educationally backward classes".[7] Given the constitutional recognition of this last category, who the backward classes are became a question of pan-Indian scope.[8] This was because the Constitution left the category undefined, without providing any exclusive method or agency for their designation.[9]

The 1951 debate which added Article 15(4) to the Constitution had made it clear that the Backward Classes, by whoever designated and according to whatever criteria, were expected to be a list of castes and communities. Castes and communal units remain the predominant "classes" deemed backward. The level of benefits (scholarships, fee concessions, reservation in government posts and admissions in technical institutions) vary from state to state.[10]

Significantly, the doubts expressed by Kaka Kalelkar, chairman of the Backward Classes Commission in 1955, regarding the caste criterion in identifying the Backward Classes were attributed by him to his discovery that it would have had a "most unhealthy effect on the Muslim and Christian sections of the nation". It was this, he wrote, that had got him "thinking anew" and to conclude that backwardness could be tackled on a number of bases other than caste. His argument was that Indian Christians and Muslims ought to have been helped "without their being driven to accept the fissiparous principle of caste".[11]

Several representations on behalf of "some" Muslim organisations had been sent in to the Kalelkar Commission requesting that *all* Muslims be treated as backward and given educational aid and adequate representation in government service.[12] The Commission's position, however, was that accepting the demand would be unfair as "officially" Muslims did not recognise caste. But recognizing that "gradually" "Islamic society in India (had)... succumbed to the influence of caste and lost its pristine purity" it added the names of such backward Muslim communities to the list of other Backward Classes. However, unlike several state governments which mentioned these communities under separate heads of Hindus and Muslims the Kalelkar Commission pointedly did not make "any such distinction on the basis of religion in determining the backwardness of any community".[13]

Unlike the Kalelkar report, the Mandal Commission Report (1980) explicitly recommended "caste as a criterion" for identifying backward classes. Its emphatic observation was that there was no doubt that social and educational backwardness among non-Hindu communities "is more or less of the same order as among Hindu communities". For while the caste system was peculiar to Hindu society, in practice it pervaded the non-Hindu communities "in varying degrees", with Hindu converts "inadvertently" acting as "Trojan horses" of the caste system among the "highly equaltarian" religions such as Islam, Christianity and Sikhism. In addition, there was no escaping from the "dominant social and cultural practices" in "predominantly Hindu India".[14]

However, given that Islam, Christianity and Sikhism "proclaimed absolute equality of all co-religionists" the Mandal Commission decided that caste could not be made the basis for identifying socially and culturally backward classes among non-Hindu communities. Instead it opted for the following guidelines. First, all untouchables converted to any non-Hindu religion. Second, such occupational communities which were known by the name of their traditional, hereditary occupation and whose Hindu counterparts had been included in the list of Hindu Other Backward Classes, for example Dhobi, Teli, Nai, Dheemar, Lohar, etc. In its estimate the total population of Hindu and non-Hindu Other Backward Classes added up to nearly 52% (43.70% + 8.40%) of the Indian population.[15]

While Backward Classes groups themselves differ in their definitions of the Backward Classes and their population estimates, they tend to be "rather expansive" . . . often including all religious minorities as well as Hindu groups. Thus for example the figure constantly used at the All-India Backward Classes Federation for this category in 1966 stood at 85% of the population.[16]

II

In the north the backward classes movement has been most active in Bihar and this since the 1940s.[17] However, it was only in the late 1970s[18] during the chief ministership of the Janata leader Karpoori Thakur, that what has been described as "Backward

Raj"[19] was inaugurated. However, a decade old study on Bihar which makes this point even as it notes that a part of the Muslim community has been included in all the listings of the backward classes proceeds to exclude the Muslims from the study on three unconvincing grounds.[20]

First, that the census while it does count Muslims does not distinguish between Muslim castes and so it is "impossible" to say which Muslims are backward and which are not. Second, that Muslims are "generally" thought of in Bihar "simply as Muslims" rather than as belonging to caste groups within their religion and that the entire community is thought of as either "backward or not backward". Third, that it is "relatively easy" to keep track of Muslims as a single group in the analysis without having to "add portions of them to the Forward and Backward groups".

Clearly the first argument should apply to Hindu castes as well. What is important is documenting that Muslim *biradaris* do not perceive themselves as being Muslims alone. Notwithstanding the fact that the history of Backward Classes annexures is a "tangled one"[21] it is equally important to map the mobilizations of Muslim *biradaris* for social justice via inclusion in specific lists/annexures for an entry into the narrative of the *biradari*[22] which tends to get concealed under the homogenous categories "Muslims"/ "Minorities".

But first a backgrounder of the Backward Classes movement in Bihar. The entire matter of reservations, as is well known, was left to the states after the Kalelkar Report had evoked an uproar when it finally came for parliamentary discussion in 1964. This was on the issue of the criterion for reservations. Until the late 1970s the state governments of Bihar and U.P. adopted only marginal fee concessions for post graduate students of the Backward Classes.[23]

It was the 1967 election that produced in Karpoori Thakur a popular leader of the Backward Classes. Thakur who was a Socialist came from the low-ranking Nai (barber) caste. His election slogan was true to Rammanohar Lohia. "*Socialists ne bandhi ganth/Pichchra Pavé Saumé Sath*" (Socialists have given the pledge the Backwards will get 60% reservation).[24] Later when Karpoori Thakur became chief minister of the Janata government in 1977, he acted on the Mungeri Lal Commission (1971) Report of 1976. A government order of November 1978 accepted its classification of Other and Most Backward Classes (Table 1). For the purpose of recruitment to jobs it announced the following reservation quotas: 8% for Other Backward Classes, 12% for Most Backward Classes, 14% for Scheduled Castes, 10% for Scheduled Tribes, 3% for women and 3% for the economically backward.[25] This evoked a backlash from the upper castes.

Table 1, based on the annexures of Other Backward Classes between 1951-93 reveals that following Thakur's reservation decision the number of Most Backward Class Muslim communities rose from 6/17 in 1955 to 14/20 in 1978. Columns three and four show that Thakur followed Mungeri Lal's classification in toto. By 1992 only 4/19 Muslim *biradaris* remain in the Other Backward Class category.

Both Table 1 and Section III (below) tie up with the findings of two other studies. Significantly, in the 1980 elections though the Congress rebound to power in Bihar getting 36% of the vote, Charan Singh's Lok Dal led by Karpoori Thakur emerged as a powerful political force among the Muslims. The Bihar Lok Dal did better in the Muslim constituencies where they got 23% of the vote as against 16.6% won by the party in the whole state.[26] Likewise the return of 2 Lok Dal M.L.A.s in 1980 was an indication of the "increasing impact" of Muslim (as also the Hindu) backward castes in the electoral process in Bihar.[27]

Once the social justice schemes for the Backward Classes, other than the Scheduled Castes and Scheduled Tribes got off the ground, it was the upper Backwards, more advanced economically and better organised who gained important leadership positions.[28] This should be seen together with the post-47 shift in the leadership structure among the Muslims in Bihar. In this regard the strong position occupied by the Momins has been attributed to the "social awakening, political organisation, economic consolidation and educational advancement of the backward castes".[29] Detailed studies of backward Muslim *biradaris* are however, yet to be undertaken.[30]

III

It was in the context of the *razil-sharif* (labouring and non-labouring) divide that the Momin (weaver) Conference had contested the monolithizing discourse and politics of the Muslim League in the pre-47 Bihar.[31] The 1937 Congress ministry which pitched at this community which bulked large (over 20%) among the Muslims had provided it with scholarships and aid to the handloom industry. After independence the Momin Conference worked on getting free studentships and stipends extended to "various" backward Muslims.[32]

It may be mentioned that Abdul Qaiyum Ansari, the pre-47 Momin Conference leader was the Congress nominee to the Constituent Assembly and served on its advisory committee on Fundamental Rights and Minorities and Tribals. Ansari was also one of the 11 members of the Kalelkar Commission and president of the All India Backward Muslim Federation for 1952.[33] The working committee of the All India Momin Conference, held in Patna on 18 June 1966 had appealed to the government to draw up a comprehensive scheme towards bringing the Muslim Backward Classes on par with other citizens, for the backwardness of a sizable population, it pointed out, did not conform with the "prestige" of the country.[34]

When in 1984 the Bihar State Momin Conference negotiated for the Momins to be moved from Other Backward Class (Annexure 2) to Most Backward Class (Annexure 1) category the language was not merely that of backwardness but of enumerating the *biradari.* It claimed to be more than half the entire Muslim population not only in Bihar but in India. The Momin Conference also foregrounded that Momins had been "traditional nationalists" since the pre-47 days and were indeed "pillars of strength to secularism and democracy and the unity and integrity of the country".[35] The acceptance of the demand was announced by Rajiv Gandhi at the Bihar State Momin Conference on 1 September and seen through on 14 November 1984.[36]

By contrast, in the case of the Bihar Jamiatur Rayeen[37] (vegetable growers and fruit sellers), mobilizing for enlistment in Annexure 1 (from 2) has been more uphill. Totaling 26% of the Bihari Muslim population, "just two less than the Momins", the Jamiatur Rayeen attributes its Annexure immobility to discrimination by the Congress on account of its association with the opposition.[38] To elaborate this point the Jamiatur Rayeen underlines the following sequence. It was on 13 September 1977 that the Janata government had decided that the facility of freeships in educational and technical institutions, available to communities classified in Annexure 1 (Most Backward Classes) would be extended to all Muslim Other Backward Classes. While this was withdrawn in the case of the Muslim *biradaris* when the Congress returned to office in 1980, the Momins not only continued to avail of it but were in fact moved to Annexure 2.[39]

Apart from this demand, which is an important rallying plank, the Jamiatur Rayeen has been campaigning for easier loans for vegetable and fruit sellers, reservation of seats in technical and non-technical institutions, complete control of the Bihar State Fruit and Vegetable Development Corporation, adequate representation on public sector undertakings, co-operatives and corporations and the Legislative Council and priority in the allotment of shops by bazaar committees.[40]

Following its representation along these lines, Laloo Prasad Yadav, the Bihar chief minister, in February 1991, directed the A.N. Sinha Institute of Social Studies, Patna to document the backwardness level of the *biradari*.[41] The Institute's study made in July-August 1991, covered 350 families in 24 villages in four districts where Rayeens are concentrated – Nawada, Madhubani, Saharsa and Bhojpur. On the basis of 9/10 indices it emerged that 80% of the Rayeens were economically and socially backward. The recommendation therefore was that the *biradari* be moved to Annexure 1.[42]

Subsequently Laloo Prasad Yadav announced at a rally of the Bihar Jamiatur Rayeen in November 1991 that its demand to be included in Annexure 1 would be conceded. When that was not forthcoming, the Jamiatur Rayeen organized a massive rally in Patna on 28 December 1993. The memorandum submitted to Yadav mentioned that the Rayeens had had much expectations from the chief minister, who was himself a manifestation of the constitutional provision for social justice.[43]

The handbills circulated by the Jamiatur Rayeen on the eve of the 28 December rally provide some significant insights into the narrative of the community. Thus one of them lamented that despite being an enumerable (26%) presence, the *biradari* was neither acknowledged nor had it impacted socially or politically. The rally, it specified was an exercise in asserting and experiencing its collective self, constructing its self-image and underlining its commitment to mobilizing for access to social justice.

The second handbill has '786' printed on top, is in Urdu but in Nagri script with at least 6 key translations included in Hindi. I point this out because it perhaps is indicative of the imperceptible fading out of Urdu among Muslims that is often talked about.

It is worth mentioning that when I happened to remark that the *ishtahar* (handbill) was only addressed to Rayeen '*bhaiyon*' (brothers) the secretary mentioned that the Jamiatur Rayeen had self-consciously tried to avoid using *jati* because of its ("caste") connotations. Also a copy of an earlier press statement by a women-youth Rayeen leader was shown to allay any conclusions about gender bias.

There are other strands in *biradaris* mobilizing for social justice. Thus recently, the Mehtars, Lalbegis and Halalkhors who are catalogued as Most Backward Classes agitated to be included in the Scheduled Caste list.[44]

The Kulahias are another case in point.[45] Their mobilization case is aimed at getting them enlisted as the crucial preliminary for access to social justice. The organisation is significantly named in Hindi officialese – Kulahia Vikas Sangathan (Development Organisation).

The Kulahia Vikas Sangathan's enumerative mobilization comes in the wake of the September 1993 announcement regarding the implementation of Mandal Commission report and its decision to revise the Backward Classes lists. Their demand is that a functionary for the identification of Muslim communities, constitutionally provided for ("according to article 338") be followed up at the level of the Welfare ministry. For many Muslim castes and Scheduled Tribes in Purnea (in north-east Bihar), Sikkim, H.P. and Meghalaya remain unlisted and therefore outside the "national mainstream".

This *biradari* totaling "11,17,949" and living in "653 villages" according to a survey conducted in September 1993, live in Purnea, Araria and Katihar, has its "own culture, civilization and language". To establish its 'extreme' backwardness the Kulahia Development Organisation memorandum mentions that only 0.5% of them are in government service, thousands of them work as agricultural labourers/labourers in Delhi, Punjab and U.P., and 80% of the women have just one sari each. "Entertainment is restricted to folktales" and the community bereft of social justice is superstitious enough to drive away phosphorous gas visible during rainy nights by beating kettles, utensils and drums lest the gas ushered epidemics into the villages.

More pointedly the Kulahias refer to the fact that 45 years after Independence they remain extremely backward when in fact the Muslims of north-east Bihar who are in a majority (40% of the population) had voted against Pakistan.

IV

Given the sedimentation of the colonial discourse of enumerating Indian society[46] in post-colonial times, enumerating mobilizations[47] continue to mark the political discourse as is evident from the core of this paper. Quite apart from the narrative of the *biradari*, usually much less in focus than the narrative of nation,[48] what is significant is the documenting of the non-homogenizing political discourse among Muslims. This is also manifest in the shifts in leadership in the putative religions ('minority') community, which going by the OBC/MBC listings is anything but a "pampered" community.

I conclude with the point that it was the intervention of the communities (castes/*biradaris*) within religious 'minorities' that deflected the Kalelkar Commission's excercise in ushering in the "casteless" society that the "nation" had "decided" on. "Caste" and "religion", both of which it sought to erase bounced right back. All this despite the *biradaris* deploying the language of the "national mainstream" and the unpartitioned "nation" for access to social justice.

NOTES

1. Sudipta Kaviraj, "On State, Society and Discourse in India", in James Manor, ed., *Rethinking Third World Politics* (London, Longman, 1991), pp. 76-77. "Given different situations a pre-modern person could have said that his community was either his religion or caste or occupational group, or his village or his region. He might find it difficult to render these varying communities to all of which he belonged into some unimpeachable hierarchy, either moral or political". That is, a "fuzzy" sense of community meant that it occurred to none to ask how many of them there were in the world or to deploy their numbers for concerted assertions.
2. Partha Chatterjee, *The Nation and Its Fragments: Colonial and Post Colonial Histories* (Delhi, Oxford University Press, 1994), pp. 223-4. Briefly, the argument is that a fundamental element in the colonial conceptualization of India as a "different" society was the "fixed belief" that the population was a "mélange of communities". This was a prelude to the picking out of "natural leaders" of the various communities and affiliating them to the colonial state seeking legitimacy. Indeed this theory of representation informed the constitutional reforms of the late colonial period. If "communities" characterized Indian society in colonial thought, those communities had to be singular and substantive entities in

themselves with determinate and impermeable boundaries, i.e. incapable of merging into a "nation", which was a larger, more modern political identity.

3. *Ibid.*, pp. 224. Thus "virtually every discussion on Indian elections looks for supportive evidence in the complicated political arithmetic of caste and communal alliances". Such calculations are reflected in both the electoral strategies of political parties, as well the choice of candidates.
4. *Ibid.*, pp. 224-6. Chatterjee makes the following important points that provide an insight into the discourse and politics of caste and religion during the past four decades. The fuzziness which enabled a wide variety of solidarities ranging from subcastes to gender to nation to be encompassed under the single rubric of *jati* (see pp. 220-3 for an elaboration) came under a great strain when those solidarities came to be forcibly inserted into the grid of the modern regime of power. Yet, the modern disciplinary regime is itself limited by the numerous resistances to its hegemonic sway. Chatterjee contends that the imaginative possibilities afforded by the fuzziness of the community have not disappeared from the domain of popular political discourse. What is ironical is that the "zone of pure politics" in the "domain of high discourse", while rejecting the colonialist dogma that Indian society was unfit to have a modern state, perceived at the same time the cultural realities of the domain of mass politics as polluting and corrupting the rational processes of state. At least some of this gets reflected in Kalelkar and Nehru's (see endnotes 10 and 11) paranoia about the "casteism" potential of project social justice
5. Moonis Raza, "Communalism in Contemporary India: Preliminary Enquiry Into Its Structure, Forms and Characteristics", *Mainstream,* vol xxxii, no. 11, 29 January 1994, p. 33.
6. Mushirul Hasan, "In Search of Integration and Identity: Indian Muslims Since Independence", Occasional papers on History and Society, Nehru Memorial Museum and Library (NMML), New Delhi, no. LII, March 1988, p. 21.
7. See *GOI Report of the Backward Classes Commission*, 1980 (Delhi, 1981), vol. i, ch. vi, "Social Justice, Merit and Privilege", for a supportive explication.
8. Marc Galanter, "Who Are the Backward Classes?: An Introduction to a Constitutional Puzzle", *Economic and Political Weekly,* vol. xiii, nos. 43 and 44, 28 October 1978, p, 1812.
9. Marc Galanter, *Competing Equalities: Law and the Backward Classes in India* (Delhi, Oxford University Press, 1984), p. 154.
10. *Ibid.*, pp. 166 & 181. fn. 59; p. 166 elaborates Nehru's "extraordinary reticence" about using the word "caste" in the course of the debate to insert article 15 (4).

11 *GOI Report of the Backward Classes Commission*, 1955, vol. i, pp. vi-vii. The background was that when the GOI recognised certain Hindu castes as backward and offered special scholarships and concessions, it led many Muslims and Christians to assert that although their religion was theoretically opposed to caste, in practice their society was more or less "caste-ridden". Muslims had also approached the Kalelkar Commission to prove that "except" for the four upper castes (Syed, Sheikh, Mughal and Pathan) all other Muslim castes were inferior and backward. Following up similar memoranda from Christians the Commission discovered that caste was indeed "rampant" in the "extreme south".

However, Kalelkar's bottom line. p. xiv, was that "the nation" having "decided to establish a classless and casteless society", backwardness ought to be studied from the point of the "individual" and "at the most of the family. Any other unit will lead to caste and class aggrandizement".

12. *Ibid.*, p. 27. This is a point of view occasionally floated in political circles. An interview with U.N. Sinha, (Chairman, Creamy Layer Committee), 25 January 1994, in Patna revealed that when the Karpoori Thakur government was working out its reservation formula (see below) Ghulam Sarvar, a Rayeen ("at that time the most significant (Muslim) leader" and at present the Bihar Assembly Speaker) had categorically shot down the proposal, contending that not all Muslims were backward.

More recently the Janata Dal has demanded that the Muslim community be declared backward. See *The Telegraph*, 15 August 1993. The stand is shared by Jabir Hussain, Chairman, Bihar State Minorities Commission, as mentioned in a telephone conversation on 29 January 1994, in Patna.

13. *GOI Report of the Backward Classes Commission*, 1955, vol. i, p. 27; p. 160 mentions that though Christianity had "consistently refused to recognise caste" the Commission decided to include Scheduled Caste converts to Christianity in the Backward Classes category in view of the ground reality of their segregation. Also see Jose Kananaikil, *Christians of Scheduled Caste Origin* (New Delhi, Indian Social Institute, 1986).

14. *GOI Report of the Backward Classes Commission*, 1980, Part I, p. 55.

15. *Ibid.*, pp. 55-6. Also see Appendix vii, p. 91. The members of non-Hindu communities are to be deemed educationally backward if neither the father nor grandfather have studied beyond the primary level.

16. *Competing Equalities*, p. 178, fn. 125.

17. "Who Are the Other Backward Classes?", p. 1814 and fns. 40 and 43, p. 1822.

18. See Francine R. Frankel, "Middle Classes and Castes in India's

Politics: Prospects for Political Accommodation", in Atul Kohli, ed. *India's Democracy: An Analysis of Changing State-Society Relations* (Hyderabad, Orient Longmans, 1988), pp. 236-43 and 249-61; Paul R. Brass, *The New Cambridge History of India: The Politics of India Since Independence* (Cambridge, Cambridge University Press, 1990), p. 214 and Atul Kohli, *Democracy and Discontent: India's Discontent: India's Growing Crisis of Governability* (Cambridge, Cambridge University Press, 1991), Ch. 4.

19. Harry W. Blair, "Rising Kulaks and Backward Classes in Bihar: Social Change in the Late 1970s", *Economic and Political Weekly*, vol. xv, no. 2, 12 January 1980, p. 72.
20. *Ibid.*, p. 65.
21. *Ibid.*, p. 64; Annexure 1 listed the Most/Extreme Backward Classes and Annexure 2 the Other Backward Classes, see table 1.
22. I base the term on Partha Chatterjee's usage "the narrative of community", *The Nation and Its Fragments*, pp. 234-9.
23. Frankel, op.cit, pp. 242, 256.
24. *Ibid.*, p. 251. For a general contextualizing of the backward class movement see Brass, op. cit, pp. 206-7. He mentions universal suffrage, zamindari abolition and the linguistic reorganisation of States which eliminated language as an alternate source of mobilization.
25. *GOI Report of the Backward Classes Commission Report*, 1980, Second part, vol. vi, pp. 157-8 comments that Thakur attempted grafting the Karnataka model in Bihar without following Devraj Urs' example of a long and adequate mobilization of the backwards' solidarity.
26. "In Search of Integration", pp. 33-34. See Frankel, op.cit p. 257 for an explanation of the Lok Dal's returns: the Backward Classes had miscalculated in believing that it was possible to use the reservations issue for raising political consciousness among all the backward communities to mobilise the poor. Moreover the Congress line was that Thakur's approach was "casteist" and would only strengthen the Yadavs and Kurmis in becoming the new Brahmans.

    See Brass, op.cit, p. 214, for the comment that the equation that emerged subsequently was an alliance of the upper castes and lowest castes against the backwards.
27. Ali Ashraf, *The Muslim Elite* (New Delhi, Atlantic Publishers, 1983), p. 48.
28. Blair, op.cit., p. 71.
29. Ashraf, op.cit., pp. 64 and 88.
30. *Ibid.*, p. 64; One may mention Mohammad Aslam, "On Muslim Identity and Politics" in A.D. Pant and S.K. Gupta, eds., *Multi-Ethnicity and National Integration: A Politico-Anthropological View*

(Allahabad, Vohra, 1985), pp. 284-6 for a reference to a similar leadership shift in U.P. Also see his "Elites Versus Artisan Leadership: Muslims and Politics in U.P. 1947-92". Ph.D thesis, submitted to La Trobe University, February 1993. I am grateful to the author for letting me go through it. The *biradari* question is taken up by E.A. Mann, *Boundaries and Identities* (London, Sage, 1992).

31. Papiya Ghosh, "Contesting the *Sharif:* The Momin Conference – Muslim League Interface in Bihar, 1938-47", paper presented at the seminar on "Caste and Class in India", Joshi-Adhikari Institute of Social Studies, New Delhi, 4 April 1992. Also "The Discourse and Politics of *Qaum, Mazhab and Biradari* in 1940s Bihar", paper presented at the workshop on "Northern India and Indian Independence" N.M.M.L., New Delhi, 9 December 1993.
32. Hasan Nishat Ansari, *The Momin-Congress Relations: A Socio-Historical Analysis* (Patna, Bihar Momin Intellectuals' Forum, 1989), p. 19.
33. Ashraf, op.cit., pp. 108-9; *GOI Report of the Backward Classes Commission, 1980* Part I, vol. 2, appendix I, p. 67.
34. Ansari, op.cit, p. 28. The working committee emphasized the insufficiency of upliftment programmes for backward Muslims in India.
35. *Ibid.*, 51.
36. *Ibid.*, pp. 51-2, significantly subtitled, "Congress Enlists Momins in Annexure I"; see Govt. of Bihar, Dept. of Personnel and Administrative Reform, resolution No. II/S, 1-105/84, 14 November 1984 for the enlistment. The resolution justifies the change in the light of having received "several" representations to that effect.
37. See "Contesting the *Sharif*" for a background of the pre-'47 Jamiatur Rayeen. Significantly this *biradari* as also the Mansoors (cotton carders) had not been keen during the 1940s to be part of a collective' together with the Idrisis (tailors) and Quraishes (butchers), that the Momin Conference had tried to float.
38. Interview with Zafar Ahmad, secretary, Bihar Jamiatur Rayeen (BJR), 29 December 1993, Patna. The reference is to Ghulam Sarvar (see above) being active in the J.P. movement. Also see the BJR representation to Laloo Prasad Yadav, February (n.d.) 1991, "*Yeh poori abadi vipaksh ké khémay mein rahi hai*".
39. BJR, representation, February 1991.
40. *Ibid.* and BJR memorandum; 28 December 1993.
41. "*Rayeen Jati Par Ek Shodh Prativedan*" (A Research Survey on the Rayeen Biradari), Director, A.N. Sinha Institute of Social Studies, Patna. I am grateful to Zafar Ahmad for a copy.
42. The report mentions that barring a few success stories the *biradari* is extremely backward, its members are derisively referred to as

Kunjras. The survey team encountered labouring women in 95.7% of the families. (There is a mention of a "joke" about the Kunjras massaging the tired Kunjarins at day end). The community had over the years lost land near Biharsharif and had been edged out of the fruit marts of Calcutta which they once dominated.

43. The chief minister gave a positive assurance yet again. See *Aaj*, 29 December 1993.
44. *The Hindustan Times* (Patna), 12 January 1994.
45. What follows is based on a press statement of the Kulahia Development Organisation addressed to *Jansatta* to coincide with a day long fast by 300 Kulahia students in Patna on 29 December 1993. I am grateful to Surendra Kishore for a copy.
46. Sudipta Kaviraj, "The Imaginary Institution of India", in Partha Chatterjee and Gyanendra Pandey, eds., *Subaltern Studies VII* (Delhi, Oxford University Press, 1992) comments on the enumeration fetish.
47. See Gyanendra Pandey, *The Construction of Communalism in Colonial North India* (Delhi, Oxford University Press, 1990); Papiya Ghosh, "Articulating Community Rights: The Muslim League and Hindu Mahasabha in Congress Bihar, 1937-39", *South Asia,* vol. xiii, no. 2, December 1991 and "Enumerating The *Aqliat*: The Bihar Provincial Muslim League 1937-47" (unpublished paper), presented at I.I.T., New Delhi, 3 November 1992 for pre-47 transitions from fuzzy to enumerated communities.
48. Partha Chatterjee, op.cit, pp. 234-9 argues that the narrative of capital in which the modern state is embedded seeks to suppress the narrative of the community but cannot really do so.

TABLE 1

Annexures of Bihari Muslim Other Backward and Most Backward Classes 1951 - 1993 *

Names	1951	1955	1976	1978	1980	1992	1993
Bhat			O&M	O&M	O	M	O
Bhathiara	M	M	O&M	O&M	O	M	O
Chik	M	O	O&M	O&M	O	M	O
Churihara	O	M	O	O	O		O
Dafalange					O		
Dafale	M	M	O&M	O&M	O	M	O
Dhobi	M	O	O&M	O&M		M	O
Dhunia	M	M	O&M	O&M	O	M	O
Faqir					O		
Gadihar				O			
Hima, Karanjia, Qassar					O		
Ibrahimi		O					
Idrisi	O	O	O	O	O	O	
Kassab	M	O	O&M	O&M	O	M	O
Mehtar, Lalbegi Halalkhor, Bhangi	M	M	O&M	O&M	O	M	O
Madari	M		O&M	O&M	O	M	O
Miriasin	M		O&M	O&M	O	M	O
Mirshikar	O	O	O&M	O&M	O	M	O
Momin	O	O	O	O	O	M	O
Mukero	O				O	O	O
Nalband	O		O	O	O	O	
Nat	M	M	O&M	O&M	O	M	O
Pamaria	M	O	O&M	O&M	O	M	O
Rangrez	O	O	O	O	O	O	O
Rayeen	O	O	O	O	O	O	O
Sayee	O	O	O&M	O&M	O	M	O
Thakurai					O		

Key: O : Other Backward classes; M : Most Backward Classes.

Note: There was a common list in the years 1980 & 1993 i.e. there was no O and M classification in these years.

**Source*:

1. 1951 & 1976: Mungeri Lal Commission Report, pp. 114-5 and 118-9 respectively.
2. 1955 : GOI Report of the Backward Classes Commission (1955), vol ii, pp. 16-23.
3. 1978 : Govt. of Bihar, Dept. of Personnel & Administrative Reform: Circulars etc. upto 1988, (10 November, 1978)pp.118-23.
4. 1980 : GOI Report of the Backward Classes Commission (1980), vol vi, pp. 178-9.
5. 1992 : Govt. of Bihar Gazette, 10 March 1992, pp. 9-12.
6. 1993 : GOI, Extraordinary Gazette, 13 September 1993, pp. 40-3

28 दिसम्बर को राईन भाईयों का विराट प्रदर्शन

राईन भाईयों ।

जिन्दगी के समस्त क्षेत्रों में हमारी स्थिति दयनीय है । इस दयनीय हालत के लिए एक ओर जहाँ हम स्वयं जिम्मेदार हैं, वहीं दूसरी ओर यह भी एक निर्विवादित सत्य है कि स्वतंत्रता, के पूर्व और उसके बाद भी हमारी प्रजातांत्रिक सरकारों की ओर से लगातार हमारे सामूहिक वजूद की अपेक्षा होती रही है । हमारी अत्यन्त दयनीय स्थिति और पिछड़ापन के बावजूद न तो सरकारी स्तर पर हमें कभी कोई सुविधा मिली और न ही हमारी सामाजिक उत्थान के लिए हमारी किसी भी माँग की पूर्ति हुई । बिहार में मुसलमानों की कुल आबादी का 26% होने के बावजूद हमारी न कोई पहचान है और न ही कोई सामाजिक एवं राजनैतिक छाप !

यह समझने और समझाने के लिए कि हमें भी एक अभिमाणित नागरिक की तरह जीवन व्यतीत करने का हक है ।

28 दिसम्बर को बिहार विधान सभा के समक्ष विराट प्रदर्शन का कार्यक्रम है ।

- ☛ अपने आत्म सम्मान की रक्षा के लिए,
- ☛ अपनी पहचान बनाने के लिए,
- ☛ सामाजिक असमता और अन्याय के विरूद्ध अपनी कटिबद्धता को दुहराने के लिए,
- ☛ अपने अस्तित्व का एहसास दिलाने के लिए,
- ☛ मुख्यमंत्री को उनका वायदा याद दिलाने के लिए,

हजारों हजार की संख्या में पटना के गाँधी मैदान में **28 दिसम्बर 93'** को **11 बजे दिन** में जमा होकर अपनी एकता और जागरूकता का परिचय देते हुए इस ऐतिहासिक प्रदर्शन को सफल बनायें ।

बिहार जमिअर्तुराईन
गोलारोड बाक़रगंज, पटना-4
दूरभाष-657791

मनव्वर प्रिन्टिंग प्रेस, सब्जीबाग, पटना-४

Scheduled Tribes And Broken Promises

JAGANATH PATHY

The constitutional and legal status of the tribes in India has many facets. It includes individual rights as Indian citizens, and special rights for the Scheduled Tribes residing in tribal majority States and Union Territories, in the Vth and VIth Scheduled Areas, and those who live outside the Scheduled Areas and tribal majority States and Union Territories. In addition, there are special provisions for the so-called "primitive groups" and denotified communities.

Of course, the special privileges and protection for the tribals have had a long history. Wherever colonialism faced the strongest oppositions to its annexation and administration, a number of protective and preventive acts were introduced, especially to restrict entry of non-tribals, to provide special agrarian laws and to restrict jurisdiction of colonial courts, laws and regulations. The most significant efforts in this direction were the introduction of the Agency system in some tribal tracts during 1825-65, the Scheduled District Act of 1874, the concept of Backward Areas in the Government of India Act, 1919, creation of partially and fully excluded Areas under the Government of India Act, 1935, various provisional laws making tribal land inalienable, as well as recognition of some forms of communal systems of land control in certain tribal regions. These concessions were primarily directed as *quid pro quo* for the numerous tribal struggles.

In North-east India, colonialism largely followed a policy of non-intervention in the customary ways of life and economy of the tribal peoples. The first Inner Line Regulation was introduced in 1873 for all the districts of the eastern frontiers of Bengal. Land was allowed to be governed by customary laws and customs, and outsiders were prohibited to acquire any land. The Jhumland Regulation recognized both collective and individual land rights of swidden cultivators. Needless to emphasize that this strategy was primarily dictated by the fact of British inability to bring the region under its direct control, and secondarily, to build buffers against the Burmese and the Chinese with local.

The leaders of the Indian National Congress were very critical of these special provisions, and considered them as integral to the British policy of "divide and rule". They however failed to comprehend why such concessions were made much before the freedom movement revealed any sign of threat to the colonial domination, nor ever evaluated how effective these provisions were to pose as obstacles to the unity of the peoples of India for independence (Pathy 1984: 165-66), and much less realised that the special provisions for the tribals conveyed the inbuilt weakness of colonial capital and power.

With independence, the Indian leadership was compelled to provide special privileges, preferences and concessions to the members of the Scheduled Tribes. There are as many as twenty Articles and two special Schedules in the Indian Constitution concerning the welfare of the tribals and tribal areas. This is unique in the whole world. Besides the Fundamental Rights to equality (Articles 14, 15, 16, and 17) and rights against exploitation (Articles 23 and 24), there are several Articles (38, 39, 41, 43, 46,47 and 48) in the Directive Principles of State Policy – which of course cannot be enforced by law. In addition, there is a provision for a minister of tribal welfare in some states (Article 164); special provisions for reservation (affirmative action) in the legislatures (except in tribal states and only for ten years in instalments) education and employment, as well as appointment of special officers and commissioner (Articles 330, 332, 334, 335 338, 339 and 342). The Scheduled Tribes are constitutionally identified under Article 366, and Article 275 provides for special grants of the Union to certain states for tribal development. Further, Article 371 upholds the customary law, justice and socio-religious practices in Negaland, Manipur and tribal areas of Assam.

Among the most important provisions for the tribals, Article 46 is often repeated as the constitutional commitment for the advancement of the tribal peoples. The Article holds: "State shall promote with special care the educational and economic interest of the weaker section of the people, and in particular of the Scheduled Castes and Scheduled Tribes, and shall protect them from social injustice and all forms of exploitation". The ideal is laudable. But when the social system is itself based upon the premise of exploitation, "one particular section among the people cannot be freed from 'all forms of exploitation' as long as their co-workers who do not belong to their caste or tribe continue in their old (exploited) condition" (Bose, 1972:95). Small wonder, despite the Article 46, social injustice and exploitation has accentuated phenomenally in post-independent India. In fact, acceptance of GATT and the Dunkel proposals are geared to annul any special favours for the disadvantaged peoples.

Reservations in education, employment and legislatures are considered the next conspicuous and meaningful provisions of the Indian constitution. Perhaps this is true, but it needs assertion that it is not the tribal collectivities but the individuals belonging to them who are entitled to such benefits. They, in turn, cannot but eventually get coopted in the system, and thereby, tend to alienate themselves from the community. In other words, their emergence is of limited significance for the general strategy of emancipation of the oppressed and exploited tribal peoples. True some may work for the upliftment of their brethren, but the system and its culture cannot but constrain them. Put simply, they can hardly become the spokespersons of the marginalised tribal peoples.

The next best provisions are the two special schedules. The Fifth Schedule (244-i) applies to most of the predominantly tribal areas, provides for Advisory Councils, three-fourths of whose members being from tribal background and expected to advise the respective states on the welfare and advancement of the Scheduled Tribes. The Governor, in consultation with the council, is empowered to direct that any particular Act or any part thereof, of the Parliament or of the state legislature, shall not apply to the Scheduled Areas. He can also formulate special regulations with respect to prohibition or restriction of land transfer by or among the members of the Scheduled Tribes, control of moneylending, bondage, land redistribution and allotment. Regrettable as it is, the Vth schedule has so far remained ineffective or inoperative in practice. Many States have either not formulated special regulations or have not enforced them, council meetings are rare, annual reports are routine, and the tribal leadership has failed to make the council a powerful voice in favour of the suffering tribals. In addition, it may be stressed that the Vth Schedule does not recognise group rights in land and land-based resources, and customary political institutions, with the sole exception of the Munda and the Manki, the village and inter-village headmen – under the Chotanagpur Tenancy Act, 1908, and the Santal Pargana Tenancy Act, respectively.

In contrast, the VIth schedule [Articles 244(2) and 275(i)] is a very powerful legal instrument towards tribal self-management and self-development. It is applicable to the tribal areas of Assam and Tripura (since 1985) and the tribal states of Meghalaya, Mizoram, Nagaland and Arunachal Pradesh. This Schedule authorises the autonomous district and regional councils to frame laws relating to use of land for agriculture, grazing, residential or non-agricultural purposes – with the exception of the reserved forests and lands acquired by the State for public purposes. The councils enjoy the power to frame laws for management of unreserved forests, use of water resources, regulation of shifting cultivation, establishment of village and town councils and their administration, appointment or succession of chiefs or headmen, establishment of local courts, inheritance of property, marriage, divorce, social customs, public health and sanitation. The courts however have not performed up to the expectations, due to diverse heritage and practices in given areas.

The autonomous district councils are empowered to administer justice which can only be challenged in the High Court or the Supreme Court. These councils are expected to manage schools, dispensaries, markets, ferries, fisheries, roads etc., and decide the medium and content of instruction in primary schools. They are also authorised to assess and collect revenue and to impose taxes on profession, trade, animals, vehicles, tolls on passengers and goods and taxes for maintenance of welfare institutions. They have the power to control and regulate non-tribal trading and money-lending. In addition, the councils are entitled to an agreed upon share of royalties with the state from mining as well as a reasonable share of the grant-in-aid received by the state government from the Union government under Article 275 of the Constitution. Besides, there are restrictions on application of Acts of Parliament and of state legislatures to the autonomous districts and regions.

In sum, the autonomous district councils not only have the power to manage their land and landbased endowments as per their own customs but also constitute an essential structure for internal self-determination. Such an overriding autonomy through the VIth Schedule has no parallel in the Constitution, except to some extent enjoyed by the peoples of Kashmir through Article 370.

But unfortunately, over the years, the autonomous district councils have been, more or less, reduced to mere administrative entities, almost like the panchayats and municipalities. Needless to mention that panchayati institutions do not have legislative powers, whereas the autonomous district councils have executive, legislative and judicial functions. Hence if the 73rd amendment to the Constitution pertaining to the three-tier Panchayat raj, is extended to the VIth Scheduled Area (currently it does not apply to the Scheduled Areas), the Councils would be deprived of their legislative powers. Already, Arunachal Pradesh and Tripura have only elected Panchayat bodies without a proper relationship with district councils. In Nagaland, though the traditional village and inter-village councils are recognized under the Nagaland village and Area Councils Act, 1978, and they are authorised with both executive and judicial functions and control of village development boards, the Deputy Commissioner is always made the chairperson of the boards. Similarly in Khasi and Jaintia hills of Meghalaya, the traditional chiefs by virtue of treaty arrangements have enjoyed judicial powers at the local levels on behalf of the district councils, the nature of district councils have changed from the principle of consensus to majority rule and are under bureaucratic guidance and control. In fact, over the years, tribal institutions and leadership have been losing ground.

Moreover the series of amendments of the VIth Schedule in 1971, 1972 and 1988 have eroded the legislative powers of the district councils in Mizoram, Meghalaya, and the VIth Schedule areas of Tripura respectively, and the councils have since been subjected to the overriding law-making powers of the concerned legislatures. The Assam Reorganization (Meghalaya) Act, 1969, has curbed the law-making powers of the district councils of judicial administration. In addition, the Governors' discretionary powers; non-effective implementation of the VIth Schedule and its dilution through several amendments; imposition of modern notions of decision making and party structure; the State's right to extinguish the tribal customary corporate rights over land, water and forest for stated public purpose or interest; frequent delay in payment of royalty to the district councils on mining and in grants-in-aid from the Union government; creation of a new oligarchy and more and more people of the Northeast demanding autonomy have limited the significance of this unique schedule of the Constitution (Roy Burman 1989).

Nonetheless, it is only the VIth Schedule in the Constitution that honours customary corporate rights of tribals in land, landbased and sub-surface endowments as per the tradition of the concerned tribal groups. This schedule alone provides a scope for maintenance and development of cultural diversity, sustainable self-development, self-management and self-reliance of the tribal peoples. It is beyond the conception of individual civil rights of equality and non-discrimination. What is required is to strengthen the thrust of the schedule and effectively implement its provisions in conformity with the tribal ethos.

II

Constitutional concern for social justice for the Scheduled Tribes notwithstanding, the tribal problematique has become exacerbated in the post-colonial India. The following briefly argues that the crisis is rooted in the uncritical imposition of individual proprietorship, the onslaught of opprobrious development, and the strategies of nation building.

Towards the end of the nineteenth century, colonialism began the process of conferring legal titles of landownership to individuals in some tribal regions, and treated the rest of the land as *res nullius*. But it became all pervasive only after Independence. Except in the VIth Schedule area, no consideration is given for the specific land systems in tribal societies and the fact that individuals enjoyed secure customary rights to land resources as members of their respective social and/or spatial groups is overlooked. Instead of the generic conception of land in the tribal system, the modern system treated it as a mere factor of production and profit under legal proprietorship of individuals. This has consistently impugned tribal customary corporate rights over land and landbased resources.

To ensure individual proprietorship, it is essential to survey the agricultural lands and settle the ownership with individuals. But a large part of tribal habitat is not yet surveyed and in many parts, the records of rights are either faulty or dated. A recent study found that in some Orissan villages between 2 to 23 per cent of tribal cultivated land has been recorded in their favour and with regard to the unrecorded lands they are treated as encroachers by law (Planning Commission 1987). Incidently the cheap plane table method used for the survey precludes measurement of lands beyond 9° slope and hence lands above this slope are simply recorded in a single entry as state land. Roughly between 25 to 40 per cent of cultivated land of tribals is located above 10° slope. Instead of improving the method of cadastral survey and settlement, the State has conveniently denied traditional ownership rights on upland resources. Simultaneously, not finding individual owners in many tribal areas, the village or lineage headmen or chiefs are suddenly metamorphosed as the real owners of land and the peasants are demoted to the level of tenants.

Moreover, as no individual exercises exclusive property rights over landbased resources like pastures, village forests, sacred groves, water sources, hunting places etc., the Indian legal system has derecognized these corporate land-based endowments. Roughly between 40 to 80 per cent of the total land in tribal regions belongs to this derecognized category, which has been usurped by the State without any compensation whatsoever. Though all the tribal peoples have lost much of the corporate resources, the denial of group rights over landbased resources has proved calamitous for the so-called 72 'primitive groups' with over 1.5 million persons. Similar is the suffering of pastoralists and artisan communities whose survival depended upon landbased resources.

Not only have landbased resources been derecognized, but agricultural lands which are not continuously cultivated are also treated as under illegal occupation. Much of the shifting land is recorded as waste land and reserved forest. It has adversely affected some 12 per cent of the tribal population, and they have more or less lost their meagre land, livelihood and culture.

In short the capitalist assumption of private property in land as the only recognizable right and *sine qua non* of development has imperilled the survival of the tribal peoples and made them susceptible to silent and subtle forms of ethnocide.

A common feature shared by most of tribal habitats is their remoteness and marginal quality of territorial resources. In the past, exploitation of such poor regions was found difficult or uneconomic. But recent rapid technological development and the unrivalled strength of world capitalism have created favourable conditions for the invasion and extraction of natural resources from the ecologically fragile territories of the tribal peoples. Forced evictions of tribals to make way for mammoth capital intensive development projects have become a distressingly routine phenomenon.

Since Independence, a large number of massive irrigation and power projects, all the steel plants, NALCO, mining complexes, heavy engineering complexes, a chain of forest based industries, refugee settlements, industrial and cash crop plantations, forest and wildlife projects and transport systems have come up in tribal inhabited areas. In the past, the dispossession of tribal lands was largely due to alienation by non-tribals, but currently, though the earlier process still continues under various subterfuges like benami transactions, usufructuary mortgages, surreptitious use of the provision of "voluntary surrender" and on grounds of religious, charitable, educational housing and other purposes, the State has emerged as the single biggest alienator of tribal lands and other survival resources in the name of national development and "public" interest.

The colonial law, Land Acquisition Act, 1894 as amended in 1984, freely permits the State to alienate tribal land for "public" purposes. There are also outrageous Acts like the Coal Bearing Areas (Acquisition and Developoment) Act, 1957 which deny compensation to displaced persons. There is no satisfactory account of the number of tribals displaced by different development projects. Nonetheless, one can safely assume that at least five million out of the total displaced 22 million, or approximately one in ten tribals have been displaced by different development projects in the last four decades. The dam projects alone have displaced nearly one million tribals. The Scheduled Tribes Commission reported in 1986 that out of the 1.7 million oustees from 119 public sector projects, a staggering 0.8 million belonged to the Scheduled Tribes. The World Bank has estimated that nearly two million tribals are currently facing resettlement to make for hydroelectric projects alone. Incidently many of these mega river basin and dam projects are funded by the World Bank.

Despite intense industrial activity in the central Indian tribal belt, tribal employment in modern enterprises is negligible. Apart from the provisions of the Apprenticeship Act, there is no stipulation for private or joint sector enterprises to recruit a certain percentage of dispossessed tribal workforce. The public sector too ignores their recruitment under the pretext of lack of skill, alleged irregularity and the like. Consequently the tribals are forced into the ever-expanding low paid, insecure and destitute labour market, and/or slowly crushed into oblivion in their homelands or in urban slums. Similarly, though a large number of irrigation projects are established in the tribal habitats and some of the major rivers originate in the area and receive highest rainfall, no more than five per cent of their lands are assured of irrigation. In fact, their customary methods of water harvesting and spreading have been rendered non-viable.

The Indian government has a notoriously poor record in rehabilitating the displaced. It has no national policy of relocation and rehabilitation of the oustees. In 1986, the Bureau of Public Enterprises had issued orders to the effect that it would be mandatory for all development projects to include a rehabilitation cost in projects. But ironically almost all the public sector units have ignored the directive. At best one-fourth of the displaced have received alternate lands, most of dry and infertile quality. In 1968-73, over 10,000 tribal families were displaced from 58,000 acres of private land but less than 4,000 families were rehabilited on about 6,000 acres of land. The pastoralists, hunters, food gatherers, forest land cultivators, swiddeners, landless artisans, forest produce collectors and others who lack individual titles to lands – constituting at least one-third of the total displaced tribals – neither received any compensation nor alternate employment. The rest received meagre cash compensation, in several instalments, calculated on the basis of local market value of land, which happens to be lowest due to the restrictions on land transfer in Scheduled Areas.

Indiscriminate involuntary displacement for national development violates several instruments of the United Nations system. For instance, the 1966 U.N. Convention on Civil and Political Rights (Art. 2) holds that ". . . in no case may a people be deprived of its own means of subsistence". Likewise the 1978 U.N. Declaration on Racism and Racial Discrimination (Art. 21) endorses, ". . . the right of indigenous peoples to maintain their traditional structure of economy and culture", and stresses that their "land rights and natural resources should not be taken away from them". Of course, the Indian Government has categorically denied before the U.N. Sub-Commission (ECOSOC) on Prevention of Discrimination and Protection of Minorities as well its working Group on Indigenous Peoples to treat the Scheduled Tribes, locally called "Adivasis", as indigenous peoples. Nonetheless India is one of the 27 countries which ratified the

International Labour Organization Convention No. 107 on Tribal and Indigenous Population, 1957, which states (Articles 11 and 12) that when in "exceptional" circumstances in the "national interest", the tribals are displaced they shall be provided with lands of quality, at least equal to that of the land and landbased resources, both collectively and individually occupied by them, suitable to their present needs and future development. Though India ratified it as early as 1962, it has never recognized corporate rights over land and landbased endowments, and indiscriminately uprooted tribal peoples at will. Anyway ILO has recently revised the convention (169) which is far more progressive than the earlier one and the process of ratification began in 1991. Even if India does not ratify it, the earlier convention remains legally in force for India unless it denounces it, and that is possible only in 2002.

It is not too much to ask from the world's largest democracy that it ought to have a comprehensive national policy on rehabilitation (social, economic and cultural) of displaced persons, instead of leaving it to the discretion of government; define "public purposes" so as to include the affected persons, consumers, NGOs, and the society at large, where the burden of proof rest on the promoting agency; that regulations applicable to non-tribals on alienation of tribal lands be made applicable to public and private enterprises; the quantum of compensation be based on both individual and corporate rights over land and land-based survival resources; provision of royalty on the value of extracted surface and sub-surface resources, and resettlements be in terms of groups rather than individuals. Whereas many may not hesitate to admit that derecognition of corporate rights over survival resources and indiscriminate uprooting for development projects have wrecked the tribals, a few continue to argue that the special welfare measures for them have compensated for the deprivation, especially through the Tribal Sub-plan since 1975 (181 ITDP, 245 MADA, 72 projects for primitive group). Without going into detail, it is suffice to note that even the Eigth Plan acknowledges that no more than 20 per cent of the tribals have received any benefits from special welfare schemes and 85 per cent of the tribals remain below the poverty line. Of course, it needs to be emphasized that the welfare system is primarily a product of tribal peoples' long drawn struggles, and largely represents a *quid pro quo* in exchange for political quiescence.

Notwithstanding Nehru's five benevolent principles for Indian tribes guaranteeing preservation and promotion of their rich identities and cultures, in practice, the cultural policy towards tribal peoples, has been deeply rooted in cultural prejudices, and the view that their cultures should be assimilated into the "mainstream" has already been consolidated. Tribal peoples are made to feel inferior in the matters of their own lifestyle, art, craft, custom, architecture etc. Their cultures are degraded and stigmatised, their values are rejected as obscurantist, their beliefs demonised, rites and symbols ridiculed, and religions are treated as superstitions or sorcery. They are given fictitious and derogatory exonyms. What is however allowed to survive are opaque signs, parody of ceremonial dances and overwhelmed exoticism in the national festivals, *apana Utsavas*, tourism brochures etc. for the non-tribal national and international consumers.

Though the Indian Constitution lays down that adequate facilities for instruction in the mother tongue at the primary level shall be promoted, not even a single tribal language is recognized (with rare regional exceptions) under the pretext that these are spoken by a small number of people and have no scripts. Tribal religions are not only derecognized but are officially included under the rubric of Hinduism. Since Independence, there is no category of tribal religion in the Indian census. The converted tribals face formidable challenges from the dominant religious vandalism and pillaging of ancestral tombs and sacred sites. A few tribal groups, after prolonged and protracted struggle with enormous sacrifices, have been granted regional political administrative autonomy but many more are denied similar autonomy. The process of nation building and cultural domination have emaciated the tribal cultural, linguistic and local self-rule.

In sum, the current tribal problematique is essentially a product of a borrowed capitalist model of growth, domination of reactionary forces, incomplete democratization of the Indian State, and the strategies of nation building, national security and national mainstream. Meanwhile the key to survival of the tribal peoples with dignity rests in their struggles for recognition of collective rights over survival resources and internal self-determination in the legitimate cultural, linguistic and political spheres, as well as a dynamic strategy for sustainable development.

III

Fortunately the tribal peoples, though traumatised by deculturation, acculturation and negative identity, have managed to preserve their self-identity and are rediscovering their philosophical and cultural uniqueness and potentialities. And during their rising struggles, there is an increasing trend towards inter-tribal unity. Their struggles are largely directed towards recuperating their inalienable customary rights to control, use and manage their land and land based resources in their own territories; to defend their languages, customs, law and authority, cultural system and epistemology in the management of their own affairs; and for cessation of subtle forms of discrimination as well as strategies of cooptation and coercion. In fact these constitute a better form of the Sixth Schedule of the Constitution at its operational best, put simply, sustainable self-delvelopment where the terms of dynamics are defined by the concerned peoples themselves. It does not mean separatism, autarchy or anthropological romanticism, nor a plea for non-change or rejection of all influences of external institutions and values. It would be a new democratic and dynamic culture that emancipates groups as well as individuals from colonialism and cultural assimilation.

Besides with endemic crisis in the capitalist system, an increasing number of conscious people are searching for alternative visions of future and look for guidance to the tribal peoples' survival as viable societies who have retained ecological balance in inhospitable regions for several centuries. They may provide insights into the very survival of this imperiled planet itself.

In short, while the provisions in the Indian Constitution appear quantitatively enormous and in fact until the 1970's they were much ahead of others, the derecognition of corporate rights of survival bases (except to an extent in the Sixth Schedule Area), the oft used undefined "public interest" and the notion of mainstream, have been unjust to the tribal peoples. The U.N. Declaration on Indigenous Peoples (1993) should be the guide for the democratic resolution of the tribal problematique, and consolidation of social justice. This declaration is much superior to the Indian constitutional rights for the Scheduled Tribes. It recognises the indigenous as peoples, defined by the concerned themselves with implied rights for self-determination within the existing state systems. Adopting this will be a conflict resolution effort and will establish a trend in the right direction to strengthen the parameters of democracy, federalism and social justice (Pathy 1991:18-26). And the resultant scenario would be a contribution to the emergence of multiple coexisting civilizations that respect both peoples and the nature. Ultimately this is a political question, but also a historical imperative of our times.

REFERENCES

Bose, N.K. 1972. *Anthropology and Some Indian Problems,* Calcutta: Institute of Social Research and Applied Anthropology.

Pathy, Jaganath, 1984. *Tribal Peasantry: Dynamics of Development.* New Delhi: Inter India Publication.

——, 1991. "What is Tribe? What is Indigenous? Turn the Tables Towards the Metaphor for Social Justice", *Religion and Society,* 38(4): 18-26.

Planning Commission. 1987. *Study Group on Landholding Systems in Tribal Areas* (mimeo). New Delhi: Government of India.

Roy Burman, B.K. 1989. "Self Management Systems in NE Region", *Mainstream.* September 23, pp. 19-22.

Injustice to Tribals in Tamil Nadu

JAKKA PARTHASARATHY

The birth of the Constitution of India on 26 January 1950 marks the origin of the term 'Scheduled Tribe'. Earlier, the term 'tribe' referred to a cultural and historical concept. 'Tribe' was used, at one time, for a certain population, to denote a bewildering variety of social categories that were neither analogous and comparable. In later usage it tended to be restricted only to the autochthonous, the aboriginals, and the primitive groups. In the Indian context, 'tribe' has never been defined precisely and satisfactorily. It may be best now to view it as an ethnic category defined by real or putative descent and characterised by a collective self-image or identity and a wide range of commonly shared traits of culture. The difficulty in defining a tribe arises from the fact that in India, tribes are in transition.

In the Constitution of India, Article 364(25) provides that 'Scheduled Tribes' means such tribes or tribal communities or parts or groups within such tribes or tribal communities as are deemed under Article 342 to be Scheduled Tribes. The President of India is empowered to specify, after consultation with the Governor of a State, 'tribes or tribal communities' to be Scheduled Tribes. Now the term 'Scheduled Tribe' has become an objective one. Today in India, administrators and anthropologists refer to the list of Scheduled Tribes for the purpose of recognising a 'tribe'. According to Piarey Lal Mehta (1991:29), "in order to achieve the objective test, the State-wise list of Scheduled Tribes prescribed under the Constitution has been evolved from the list of 'Primitive Tribes' prepared in the 1931 census". The Backward Classes Commission observed that, 'the Scheduled Tribes can be ascertained by the fact that they live in the forests, they lead a separate 'excluded existence and are not fully assimilated in the main body of the people'. The general opinion was that the Scheduled Tribe people suffered social injustice at all levels.

The Constitution categorises the Scheduled Tribe communities as a weaker section. Humanness of a society is determined by the degree of protection it provides to its weaker members. The founders of the Constitution conceived this as a wise measure to give the downtrodden Scheduled Tribes some sort of special assistance, to secure justice – social, economic and political. The need was to evolve ways and means of gradual adjustment of the tribal population to changed conditions and their slow integration in the general life of the country without undue and hasty disruption of their way of living. The Constitution, accordingly devised suitable safeguards to meet the needs and aspirations of the Scheduled Tribes. Provisions were made in the Constitution under the Fifth and Sixth Schedules to protect the Scheduled Tribes' interests to save them from outside exploitation. Protecting the Scheduled Tribes from injustice and exploitation has been enshrined as an important directive in Article 46 of the Constitution.

This paper seeks to examine the anti-exploitative steps for tribal development and the results of these steps among the scheduled tribe communities, the Malayali, the Irular, the Kanikaran and the Paniyan, inhabiting Tamil Nadu.

I limited my study to four tribal communities, i.e., the Malayali of South Arcot district, the Irular of Chengalpattu M.G.R. district, the Kanikaran of Kanniyakumari district and the Paniyan of Nilgiri district in Tamil Nadu, because these communities represent 70.88 per cent of the total Scheduled Tribe population of the State. The Malayali and the Irular are major tribes and the Kanikaran and the Paniyan are minor tribes. They represent different geographical areas of the State. For collecting field data on the communities, I used the standard anthropological technique of participant observation, i.e., to be present with the people as an important tool make the intensive study. I lived with the people continuously for many days during the years 1990-92 in the selected tribal settlements. The information so gained was supplemented through interviews with carefully chosen informants. The type of interview was closed. The secondary data was based on the government records and other academic research reports.

Tamil Nadu, one of the major states of the southern zone in India, consists of important tribal groups. According to the 1991 Census, the Scheduled Tribe population in Tamil Nadu was 574194 constituting 1.02 per cent of the total population. There are 36 scheduled tribes of varying numerical strengths. The Malayali and the Irular are the largest tribes; Kuruman, Kurumba, Paniyan and Sholaga etc., come under the middle range and the

Toda, the Mudugar etc., are small in numbers. Concentration of Scheduled Tribes is found in the Northern districts of the State. Most of the Scheduled Tribes live in hilly and remote areas by primitive subsistence living, and a large number of them are food gatherers by tradition. The literacy rate of the tribals is 20.45 per cent as against the general literacy rate of 46.7 per cent (1981 Census). The literacy level among tribal women (14.00 per cent) is much less than that of tribal men (26.70 per cent). 90.31 per cent of the tribals live in rural areas and 9.69 per cent live in urban areas.

The present paper is based on the data collected from four scheduled tribe communities in Tamil Nadu. Four settlements of the Malayali group comprising 150 households in Kalrayan hills of South Arcot district; nine settlements of the Irular comprising 150 households in Chengalpattu M.G.R. district; eleven settlements of the Kanikaran group comprising 237 households in Kanniyakumari district and nine settlements of the Paniyan comprising 150 households in Nilgiri district are studied. Brief ethnographic details of the Malayali, the Irular, the Kanikaran and the Paniyan are given to understand their culture and society.

Malayalis are one of the major tribes of Tamil Nadu. Their total population in Tamil Nadu, according to the 1981 Census is 209040, out of which 106826 are males and 102214 are females. The Malayalis who are classified as a Scheduled Tribe in Tamil Nadu form 45.60 per cent of the total Scheduled Tribe population of the State. In Tamil Nadu they are scattered in six districts namely North Arcot Ambedkar, South Arcot, Salem, Tiruvannamalai Sambuvurayar, Tiruchirapally and Dharmapuri. Their population in South Arcot district in 27355.

Etymologically the word Malayali is derived from the words *malai* and *ali*, which means inhabitants of the hills. They are Hindus and profess Hindu religion. They observe all the Hindu festivals and pay pilgrimage to distant sacred centres. A few of them converted to Christianity. Their traditional political organisation is maintained by *thalamai nattan*, *nattans* and *oorgoundans*. They are also participating actively in the statutory Panchayat Raj System.

The Irular are one of the major tribes of Tamil Nadu. They are also found in Karnataka and Kerala states. Their population in Tamil Nadu, according to 1981 census, is 105857, out of which 54229 are males and 51528 are females. The Irular, who are classified as Scheduled Tribe in Tamil Nadu, form 23.09 per cent of the total Scheduled Tribe population of the State. In Tamil Nadu, they are distributed in ten districts, namely, Chengalpattu M.G.R., North Arcot Ambedkar, South Arcot, Tiruvannamalai Sambuvurayar, Coimbatore, Salem, Tirchirapalli, Thanjavur, Kanniyakumari and Nilgiris. Their population in Chengalpattu M.G.R. district is 33943.

The Irular are known by several names like Irulas, Irulon, Iruliga, Kattakarar, Poosali, Villiar. Their life cycle rituals are markedly different from neighbouring non-tribal communities. The Irular had animistic tendencies but now they worship local Hindu deities. Their tribal goddess is Kanima. They go on pilgrimage to Tirupati, Palani and Sabarimala. Their tribal council is headed by *moopan.*

The Kanikaran are found in Kanniyakumari district of Tamil Nadu. They are also found in Trivandrum and Quilon districts of Kerala. Their total population in Tamil Nadu, according to 1981 census, is 3698, out of which 1878 are males and 1820 are females. The Government of India recognized them under the name 'Kanikaran or Kanikkar' and gave them the status of Scheduled Tribe. They call themselves as Kanikkar, while other community people refer to them by the name 'Kanis'. The literal meaning of the word Kanikaran means 'hereditary proprietor of land'. They mostly depend on the forest and the land in the forest for subsistence. A few of them become self-cultivators.

The Kanikaran were said to be the original inhabitants of the mountains of South Travancore. They followed the religious cult of animism. Now they have three kinds of deities – spirits, minor deities and superior divinities. Nowadays, they profess Hindu religion and a few profess Christianity. The Kanikaran have headman called *muttukani,* who presides over tribal council called *sabha.* The *pilathi,* a magician or *mantravadi* is the religious head of the Kanikaran settlement.

The Paniyan are one of the primitive tribes of Tamil Nadu found in Nilgiri district. They are also found in Kerala. Their total population in Tamil Nadu, according to 1981 census is 6391, out of which 3177 are males and 3214 are females. The Paniyan who are classified as a Scheduled Tribe in Tamil Nadu form 1.39 per cent of the total Scheduleld Tribe population of the state. In Tamil Nadu, they are scattered only in Gudalur taluk of Nilgiri district. Their population in Nilgiri district is 6210. The

Government of India identified the Paniyan as one of the six primitive tribal groups of Tamil Nadu.

The life cycle rituals of the Paniyan are markedly different from that of the other tribal communities of the Nilgiris. They follow the religious cult of animism. The priest, *attali,* who is assisted by a *komaram* acts as a middle man between spirits and the Paniyan devotees. The Paniyan tribal council, called *kottani,* is a permanent body with a group of elders called *muppanmars* and for every one or two Paniyan *paddis* (settlements) there is a Paniyan headman called *kuttan.*

The Constitution, though it has abolished representation on communal lines, has included safeguards for the advancement of the backward classes amongst the residents of India (irrespective of their religious affliations), so that the country may be ensured of all-round development. These provisions fulfil the assurance of "justice, social, economic and political" which has been held out by the very Preamble of the Constitution. A major section of such backward classes has been specified in the Constitution as Scheduled Castes and Scheduled Tribes because their backwardness is patent (Durga Das Basu: 1993: 59). Thus a number of special provisions have been made in the Constitution for safeguarding the rights and interests of Scheduled Tribes. Special safeguards have been spelt out in 24 Articles in the Constitution. The following are a few important Articles.

Article 46, under the Directive Principles of State Policy, in Part IV of the Constitution reads that, "The State shall promote with special care the educational and economic interests of the weaker sections of the people, and, in particular, of the Scheduled Castes and the Scheduled Tribes, and shall protect them from social injustice and all forms of exploitation".

Article 15 says that measures for the advancement of the Scheduled Castes and Scheduled Tribes are exempted [Article 15 (4)] from the general ban against discrimination on the grounds of race, caste and the like. It means that if special provisions are made by the State in favour of the members of the Scheduled Tribes, other citizens shall not be entitled to impeach the validity of such provisions on the ground that such provisions are discriminatory against them.

Article 19(5) prevents the alienation or fragmentation of their property except with the concurrence of a specified administrative authority or under specified conditions.

Article 338 of the original Constitution provided for the appointment of a Special Officer to investigate all matters relating to the safeguards provided for the Scheduled Castes and Scheduled Tribes under this Constitution and to report to the President upon the working of those safeguards. Article 338 has been substituted by the Constitution (65th Amendment) Act, 1990, to set up a National Commission for Scheduled Castes and Scheduled Tribes in place of a Special Officer, with some additional duties, e.g. to inquire into complaints with respect to determination of the rights and safeguards of the Scheduled Castes and Scheduled Tribes.

Article 339(2) states that the executive power of the Union shall extend to the giving of directions to any State as to the drawing up and execution of schemes specified as essential for the welfare of the Scheduled Tribes in the State.

Article 275(1) provides financial aid for the implementation of various welfare schemes, which requires the Union to give grants-in-aid to the States for meeting the costs of schemes of welfare of the Scheduled Tribes and for raising the level of administration of the Scheduled Areas in a State.

Article 244, in the Fifth and Sixth Schedules of the Constitution prescribes special provisions for the administration of areas inhabited by Scheduled Tribes.

Besides, there are temporary provisions in Articles, 330, 332 and 334 for special representation and reservation of seats for Scheduled Tribes in the Legislatures.

Thus the scheduling of tribes and tribal areas which derives authority from the Constitution of India, has the following advantages:

(1) Political – reservation of seats in Legislatures and local bodies.

(2) Protective – special Legislation for protecting economic interests and eliminating exploitation.

(3) Development – Implementation of special programmes for education and socio-economic development.

State governments, on the basis of the reports of Commissions, have undertaken tribal development programmes as part of Five Year Plans. These programmes are meant to supplement the general development efforts for Backward Classes, including Scheduled Tribes.

The Fifth Five Year Plan 1974-79 is a watershed in the history of tribal development in Tamil Nadu, in 1976, the concept of Tribal sub-plan was evolved with an observation that, 'the immediate objectives will be to eliminate exploitation in all forms, speed up the process for social and economic development and improve the organisational capacities of the Scheduled Tribes. The authorities realized that the schemes drawn up by them would have better results if they were implemented in those areas where the tribals lived in large numbers. This new strategy envisaged the preparation of a sub-plan for tribal areas. The Tribal sub-plan area in Tamil Nadu is divided into nine viable Integrated Tribal Development Projects (ITDP) areas. The total sub-plan area covers 210057 tribals. The rest of the Scheduled Tribes are scattered in various areas. The Scheduled Tribes who live outside the Tribal sub-plan areas are being covered under various ongoing programmes of the State government as well as under the Special Programmes for Primitive Tribal Groups. The assistance provided for them as grants under provision to Article 275(1) of the Constitution. In the ITDP areas, funds are pooled from the State Plan, central and centrally-sponsored schemes, Special Central Assistance and institutional finance so as to ensure that the optimum benefits reach the tribals. Economic development programmes are family-oriented and aimed at enabling them to cross the poverty line. According to Tribal Sub-Plan 1985-1990 (1986), in Tamil Nadu, the size of the Tribal Sub-Plan is increasing yearly. During the year 1976-77 the outlay was Rs. 101.82 lakhs, but it increased for the years 1985-90 to Rs. 69.00 crores.

The Kalrayan hills of South Arcot district (recently bifurcated into two districts) extending over an area of 571 sq. kms (57105 hectares) with an elevation ranging from 1000 to 3800 feet, is formed into one Integrated Tribal Development Project area (ITDP). The Kalrayan hills were divided into three Jagirs called Ariya Gounden Jagir, Kurumba Gounden Jagir and Sadaya Gounden Jagir. Each Jagir was held and controlled by a Jagirdar. These three Jagirdars were assisted by the Malayali tribal council heads. There were number of unusual taxes collected from the tribal people by the Jagirdars. They were – plough tax, bachelor tax, widow or widower tax, marriage tax, tax for cutting trees and wood, grass tax, Jagir citizenship tax, house tax, tax for shifting cultivation, goat tax, tax for cattle etc. The tribal people were also doing bonded labour free of cost on the lands of Jagirdars. The tribal people were compelled to sell their produce only to contractors appointed by the Jagirdars and were prevented from marketing their produce profitably to anybody else. They were not allowed to get fundamental basic amenities. Since the tribal areas in Kalrayan hills were solely under the control and enjoyment of the Jagirdars, the Panchayat Act 1958 could not be enforced in the tribal villages and there was no agency of the government administration at the tribal village level. Action was taken in 1965 by the then Madras Government for taking over Jagirs under the Inam Estate (Abolition and conversion into Ryotwari) Act 1963. The Jagirdars in the first instance resisted the move and obstructed the proceedings by resorting to writs in courts of law but later on withdrew their suits against the government. On 25 August 1976, the Jagirs of Kalrayan hills were taken over by the Government of Tamil Nadu and Ryotwari system was introduced to set free the tribal people from the cluches of Jagirdars.

In Kalrayan hills, though the Inam Estate Act 1963 helped the Malayali tribal people to some extent, but in the process of transition from Jagirdari to Ryotwari, hundreds of the tribal families lost thousands of hectares of the lands they had been cultivating for several decades. The Malayalis of Kalrayan hills had been practising shifting cultivation locally called *punal kadu* in addition to settled cultivation. The Jagirdars who were collecting land revenue from the tribal people never maintained any land records nor gave receipts for land revenue. The government therefore ordered survey and settlement of the Kalrayan hills. As a prelude, the district and local revenue administration prepared village land registers for each village to determine the rights of occupants of lands for the grant of *ryotwari pattas*. In 1978, *ryotwari pattas* were granted to the tribals with reference to sections 10,11 and 12 of the Inam Estate Act of 1963, but many tribals were denied *pattas* for thousands of hectares of lands they had been holding for several decades on the ground that these lands consisted of shrub jungle. The data shows that 10,112 hectares of land cultivated by the Malayalis, constituting 55 per cent of their original holdings were transfered to Forest Department on the recommendation of survey and settlement reports. Thus in the process of transition, the non-*patta* lands of Malayalis were declared as forest. In the Constitution, Article 48-A (42nd Amendment) Act of 1977 states that the State shall endeavour to protect and improve the environment and safegurad the forests and wild life of the country. The Forest Act of 1980 prohibits conversion of notified forest area to non-forest purposes. In this juxtaposition, most of the Malayali people of the Kalrayan hills who lost land felt exploited. The *ryotwari* system thus gave more forest to the Forest Department.

In the Tribal sub-plan area of the Kalrayan hills, the bonded labour system has been identified. With the promulgation of the Bonded Labour System (Abolition) Act 1976 (Central Act 19 of 1976) in the Kalrayan hills, the Government of Tamil Nadu identified 5628 tribal families as bonded labourers and set them at liberty from bondage.

In reality, the three abolished Jagirdars have become dominant landlords and are indirectly and unofficially ruling the Kalrayan hills through their agents, who are mostly contractors. Tribal heads who still fear the Jagirdars encourage people to do free and bonded service to the Jagirdars and their agents. Even today, the Malayalis are involved in three types of bonded labour. One is customary bondage; the services rendered are customary and traditional. Second is trade bondage, under which the employees, particularly forest contractors and non-tribal money lenders, lend small amounts to the Malayalis but get much more throughout year in return either by labour or by way of other services. The third is *padiyal* bondage; under this agricultural labourers are not given a reasonable return for their labour but are bound by custom and indebtedness to continue to work for the powerful Jagirdars and contractors.

The following laws are in force in Tamil Nadu to control money lending, debt redemption and abolition of debt bondage in tribal areas – The Tamil Nadu Debt Conciliation Act (1936); The Tamil Nadu Pawn Broker's Act (1943); The Tamil Nadu Indebted Agriculturist's (Repayment of Debts) Act 1955; and The Tamil Nadu Money Lenders Act (1957). With the promulgation of Money Lenders Act 1957, the government freed 9 per cent of the sample tribal house-holds in the Kalrayan hills.

But, in reality, the Debt Relief Act is not being enforced; it is helping the money lenders. Data shows that 91 per cent of the Malayali families are in debt. The interest charged by money lenders is 8 per cent per month.

In India, the cooperative movement took concrete shape in 1904 with the passing of the Co-operative Credit Societies Act to combat rural indebtedness and to provide credit to farmers. The Scheduled Areas and Scheduled Tribes Commission (popularly known as the Dhebar Commission 1961) made an elaborate study of cooperatives in tribal areas. In 1971, the K.S. Bawa Commission examined the working of cooperative organisations in the project area of the eight tribal development agencies (TDAS) and recommended "organisation of large sized multi-purpose cooperative societies (LAMPS) in tribal areas to provide production as well as consumption credit, undertake marketing of agricultural and minor forest produce (MFP) and distribute consumer goods as well as agriculture inputs so that the tribal could secure all facilities under one roof. By the middle of 1981, 2558 LAMPS were organized in various states in India. In order to free the tribals from the clutches of exploiters, the Government of Tamil Nadu introduced LAMP Societies in its ITDP as well as Non-ITDP areas in the year 1976. In Tamil Nadu, there are 12 LAMP Societies in ITDP areas and one LAMP Society in non-ITDP area.

In the Kalrayan hills, the Government of Tamil Nadu started three LAMP co-operative societies in the year 1981 at Vellimalai, Kilakkadu and Mottampatti villages. As on September 30, 1991, the total tribal members in these three LAMP societies were 3226, 1635 and 1792 respectively. But in reality, the LAMP objectives failed to be achieved in the Kalrayan hills because of non-functioning of the three LAMPS. Though they are to some extent functional at the consumer goods distribution level, at the market and credit loan level these remain defunct. Traders living in the foothills purchase rich minor forest produce and agricultural produce from the tribals at cheap rates and also cheat them with improper and unauthorized measuring standards.

Adjacent to Madras city lies the district of Chengalpattu M.G.R. The district derives its name from Chengalpattu town, a part of the ancient kingdom of the Pallavas, and from the name of the former Chief Minister of Tamil Nadu, M.G. Ramachandran. This region comes under the non-ITDP area, i.e., outside the Tribal sub-plan. Tribal development schemes are implemented through the Integrated Rural Development Project (IRDP). The Government of Tamil Nadu identified the Irular tribals of this district as a 'dispersed tribal group' and declared them extremely poor illiterate and unskilled. Except in providing housing facilities for tribals and trade cooperative societies, the other protective measures have not been taken by the government. The

Forest Department promulgated the Wild Life Protection Act 1902, but just to save a variety of snakes.

Traditionally the Irular of Chengalpattu M.G.R. district were hunters and trappers of porcupines, rats and snakes; now they are involved in different occupations – mainly agricultural labour, husking paddy in rice mills and selling firewood. They were also cultivators of cereals, but due to continuous exploitation by dominant peasant caste groups, they have become low wage labourers. The status they enjoyed as cultivators towards the end of 18th century (Thurston: 1909) has been reduced to that of agricultural labourers and low wage earners today. Data shows that 16 per cent of them are working as bonded workers in rice mills, owned by dominant caste people. 42 per cent are earning their livelihood as wage earners through tree cutting and agricultural labour at Rs. 11 per day. A few are earning through stone cutting and work in brick making factories for low wages. The scope of snake catching too has reduced due to the restrictions imposed by the Forest Department. Data shows that 93 per cent of Irular families are in debt.

The Scheduled Tribe population in Kanniyakumari district belong to the Kanikaran group. The Kanikaran settlements are near river beds and fresh-water lakes. This region is a non-ITDP area, but programmes under the Integrated Rural Development Project and Forest Department are trying to help the Scheduled Tribes. The Kanikaran of Kanniyakumari district are facing the self-identity crisis of 'Scheduled Tribe' status. Government officials are confused as to of who are 'Kanis' and who are the Kanikkar or Kanikaran. Though anthropologists and social workers have clarified that Kanis, Kanikkar and Kanikaran are one and same, but the problem of government officials have problems in issuing 'Scheduled Tribe certificates to original Kanikaran'. The dominant caste groups have a selfish interest in this matter. Kanikaran dwelling places are mostly occupied by dominant agricultural caste groups and traders from Kerala State. Most of the Kanikaran have mortgaged their lands to neighbouring Hindus and Christians. The Government of Tamil Nadu through their District Adi Dravidar and Tribal Welfare department is not trying to restore tribal lands from non-tribal landlords. Money-lending is at its peak. The data shows that 32 per cent of the family ration cards of the Kanikarans are in the possession of the outside money lenders.

Another exploitative element from outsiders is religion. The Kanikaran followed the religious cult of animism. Animism is that view of the world which ascribes life and thought to inanimate things. It is belief in the existence of souls or spirits, who take their abode, either permanently or temporarily, in objects, whether lifeless or living, and this object as endowed with higher power is worshipped or employed to protect individuals or community. The Kanikaran who believe in animism are facing external influence on their belief system. Preachers from the Hindu and Christian faiths are trying their best to convert the animistic Kanikaran. This is creating conflicting tensions in the Kanikaran world view and in the family structure. There are cases of a wife following the Hindu faith and her husband the Christian.

The Government of Tamil Nadu implemented the Bonded Labour System (Abolition) Act 1976 under the direct control and supervision of the Collector of Nilgiri district for the Paniyans. This Act is intended to release labourers from bondage and rehabilitate them in government colonies. The bonded labour system is a practice in which the labourers are denied freedom of work and movement and are forced to work under customary and debt conditions. The Government of Tamil Nadu released 481 Paniyan bonded labourers and rehabilitated them in Government-run agricultural farms. The Government also started 'The Paniya Welfare Land Colonization Cooperative Society' for the welfare of the Paniyans.

In Nilgiri district, the chief occupation of the Paniyan is agricultural labour. The Paniyan are subjected to a subtle form of bonded labour by local non-tribal landowners. Most of them are employed in the agricultural farms owned by the Chettis, Moplahs and the Syrian Christians. According to the data, the total number of bonded labourers of the Paniyan in Gudalur taluk of Nilgiri district in 1992 is 1112 (562 males And 550 females). The bonded contract for employment as farm servant is normally for a year, commencing from April. A Paniyan receiving five bags of paddy and Rs. 300/- on Vishu Day (Malayalam New year Day) is not expected to leave his master for the year. Usually the Paniyan takes loans from their masters and this virtually places him in bondage for the succeeding year also. The free bonded labourers are also facing problems. A few of the rehabilitated Paniyans are returning to the old bonded labour system. While evaluating the

Kappala Government Farm rehabilitated Paniyans of Nilgiris, Anand Bhanu (1986:62) expressed his views that, "The freed Paniya bonded labourers are dissatisfied with the programmes executed. They feel that the old system was far better than the present one. Now they have become bonded to the 'Government masters' with multiple problems in terms of work, wage, food, house, water, protection etc." Paniyan working on the lands of the landlords work for long hours but escape for relaxation to Gudalur town.

The Malayali informants of Kalrayan hills said that the anti-exploitative measures of the government failed because of lack of coordination between the district Adi Dravidar, the Tribal Welfare Department and the Forest Department. They further stressed that the non-tribal dominant caste people never recognize the Malayali as a Scheduled tribe, and mislead government officials responsible for tribal development. Implementation of protective measures was at the mercy of rich non-tribals residing on the foothills of the Kalrayan hills.

The Irular are of the opinion that there are many officers and offices but few approach them with a human heart. Most of the Irular said that they needed help badly from the authorities to counter the exploiters.

To avoid more exploitation from the outside landlords and money lenders, the Kanikaran formed a tribal association called 'Kanikkararkal Nala Urmai Sangam' (KNUS) to fight against injustice. In January, 1988, KNUS submitted their demands to the Prime Minister, a year later submitted a memorandum to the Governor of Tamil Nadu and threatened to boycott the General Elections to the Tamil Nadu Legislative Assembly if their demands were not met. These are: a new census of the Kanikaran tribals; implementation of constitutional justice; return of illegal mortgaged land deeds; return of ration family cards from money lenders; issue of land *pattas*; mobile ambulance to tribal settlements; right to collect reeds and bamboos from the forest; free legal aid facilities; banning religious preachers from Hindu and Christian faiths and easier arm licences.

The study found that the social justice promised by the Constitution remained a mere promise and social reality was different. The privileged non-tribal elites were exploiting the Articles designed to protect Scheduled Tribes for their own benefit. The tribal people have limited access to justice.

REFERENCES

1. Basu, Durga Das, 1993. *Introduction to the Constitution of India,* Prentice-Hall of India, Pvt., Ltd., New Delhi.
2. Bhanu, Anand B., 1986. *Evaluation of Paniya Bonded Labourers: A case study of Kappala farm in Gudalur taluk, Nilgiri district, Tamil Nadu,* Tribal Research Centre, M.Palada, Udhagamandalam.
3. Fuchs, Stephen, 1973. *The Aboriginal Tribes of India,* MacMillan India, Ltd., New Delhi.
4. *Imperial Gazetter 1911.* Government Press, Madras.
5. Mehta, Piarey Lal, 1991. *Constitutional Protection to Scheduled Tribes in India, in Retrospect and Prospects,* H.K. Publishers and Distributors, Delhi.
6. Parthasarathy, Jakka, 1990. *The Kanikaran Women: A Study on Socio-economic Changes,* Tribal Research Centre, Tamil University, M.Palada, Ooty.
7. Parthasarathy, Jakka. 1992. *Tribal Women and Development : a cross cultural study among the Irular and the Malayali,* Tribal Research Centre, M.Palada, Ooty.
8. Parthasarathy, Jakka. 1992. 'The Paniyan of Tamil Nadu: A tribe from Malabar,' in *Man In Asia,* Vol.V, No.11, December.
9. Parthasarathy, Jakka, 1992. *Tribal Women and Town: Looking at the Paniyan of Nilgiris, Tamil Nadu,* 79th Indian Science Congress, Baroda.
10. Thurston, E., 1909. *Castes and Tribes of Southern India,* Vol.VI, Government Press, Madras.
11. Tribal Sub-Plan, 1985-1990, Seventh Plan revised, Tamil- Nadu, The Director of Adi Dravidar and Tribal Welfare, Madras.

White Sahibs, Brown Sahibs

K.S. DHILLON

Constitutional or political change in a country of the size of India is by its very nature bound to be a slow, complex and carefully worked out process. Any attempt at forcing its pace beyond reasonable limits will cause social tensions, widen the gulf between different classes and may even seriously disrupt governmental functioning, sometimes even leading to a total breakdown of established norms of administration, public disorder and anarchy. Such upheavals in society are not normally conducive to public good and are best avoided. The movement for political change in India which started in an organised manner in the late 19th century was primarily of a "gradualist" kind, asking for a smooth, slow but certain infusion of an element of self government in political institutions in India. The objective was to slowly and progressively achieve for India the status of a self-governing dominion within the British Empire. The class of Indians who were in the forefont of what could be called the emerging political leadership in India were by and large, western in thought and orientation and liberal by belief and outlook, having been so shaped by their ample exposure to the prevailing European streams of thought. Not till the advent of M.K. Gandhi, was there any worthwhile attempt to involve the mass of the people in political movements – which were essentially elitist in character, barring of course, some stray departures from the general trend. Perhaps it was not conceivable at that stage of political development that there could be any other sure road to self rule except through slow constitutional reform which was being offered by the British Government in small measures starting from 1909 onwards. No demand for total freedom is known to have been voiced by the recognised Indian political leadership of the times as a definite objective, though the novels of Bankim Chandra Chatterji and some of his contemporaries had created a radical nationalist upsurge and motivated some terrorist groups to take to violence in pursuit of a revolution. There were, also, some Hindu revivalist movements who dissociated themselves from the then prevailing dominant political ideology but their formulations were vague and failed to make much headway in the ensuing political developments. The Russian Revolution had not yet happened and the fundamental lessons of the French Revolution had been formalised and idealised into concepts and precepts, guidelines and principles – but only to govern political mobilisation.

A clear break with the "gradualist" tradition of Indian political agitation, which dominated the political discourse for the first twenty years of the 20th century, seems to have occurred with the emergence of Gandhi on the political scene following the atrocious behaviour of the British Indian Government at Jallianwala Bagh and other places. Non-cooperation and civil disobedience as weapons of an oppressed nation to fight the oppression let loose by an alien power radically changed the whole scenario. In the event many of the older generation of leaders were marginalised and a new partnership in political leadership between Gandhi and Jawaharlal Nehru burst on the scene with tremendous impact. The goals and policies were redefined, the methods and strategies were refined and a whole new set of rules and guidelines were evolved. In 1929, the objective of the Indian political struggle was modified from dominion status to independence. However, in all the rough and tumble of political mobilisation, the central theme of constitutional change as opposed to violent revolutionary modes, was still fully upheld. Since Nehru dominated the political landscape so completely from then onwards till his death in 1964, it will be in order to dwell at length on him as a man, a political thinker and ideologue who played by far the most influencial role in the framing of the Indian Constitution. It may also not be improper, therefore, to ascribe to him whatever flaws or inadequacies it was later found to possess.

Born with the proverbial silver spoon in his mouth, much fussed over by his parents and numerous relatives as a child, educated in the West, Nehru imbided in a large measure western lifestyles and patterns of thought, also a considerable amount of woolly Fabian (socialist) ideas during his long sojourn in England and Europe. Being an only son in an enormously wealthy household he grew up to be a haughty, though shy, tempestuous, short-tempered, self-centred young man – intolerant of dissent and with a pronounced egotistical strain. Since his own background was rich and feudal, he could not get out of an exclusivist, elitist frame of mind. His so-called "love" for the illiterate and poor Indian masses was at his best when exercised from a distance, preferably from above. Their 'affection' for him was actually a form of reverence and awe which comes naturally to us Indians for the scion of a wealthy family of impeccable ancestry (including a Kotwal of Delhi under the Moghuls). For some strange reason, Gandhi soon focussed all his hopes and ambitions of a successful conduct of his struggle for freedom on the young Nehru and sort of adopted him as his political heir. No two personalities could be more unlike each other in backgrounds, life-styles, public postures, even political orientation. However they clicked as a team, complementing and supplementing each other as occasion arose, very soon coming to occupy the centre stage and dominating the Indian political scene for the next thirty years, till the assassination of Gandhi, through a period of intense political activity marked by escalating hostility between the two major communities culminating in Independence, but also, tragically, the partition of the country. It would always remain something of a historical puzzle how and why such committed opponents of partition as Gandhi, Nehru and Azad meekly succumbed in the end to the charms and blandishments of Mountbatten. Recent research has shown that the road to partition was not wholly the creation of M.A. Jinnah but was quite largely paved with many acts of omission and commission by the Congress under Nehru's leadership. However, that is not the theme of this paper.

Carried away by the adulation of the masses and the primacy accorded to him in the Congress leadership by Gandhi, Nehru started making pronouncements on all manner of issues concerning the long range objectives of the Indian political movement. One issue on which he frequently became uncommonly loquacious was the making of the Indian Constitution – not only its character and composition but also its aims, objectives and directive principles. He started elaborating the task before such a constituent Assembly in specific terms as early as 1929 together with redefining the goals of the freedom struggle. He had set his heart on a Constituent Assembly, formed on the basis of adult franchise. Further, he expected such an assembly not only to produce a constitution of his conception but also to sort out inter-alia, a large number of vexing issues with regard to worsening communal situation, the place of the

Harijans (later to be brought under the category of Scheduled Castes) and the Tribals in the larger Hindu society, the relations between the federation centre and its units and, of course, to define the form and structure of the new Government of India -- issues which were to become more and more strident and complex in the 1930's and 40's. He reverted to the subject of forming a Constituent Assembly again and again in the following years and seemed to attach a great deal of importance to such an agency to find answers to all the problems India was increasingly faced with as the Muslim League came to occupy the centre-stage so far as Muslim India was concerned. The reluctant and half-hearted acceptance of the Government of India Act 1935 by the Congress party and the subsequent whimsical working of provincial governments in the nine Congress majority provinces effectively halted the constitutional progress to a federal set-up envisaged by Irwin during the round-table conferences and the ensuing deliberations. The 'Quit-India' movement preceded by the resignation of the Congress governments in the provinces, in a major way dissociated the Congress Party from political initiatives and left the scene clear for the Muslim League under the astute leadership of Jinnah to strengthen its position among the Muslims of India, so that by 1946, this party became almost their sole representative, placing Maulana Azad and other Congress Muslims in an extremely awkward position.

The mounting intransigence of Jinnah in the crucial period between 1940 to 1947, through some very important stages of political development in India, can perhaps be easily traced to serious tactical miscalculations of the Congress leadership, almost totally dominated by Nehru at this stage of its history. The tragic sequence of events leading to partition and its aftermath were the saddest outcome of such flawed and faulty approach to the by now almost impossible communal question. With the arrival of Mountbatten on the scene in March 1947 with a clear mandate to complete the withdrawal of the British power by June 1948 (later advanced to August 1947), events started moving at a breakneck speed. It was something of a sad volte face for Nehru to accept a Constituent Assembly only indirectly elected by a limited franchise as laid down in the Government of India Act 1935, Schedule VI "mainly based on property qualifications. The total voting strength of the British Indian provinces was about thirty million against a population of 256 million, according to the census of 1931. Thus only 11.3 per cent of the population was enfranchised".[1] The people of the Indian states which formed two fifths of the country's population then also went totally unrepresented. It was this Assembly, formed in the manner earlier always disapproved by Nehru and consisting of a class of people westernised in orientation, gradualist in approach to political issues, and mildly socialistic in ideological terms (the latter under the flood of rhetoric let loose by Nehru who dominated all debates when present) who finally framed the Constitution of India – one of the lengthiest in the world, with a plethora of lofty ideas which was however to prove somewhat unequal to the task of providing social justice in the years to come – despite numerous amendments to facilitate and promote social change. There was much concern and sympathy for the masses, frequent expression of grief over the sufferings of the poor and the deprived and a commitment to accord a central position to the common man in the new Constitution. At the commencement of its monumental task the Constituent Assembly set the tone in the following manner:

> It was, therefore, only proper that as the clock struck the midnight hour and the Constituent Assembly assumed full sovereign powers, all the members of the Assembly standing took another pledge – the pledge of dedication to the service of India. Service of India, in the words of Nehru, meant 'the service of the millions who suffer'. Nehru reminded the nation and the framers of the Constitution of future India: 'the ambition of the greatest man of our generation has been to wipe every tear from every eye. That may be beyond us, but as long as there are tears and suffering, so long our work will not be over'.[2] There was no dearth of high sounding principles, turns of phrase, rhetorical flourishes in the speeches made in the Assembly – specially by Nehru. There was a large measure of agreement on what the new Constitution must aim at. There was a massive infusion of Fabian thought in its framework. The debates were full of sound and fury regarding the lot of the common man. In the words of Granville Austin, "The Indian Constitution is first and foremost a social document. The majority of its provisions are either directly aimed at furthering the goals of social revolution or attempt to foster the revolution by establishing the conditions necessary for its achievement".[3]

> At another place, the same writer says: "The Constitution was to foster the achievement of many goals. Transcendent among them was that of social revolution. Through this revolution would be fulfilled the basic needs of the common man and it was hoped, this revolution would bring about fundamental changes in the structure of Indian society – a society with a long and glorious cultural tradition, but greatly in need, Assembly members believed, of a powerful infusion of energy and rationalism. The theme of social revolution runs throughout the proceedings and documents of the Assembly.[4]

Clearly, therefore, to Nehru and the majority of his colleagues in the Assembly, the Constitution was to be an instrument of major social change. Reshaping the Indian society and redefining social relationships were, no doubt, the central issues in the making of the Indian Constitution. Its aims and promises were spelt out in the Preamble and the Directive Principles of State Policy. The social, economic and political rights of the citizens were enshrined in the Fundamental Rights. The inherent contradictions in the working of the Indian Constitution with respect to the concept of social justice soon became apparent when the Fundamental Rights of the individual tended to obstruct the implementation of policies directed at providing social justice to the landless and other deprived sections of society. That Nehru was not unaware of the flawed nature of the new Constitution is clear from his speeches in Parliament during the debates on the Fourth Amendment to the Constitution. Perhaps his views need to be quoted at length to underscore the point.

"The Constitution lays down certain Directive Principles of State Policy and after long discussion we agreed to them and they point out the way we have got to travel. The Constitution also lays down certain Fundamental Rights. Both are important. The Directive Principles of State Policy represent a certain move towards a certain objective. The Fundamental Rights represent something static, to preserve certain rights which exist. Both again are right. But somehow and sometime, it may so happen that dynamic movement and that static standstill do not quite fit into each other.

"A dynamic movement towards a certain objective necessarily means certain changes taking place; that is the essence of movement. Now it may be that in the process of dynamic movement certain existing relationships are altered, varied or affected. In fact, they are meant to affect those settled relationships and yet if you come back to the Fundamental Rights, they are meant to preserve, not indirectly certain settled relationships. There is a certain conflict in the two approaches, not inherently because that was not meant. I am quite sure. But there is that slight difficulty and naturally when the courts of the land have to consider these matters, they have to lay stress more on the Fundamental Rights than on the Directive Principles of State Policy. The result is that the whole purpose behind the Constitution which was meant to be a dynamic Constitution leading to a certain goal step by step is somewhat hampered and hindered by the static element being emphasised a little more than the dynamic element and we have to find some way of solving it.

"The essential difficulty is the whole conception of Fundamental Rights is the protection of individual liberty and freedom. If in the protection of individual liberty you protect also individual or group inequality, then you come in conflict with that Directive Principle which wants, according to our Constitution, a gradual advance, or let us put it another way, not so gradual but more rapid advance, wherever possible by a state where there is less and less inequality and more and more equality. If any kind of an appeal to individual inequality, liberty and freedom is construed to mean as an appeal to the continuation of the existing inequality, then you get into difficulties. Then you become static, unprogressive and cannot change and you cannot realise that ideal of an egalitarian society which I hope most of us share.

"I would like to draw the attention of the House to something that is not adequately stressed either in Parliament or in the country. We stress greatly and argue in courts of law about the Fundamental Rights. Rightly so, but there is such a thing as the Directive Principles of the Constitution. These are, as the Constitution says, the fundamentals in the governance of the country.

"Now, I should like the house to consider how you can give effect to these principles, if the argument which is often being used, if I may say so, with all respect, by the Supreme Court, is adhered to. You can't . . . But I say, then, if that is correct, there is an inherent contradiction in the Constitution between the Fundamental Rights and the Directive Principles of State Policy. Therefore, again, it is upto this Parliament to remove that contradiction and make the Fundamental Rights sub-serve the Directive Principles of State Policy".[5]

This realisation (about the inherent contradiction) came to Nehru and his colleagues quite early, as it would appear, in the actual implementation of policies aimed at social justice. Then why were they powerless to take effective measures to resolve, or remove, the impediments? Did they lack the will to do so or alternatively, did the mandarins of the Law Ministry fail to produce a foolproof amendment draft? A close study of the changing culture of the political class, specially that of the Congress, in the years following the illness and death of Nehru, would reveal that there was a fundamental transformation in the party's ideological moorings and a considerable dilution of its deep commitment to social justice, following the generational change in its political leadership though ceremonial lip service to the cause of the common man continued to be paid from time to time. As the Congress leadership became aware of a definite decline in its popularity, it started taking resort to political gimmicks like bank loan melas, land ceilings and slogan mongering (*garibi hatao* for instance). All these measures and slogans came to signify only vote catching devices. Every succeeding generation of politicians acquired more privileges, more power and pelf and more trappings of office. So that the Prime Minister of free India became a more formidable personage than even the Viceroys of old. The President of a country, inhabited by more than 40% of its people living below the poverty line, lives in the same Viceregal mansion as did the British Governors-General, attended upon by an even larger army of secretaries, joint and additional secretaries, military secretaries, ADC's and a whole paraphernalia of cooks and bearers, *chaprasis* and *jemadars* in starched uniforms and turbans. The bands play the same tunes with Indianised wordings and the President's ceremonial drive is as resplendent as in the days of the Raj.

The Republic's Ministers and parliamentarians have acquired privileges and perquisites unavailable in any but the richest nations, in the process over-shadowing even the executive councillors of the Imperial government in India – proving once again that the basic political philosophy motivating the Indian political class is not a popular democracy but a feudal oligarchy. In the prevailing political culture, whatever hope there may have been initially of ensuring social justice has all but vanished –

except of course in sloganeering. The debate as to whether it was the Constitution which failed in ensuring social justice or the political class who lost their direction or again the civil service which was designed to maintain its 'colonial' character, is valid at this juncture when more and more concerned people are articulating their shock and anxiety at the widening gulf between the privileged and the deprived. True, the Constitution was not a perfect formulation of operational techniques though it was high on ideology. No constitution ever is. It can only reflect the prevailing norms, ideals, aspirations and ambitions of the relevant age. The Indian Constitution has been amended many times. It was not beyond the capacity of our Parliament to remove impediments and incorporate capabilities to bring about the intended egalitarian objectives of social justice, if they really wanted to do so. Somewhere along the line, they seemed to have lost the will to do so. The friends of the poor were no longer poor themselves; the bleeding hearts shedding copious tears for the deprived sections, themselves gathered enormous power, wealth and privileges to which they became too much attached. Politics became an instrument only to achieve material well being. In the process, the flexibility of the Indian Constitution ceased to serve as an enabling facility to promote social change, though it was amended several times, instead to stifle democracy, prolong periods of Presidential rule in parts of the country and enact draconian legislation. The blame perhaps lay not with the framers of the Constitution, whose credentials were admittedly not fully unflawed, but with the operation of the Constitution in a later day politically dishonest and morally degenerate age.

The need and justification of importation of much of the 1935 Government of India Act into the Indian Constitution is a matter of debate, though it did enormously help to bring about a smooth changeover in the sphere of administration. Administrative continuity was maintained and the trauma of a sudden breakdown was averted. The Indian members of the civil service simply replaced the British members in the secretariats and the districts. The administrative culture, ethos, norms of behaviour and conduct did not change immediately. Only the rules of business in the secretariats were modified to fit in with the democratic polity. The basic unit of administration, namely, the district, remained more or less unaffected where the Collector/D.M. continued to provide a paternalistic administration in the old

'Mai-Baap' tradition (which incidentally was not a British innovation). Philip Mason's classic work on district administration remained essentially a prescribed reading for the trainees of the I.A.S. The safeguards provided for the senior civil servants of the country in the 1935 Act were wholly enshrined in the All India Services Act and related provisions. These enactments were designed to protect the Civil Services including the Police, from the whimsical behaviour of the political class much in the manner of the 1935 Act. For it was believed (rightly perhaps as became evident when a lesser breed of politicians came to occupy positions of authority in the post-Nehru era) that "a Civil Service minutely just, inflexibly upright, well enough paid to be above corruption, independent and confident because assured of a career that could only be interrupted by gross misconduct"[7] must be insulated from political pressures. The newly independent Indian political class too seemed to share that view, though latter day politicians had misgivings on that score and laid the major blame for the failure of the social revolution objectives on the 'colonial' attitudes of the higher civil service. It was thought that the latter with their elitist attitudes, values, backgrounds and inherited belief in the rule of law (a "status quo" approach in other words) were unable to implement the social justice programmes. The upshot was that the civil service itself lost its elan, autonomy and adherence to the rule of law; their attachment to the principles of fair play and natural justice which had hithertofore governed the exercise of their power became stultified and the application of power and authority became selective and a command performance. Their ability to function as an autonomous wing of the administrative structure for the implementation of policies framed by the Legislature suffered a serious erosion as a result of the political class becoming more assertive and grossly interfering in the day-to-day funtioning of the civil service. The police was specially subjected to a constant process of disruption of the chain of command and undermining of established hierarchical structure by the political class to the deteriment of discipline and obedience, without which no uniformed organisation can perform well. This process soon produced a class of police officers, subservient to the politician rather than to the provisions of law. Public services became totally politicised and manipulatable and so unable to fulfil their allotted charter of duties. Obviously, it was not the so-called "colonial" heritage of the civil services which led to the failure of the social revolution sought to be brought about by the framers of the Indian Constitution but a loss of commitment and direction which characterised the thinking and working of the latter day politicians. Given the right kind of political leadership and direction, the civil service were still capable of delivering. Unfortunately, the leadership itself failed to lead in the right direction. Their principles changed, their sense of integrity plummetted. Worst of all, they denied the civil service the requisite environment to perform their allotted functions. In the event, the civil service itself which had produced men of great strength of character, judgement and vision, soon became peopled primarily by men of straw. As the civil service ceased to get adequate space to grow in stature, its members lost their originality, initiative, brilliance, dedication, honesty of purpose and sense of integrity necessary to the premier implementation agency of government. The social and economic policies and programmes developed distortions and eccentricities of a kind which defeated the very purpose and direction of social change.

The Indian Civil Service and the Indian Police, the two premier services of the Raj had become associated in the mind of the political class with imperiousness, insolence, commitment to the interests of the colonial power, exclusiveness and insulation etc. If the adjective "colonial" in "colonial heritage" implies that the civil service was created by the British Indian government to subserve their imperial interests, it would not perhaps be a correct reading of history. For the Indian Civil Service except in rare instances, was the most liberal, the most efficient and the most dedicated of all bureacracies, India had ever known. The service was manned by some of the finest and best men of education, vision, dedication, commitment, objectivity and honesty that the age could offer. They were hard working, energetic and dynamic to an extent that defies belief today. None of their predecessors whether in the ancient or the mediaval periods in India could match them in sheer class and professionalism. What was 'colonial' in the I.C.S. was simply a qualifying phrase to indicate the period of their existence and should not be seen in a pejorative sense. In fact the very complex tasks involved in administering this country with its myriad problems after the Transfer of Power were carried out most successfully by a depleted civil service, trained and put through their paces by experienced seniors under the Raj earlier. It would not be out of place here to quote what two eminent Indian members of the service had to say about the characteristics and qualities of those officers and the way these were cultivated and nurtured.

"More important . . . was the informal part. . . of the training of a young officer. A good collector's house was often a second home to the young administrator. He was encouraged to drop in of an evening. Hardly ever was the Collector so busy or preoccupied that he would not have time with the young man . . . he might ask the young magistrate to come and have tea with him one evening a week. Seated on a comfortable sofa . . . plied with good tea and excellent home made cake, the touchiness and arrogance so characteristic of the intelligent, inexperienced young prize winner . . . would fall off like an old garment. Differences of kind or race would sink to insignificance and the young man would, sometimes to his surprise, find himself talking freely, listening with attention, pleased at the praise, not hurt at the warning and advice."

"The young man imbibed standards, sometimes even without being told. Automatically, he learned there were certain things one did not do. However awkward the circumstances . . . however grave the consequence to onself . . . one did not lie. In all emergencies it was one's duty to stand firm. However frightened one might feel, one did not show it. In all one's dealings, the rule must be probity. The throwing of one's own responsibility on one's subordinates degraded one not only in the sight of one's fellows but in one's own eyes . . . while one showed deference to one's elders, one was not frightened of them. If one differed, one expressed one's views frankly. . . It was a great merit of government in this period (that is, upto 1947) that it neither punished frank expression of opinion from its officers nor even resented it.[8]

Another member of the service, Dharam Vira, spoke in almost the same manner. "I often disagreed with my superiors. An Indian was sometimes bound to feel differently. And I usually said frankly what I thought, but I do not think it was ever held against me or taken amiss. It was curious. We were all men of the same calibre and background. Sometimes it was chance that one got into the I.C.S. and a classmate into the provincial service. There was not much in the formal training of the I.C.S. The training lay in being given a job and told to get on with it. But because we were given that trust and responsibility we soon found ourselves ready to tackle anything in the way they – the provincial service – seldom were".[9]

It was this "trust and responsibility" and the necessary professional autonomy which was denied to the successor services – the IAS and the IPS – by the later day political class which stunted the civil service. They lost their elan and vitality and in due course, their capacity to effectively carry out the policies of the government, the politician frequently encroaching in their domain ordering postings, promotions and transfers instead of concentrating on policy formulation and political direction. Not only did the politician-civil servant relationship become distorted, the qualities of integrity and probity which had so far provided the backbone and ethos of the civil service became weak and destroyed its reputation. Simultaneously, an unplanned expansion in the civil services due to faulty cadre-management as also careerism of a vicious type caused discontent and frustration among officers placed in unsatisfying slots with poor job content. Large cadres meant diffuse control and indiscipline, lack of trust and responsibility led to emasculation of vigour, initiative and morale. Since competence and efficiency became degraded, the men holding positions of power and responsibility became professional dwarfs. Policy implementation had to suffer a serious set back. Naturally.

Was it really the "colonial" heritage and the class character of the new administrators which led to failure in the achievement of social justice goals?[10] Are there inbuilt (wilfully or negligently?) obstacles in the Constitution itself which impede social change? Or has there been a systems failure caused by a loss of direction, abandonment of the noble principles of selflessness and austerity, deterioration in the leadership qualities of the political class? And, of course, the proliferation of service cadres, growing venality, loss of elan, versatility, professional efficiency and commitment, lack of trust and confidence in the civil service? These are some of the issues which need to be examined in depth in order to find answers to the questions agitating the minds of all those who are acutely conscious of the social landscope today. The dangers of the growing disparities between classes and the ever widening schisms between castes fuelled by the growing awareness of their rights by the deprived sections on the one hand and the unfulfilled promises of the Preamble and the Directive

Principles on the other can no longer be side tracked. The tensions are very close to reaching the flashpoint, massive pressures are building up and social relationships are fast changing. Our Constitution was framed in a different milieu by people imbued, no doubt, with much compassion and sentiment but without much administrative experience. Perhaps a time has come to take a fresh look at the whole scheme of our constitution.

NOTES & REFERENCES

1. Coupland R., *The Constitutional Problem of India*, Madras, 1934, Parts I and II.
2. *Constituent Assembly Debates,* Vol. V, pp. 1-2.
3. Granville Austin, *The Constitution of India - Cornerstone of a Nation,* Oxford 1966.
4. Ibid.
5. Jawaharlal Nehru speaking on the Constitution (Fourth Amendment) Bill, 1955, L.S. debates Vol II, Part II Cols 1949-57 (March 14, 1955), Vol II, Cols 4833-46 (April 11, 1955), 5116-24 (April 12, 1955).
6. In Winston Churchill's words the Government of India Act, 1935 was "a gigantic quilt of jumbled erochet work, a monstrous monument of shame, built by pigmies". (H.V. Hodson, *The Great Divide*, Oxford University Press, 1985, p. 48).
7. Philip Mason, *The Men who Ruled India,* New Delhi, 1985, p. 345.
8. A.D. Gorwala, as quoted in Philip Mason's, *The Men who Ruled India,* New Delhi, 1985, pp. 294-95.
9. Philip Mason, *The Men who Ruled India,* New Delhi, 1985, p. 295.
10. It is interesting to recall what Thomas Munro, Curzon and other British administrators thought of the application of British Parliamentary democracy to India. Arthur B. Keith writes in the Preface to his *A Constitutional History of India - 1600 to 1935,* London, 1936 as follows:

    "The result was inevitable, with steadily increasing strength the Indian intelligentsia has demanded the fulfilment of self-government, not in the form contemplated by Munro and his contemporaries, but in that of British parliamentary institutions. To men deeply imbued with the fundamental principles of democracy, such as Lord Morley of Blackburn, these demands seemed inconsistent with the structure of Indian society, which is founded on the basis of social inequality and racial and religious diversity".

    Could they be right and did we, perish the thought, opt for a wrong model of government for free India?

Social Justice and the Public Services

V.S. PRASAD

> One of the matters which we do not usually find place in a constitutional document but have been included in our Constitution is the Public Services.
>
> (DURGA DAS BASU, 1992)[1]

> The disproportion between what I would like to name as 'Social Justice' texts, as distinct from the 'governance' texts is rather conspicuous in the Corpus which we call the constitution.
>
> (UPENDRA BAXI, 1991)[2]

Indian Constitution has many distinctive features, one of which is the inclusion of detailed provisions on the apparatus of governance. The Constitution visualises an important role for the State and its instruments in achieving social justice. The Directive Principles of State Policy, which embody the constitutional philosophy of social justice expect the State to be its instrument in fulfilling the goals of justice. This paper is an attempt to examine and interrogate the role of public services, from the Constitutional perspective, in promoting the formation of an egalitarian social order.

From the analysis of the provisions of the Constitution[3] three distinct features of public services can be inferred. These are:

One: Public services under the control of people's representatives, which is ensured through provisions like;

(i) power of legislature, Union and State, to prescribe the conditions of service of public servants; (Art 309)

(ii) political executive/ministerial responsibility for the governance which results in subordinate and supportive role to public services; (Art 74-75),

(iii) political executives' power to make rules for the transaction of the business of the Government of India (Art 77).

Two: Competent, impartial and non-political civil service, which is ensured by provisions like;

(i) career service recruited on merit basis; (Art 309)
(ii) recruitment of higher civil services by an independent authority (UPSC/SPSC); (Art 315-323)
(iii) security of services; (Art 311)
(iv) rule of law governing the behaviour of public services (Art 14, 15).

Three; representative bureaucracy, which is ensured by the provisions like;

(i) equality of opportunity in matters of public employment with a provison for reservation of posts in favour of backward class of citizens to provide adequate representation in services; (Art 16)
(ii) the claims of the members of the Scheduled Castes and the Scheduled Tribes shall be taken into consideration consistently with the maintenance of efficiency of administration, in the making of appointments to the services and posts in connection with the affairs of the union or of a State (Art 335).

The Public Services under the control of people's representatives are considered an important feature of a democratic political system. The Westminster parliamentary form of government gives the final powers in governance to the Council of Ministers which is responsible to the Legislature. Administration is considered an instrument for the realisation of values set by the political system.

An impartial and non-political public service is also considered the hallmark of Westminster parliamentary democracy. After the Northcote-Trevelyan Report (1854), merit was adopted as a principle for recruitment to public services in India. It is supposed to satisfy the needs of democracy making available equal opportunity to all in public employment; and the needs of efficiency, by entrusting the job to the best qualified person. The Weberian paradigm of politically neutral career service finds support in the Constitutional provisions. It is assumed that the democratic political system which is based on competitive politics need 'neutral competence' for the survival of the system.

Representative democracy gave rise to the demands of representative bureaucracy. The essential argument has been that the civil service which includes all categories of population ensures that heterogeneous values and interests are adequately articulated and brought to bear upon the decisions taken and the policies formulated. Van Riper makes it clear that a representative bureaucracy must "(i) consist of a reasonable cross-section of the body politic in terms of occupation, class, geography and the like, and (ii) must be in general tune with the ethos and the attitudes of the society of which it is a part".[4] The case for representative bureaucracy is more strong in countries like India where the State is given a very important role and administrative positions are traditionally occupied by the upper castes/ classes of society. The constitutional provision of reservations to Scheduled Castes, Scheduled Tribes and other Backward Classes of citizens for providing adequate representation in service is a measure for achieving social justice.

The application of the normative framework raises some issues which are posed below:

(i) Do the Parliament and the political executive have the necessary competence to fulfil their obligation to control and direct the administration which is becoming increasingly technical? The incongruence between the capabilities and powers may be one of the sources and causes for the control being shifted from the system to the individual civil servants. The increasing phenomenon of politicians inflicting personal insults on civil servants partly reflects their incapacity to control the administrative system and partly their practice of browbeating the administration for partisan purposes. The oft-heard complaint of politicians blaming the bureaucracy for failure in achieving social justice, indicates both the ineffectiveness of political control over administration and the desire to shift the blame.

(ii) The increasing crisis of legitimacy of political institutions like Parliament and Cabinet makes them ineffective in using the public services for social justice.[5] Here the nature of the political system is considered a critical variable influencing the role of public services. This institutional crisis may also result in an unholy alliance between the political and the administrative systems to subserve their selfish and partisan interests.[6] The bureaucracy may justify its role in the unholy alliance on the plea that its position is that of a mere subordinate in the political system.

(iii) The Constitution mainly places the burden of controlling the public service on the Parliament and Cabinet. Public control in a representative democracy is equated with control by people's representatives. Do the people have any alternative mechanisms to control the bureaucracy in the event of failure of representative institutions to do so? The existing constitutional arrangement has no satisfactory answer to this question.

(iv) Many studies observe low levels of competence of the Indian bureaucracy.[7] Is it because of (i) failure of select persons on a merit basis and/or (ii) failure of define merit appropriately, (iii) and/or merit not being a sufficient condition for competence and/or (iv) environmental factors not allowing the realisation of potential of public services? Is it not essential to critically examine the elements 'merit' if social justice oriented public service is to be created?

(v) The particularistic orientation dominates the behaviour of Indian administration.[8] "Tell me the person I will tell the rule" is not an exaggeration. Indian administration is also infamous for its lack of respect for rule of law. As a perspective observer: put it "Governance in India is not by rule of law, but by the law of the ruler. The law in our tradition is what the ruler wishes".[9] Can particularism of bureaucracy help in achieving social justice?

(vi) Politicisation of bureaucracy in the sense of use of civil services for partisan political purposes is increasingly evident. At the higher levels of civil services a de facto spoils system seems to have come in. The senior civil servant in India today enjoys the advantage of the tenure and anonymity of the British system with the patronage, power and accelerated advancement of the American system.[10] This raises two important questions: One, is it logical and rational to assume political neutrality of an administrative system which has to work under the control of political masters located as they are in a divisive, stratified society like India? Second, does the politically neutral civil service play a significant role in achieving social justice?

(vii) Even after 45 years of the Republic, the provision of adequate representation to weaker sections has not been fulfilled inspite of all the noise about Mandalisation of services in recent years. Though in recent years opportunities are opening up to weaker sections in the public services, it is still dominated by middle and upper middle classes and castes. The working class is very inadequately represented in the higher echelons of civil service. We have to travel a long way to reach the constitutional obligation.

(viii) The assumption that the bureaucrats carry their class/caste attitudes and prejudices into their official life needs more empirical testing.[11] We should not neglect the deviants from class norms who are there both in the upper as well as lower classes. The failure of the people coming from lower classes into the public services to identify with the interests of their own class weakens the case for a representative bureaucracy as a means for social justice. This is not to argue for the continuation of upper caste dominance in civil service or to reject the demand for reservations. The question is how do we transform a representative bureaucracy into a sensitive and committed bureaucracy for social justice?

(ix) The representative bureaucracy, in the short run, may also result in growing cleavages in public services. The corridors of administration are agog with stories of caste conflict and divisions within the bureaucracy. The power struggles between officials who seek more resources, security, status of power may get further accentuated by caste divisions.

(x) The ruling classes in India, dissatisfied with the performance of the administration to serve their interests and not sure of their ability to hold on to state power for long, are advocating strategies of liberalisation, privatisation, market friendly administration etc., resulting in a retreat of the State from the arena of social justice. In this context, the demand for increasing representation to weaker sections in a defamed and disfigured administrative structure may not by itself be an adequate and effective means to achieve social justice.

The normative framework of bureaucracy provided in the Indian constitution is aimed at achieving the values of democracy, impartiality, efficiency and social representativeness. The incorporation of these diverse values resulted in several contradictions in the working of the administrative system. The contradictions are endocentric and exocentric in nature. The diverse values of political control and impartiality and efficiency and social representation may result in endocentric contradictions.

The exocentic contradiction refers to the contradiction between the Weberian framework of bureaucracy laid down in the Constitution and the inegalitarian society with its historical burden of colonial administration. The administrative culture itself has been influenced by social forces and diverse and changing social scenario engendered many models of administrators like the (a) egoistic, (b) pragmatic, (c) sympathetic and (d) lumpen.[12] Consequently, one has to look beyond the normative framework of the Indian Constitution to understand role of the public services on the one hand and the very operational feasibility and utility of the constitutional framework itself on the other.

REFERENCES

1. Durga Das Basu, 1992, *Introduction to the Constitution of India,* 14th edn., Prentice Hall of India, p. 338.
2. Upendra Baxi, 1991, 'Accumulation and Legitimacy : The Indian Constitution and State Formation', in R.V.R. Chandrasekhara Rao and V.S. Prasad (ed), *Indian Constitution and Polity,* Sterling Publishers, New Delhi, p. 34.
3. Durga Das Basu, 1992, *op.cit.*
4. V. Subramaniam, 1971, *Social Background of India's Administrators,* Publications Division, Government of India, New Delhi.
5. Atul Kohli, 1992, *Democracy and Discontent, India's Growing Crisis of Governability,* Cambridge University Press, 1st Indian edn., Foundation Books, New Delhi.
6. Kuldeep Mathur, 'Bureaucracy in India: Development and Pursuit of Self Interest', *The Indian Journal of Public Administration,* Oct-Dec, 1991, vol. XXXVII, No. 4.
7. C.P. Bhambhri, 1986, 'Bureaucracy in India', in Kuldeep Mathur (ed.), *A Survey of Research in Public Administration, 1970-79,* ICSSR and Concept, New Delhi.
8. G. Haragopal and V.S. Prasad, 'Social Bases of Administrative Culture in India', *The Indian Journal of Public Administration,* July-September, 1990, Vol. XXXVI, No. 3.
9. B.K. Nehru, 1992, 'A Fresh Look at the Constitution', in C.K. Jain (ed), *Constitution of India, In Precept and Practice,* Lok Sabha Secretariat and CBS, New Delhi.
10. B.R.R. Vithal, 1991, 'Evolving Practices and Emerging Fissures', in R.V.R. Chandrasekhara Rao and V.S. Prasad (eds), *Indian Constitution and Polity,* op.cit.
11. V. Subramaniam, op.cit.
12. G. Haragopal and V.S. Prasad, *op.cit.*

The Emerging Administrative Reality

K.S. SUBRAMANIAN

This paper will be in three sections. In the first, I develop my main arguments on the issue of social justice and constitutional imperatives – an issue which has been ably explored by Ajit Bhattacharjea in his thematic note on the seminar. The focus will be on the role of the administrative structure (at the district, state and central levels) in achieving or fulfilling the constitutional objective of delivering justice to the rural poor in the context of their increasing awareness and militancy about their human, social and legal rights. The main thesis will be that there is a built-in contradiction between the constitutional imperatives on the one hand and the political-organisational character of the administrative structure on the other which, along with other socio-economic and political factors, inhibits the achievement of this objective. The structure was created to manage the socio-political status quo in a particular historical conjucture. The qualitatively new conjuncture that has emerged after independence has eventually destroyed the administrative, managerial and policy capacity of that structure, especially in the context of accentuating social tensions in rural India. The dynamics of change in rural India have also produced an information crisis in the administration which is a particularly marked feature in the post-emergency situation. These issues have been given less attention than they deserve. In the second section, I provide evidence drawn from my recent research in support of the arguments set out in the first. Some tentative conclusions are drawn in the final section.

I

Assessment of the possibilities and efficacy of enforcement, by political or administrative action, of the constitutional provisions on social justice can be done in two ways. One can argue in a somewhat fundamentalist, though not incorrect, manner that those who struggle for social justice under the Indian Constitution will inevitably come into conflict with the basic features of the

Indian Constitution such as the power of the Central Government to dismiss state governments, especially those with a radical programme; the financial, economic and administrative dependence of the states on the Centre and so on (Namboodiripad, 1982). On the other hand, one can adopt a more gradualist, piecemeal social-engineering perspective and try to assess the impact of the various measures taken under the Constitution and under the general and specific laws to improve the lot of the weaker sections such as the Scheduled Castes (SC's) and Scheduled Tribes (ST's) and arrive at an informed judgement on the efficacy of the existing mechanisms for delivering social justice at the cutting edge level (Shah, 1993).

Shah's study is recent and comprehensive and quite useful from the point of view of the theme of my paper. I assume that not many are likely to seriously dispute his findings and observations.

The paper is titled "Development, New Economic Policy and the Deprived Communities". It is significant that virtually all the sub-headings of the paper should indicate a negative assessment of the performance so far in achieving the social objectives of the Constitution. They go as follows: "More Disadvantaged", "Sluggish Capitalist Development", "State Institutions Protect Rich Peasant", "Forest Department Officials Exploit Adivasis", "The Deprived Have A Long Way to Go", "A Small Section Benefits", "Reservation Quota Nor Fully Utilised", and "Most Atrocity Cases in Villages Unreported". The overall assessment, therefore, is that the condition of the deprived communities have, by and large, not improved, "though the country has moved on the path of development in terms of growth and resources" (p. 64). Referring to development projects in certain areas where the local tribals have not only lost their land but also got uprooted from their cultural milieu, the following observation of the Commissioner for Scheduled Castes and Tribes is cited: "The story of acquisition of land and displacement of people living in it, is a story of utter disregard of rights of common people, of injustice in the name of law, of empty promises and false hopes. The state and its representatives and under their shadow all sorts of elements have used the law of acquisition in an arbitary manner. And that is not all. They have grossly and openly misued it" (Shah, 1993: 69).

The Constitution and several policy pronouncements promise

to protect the cultural identity of the tribals and "not to disturb the harmony of tribal life". Shah notes the violation of these declarations in practice and cites the observation of the National Committee on the Development of Backward Areas in 1981: "The constitutional provisions in relation to the protection and development of tribal communities and administration of Scheduled areas, however, have not been operationalized. Law provides the basis and the frame for all administrative action. But the regulation making power under the Fifth Schedule has been used by the states to a very limited extent. It has been held that it is Parliament which can enact a law on tribal affairs. But no law has been passed so far by Parliament either for the protection or for the development of the Scheduled Tribes. Similarly, no regulation has been made for peace and good administration of the tribal areas, although there is a specific provision for this purpose under the Fifth Schedule, and administration has continued to remain the weakest spot in tribal affairs" (Shah, 1993: 73).

Similar findings are recorded in innumerable other studies. They clearly establish that mere administrative action to achieve the social justice objectives of the Constitution is at best of limited utility being partial, inadequate, incomplete and unsatisfactory and that, essentially, the problem is related to political action on a broad front. Nationalistic assumptions on the part of scholars and policy makers at independence and thereafter had led to an understanding that once the foreign rulers are thrown out, the task of development under our own leadership will proceed in a linear, unproblematic manner. Development experience of the last several decades has shattered this understanding and there is increasing awareness that the role of the State in developing societies is a far more complex affair. Intense debate on the role of the State in India and other similar countries is, therefore, a marked feature of the social science scene today (IDS Bulletins 1986, 1987a, 1987b, Bardhan, 1984; Rudolphs, 1987: Eyres, 1988, Randhir Singh; 1990; Seminar, 1990; Vanaik, 1990; Shah, 1990). It is in the light of this emerging understanding that we have to reassess the nature, evolution and impact of Government policy in the recent period in operationalising the constitutional imperative of achieving growth with social justice. Such an assessment must, no doubt, be complex and multi-sided but one can see certain clear patterns.

One such pattern, at least in the assessment of the present writer, is that of the increasing awareness, and militancy of the rural poor in relation to their human, social and legal rights and the lessening capacity of the inherited administrative structure (at the managerial and policy levels) to comprehend this militancy and awareness and the consequent aggravation of social violence in rural india. Controversially, one can even argue that civil servants under the British Raj (despite their imperial organisational and political objectives) had the capacity, at least in some cases, to perceive the public interest and reflect to their masters. The introduction of the political process after independence, and the pervasive "politicisation" of the civil services seems to have led to an undermining or dilution of this capacity. Here, we are not passing any value judgement on colonialism and anti-colonialism but merely noting certain objective developments in the civil services. A number of other factors are no doubt at work requiring more complex analysis but this debating point seems worth making in the context of the present discussion.

It is the rapid development of this increasing awareness and militancy on the part of the rural poor that has shaped, in part, the evolution of official policy in the rural sector since at least the early 70's, when the emotive slogan of "Garibi Hatao" was launched. Following the Emergency and the twenty-point programme, official efforts were made to meet, to some extent, the increasing awareness of the rural poor about their human, social and legal rights under the impact of the politics of parliamentary democracy and the competitive mobilisation of the rural poor by the ruling and opposition political parties. The Untouchability Offences Act of 1955 was tightened up as the protection of Civil Rights Act in 1976. The Bonded Labour (Abolition) Act was passed. The Minimum Wages Act was sought to be strictly enforced. Greater attention was paid to the issue of increasing "atrocities" and violence against the rural poor by the increasingly powerful intermediate castes and classes, the beneficiaries of the development process. The Atrocities (Prevention) Act recently enacted was the ultimate outcome of the official efforts from the mid-70's to analyse, study and deal with the increasing violence against the SC's and ST's (see, for an analysis of statistics and policies, Subramanian,1986).

Further, at the level of the planning process, it became

increasingly clear that reliance on growth alone would not be sufficient to achieve the basic objectives of the Indian Constitution such as the reduction of inequalities in income, wealth and economic power, removal of poverty and lessening of unemployment. The Fifth Five Year Plan launched a "direct attack" on poverty and welfare programmes were formulated to benefit well-defined "target-groups" officially recognised as having been historically exploited and victimised. The Tribal sub-plan for the Scheduled Tribes and the Special Component Plan for the Scheduled Castes emerged. The SFDA (Small Farmers Development Agency), the MFAL (Marginal Farmers and Agricultural Labourers Development Programme) were combined to form the IRDP (Integrated Rural Development Programme) which has been the major anti-poverty programme recently together with the Jawahar Rojgar Yojana. Within the existing framework and priorities, increasing budget allocations have no doubt been forced to be set aside for the welfare of the rural poor, precisely to meet at least to some extent the increasing rural poor awareness and militancy.

The patchy quality and content of the official efforts at rural poor amelioration and indeed the basic class character underlying them have been repeatedly exposed in official and non-official reports. An important official publication in the mid-eighties contains a separate chapter on "conceptual issues" which takes note of the emerging "structural dualism" in the Indian economy and states clearly: "Left to its own logic in a dynamic context, the dominant tendency of the system worked not in favour but against the interest of the masses" (GOI, 1985: 6). The report, therefore, calls for a planning strategy which would neutralise the logic of this "dualistic structure" by including "mass-oriented agrarian reform, labour-absorbing and land-augmenting technological innovation, political decentralisation, and administrative restructuring to ensure planning from the bottom and, above, all grass-roots mobilisation of the poor" (Ibid: 7).

It is the issue of the increasing awareness and militancy of the rural poor about their human, social and legal rights and the role of the administrative structure in perceiving, interpreting and formulating policy to deal with it that has been the focus of the present writer's research in the recent past. In the course of his work in the government and thereafter he has had the opportunity of extensive field observation on the role of the delivery system at the cutting edge level in meeting the expectations of the people especially the rural poor consisting mainly of SC's and ST's in the category of agricultural labourers and poor peasant numbering about 200 million. The experience led to an attempt to conceptualise the phenomenon documented in official and non-official reports, of increasing violence against the rural poor both by the rural well-to-do and by the state machinery. The former consisting mainly of the intermediate castes have gained enormously out of the development process since independence, especially after the Green Revolution. One observer has noted the emergence of an integrated class-caste alliance of the rural and small town rich with strong links and interests in the urban sector (Balagopal, 1988). The state machinery has manifold links with the rural alliance which exploits the rural poor on account of their economic dependence, social disabilities and lack of political influence. The limited official efforts aimed at the welfare of the rural poor are seen by the rural elite as well as influential elements in the state machinery as attempts by ruling political formations to woo the rural poor because of their numerical preponderance and electoral and political importance.

The key question in the research of the present writer was: how to characterise the essential nature of state bureaucratic intervention in rural India today? On the one hand, the implementation over the years of a variety of rural development programmes (however inadequate in number and inefficiently implemented), of course along with other factors, has given rise to unprecedented awareness and militancy on the part of the rural poor who attempt organised assertion of their rights to land, minimum wages, civil rights, and end to social oppression and so on. On the other hand, the inherited state machinery which has a historically "over-developed" (Alavi, 1972) character in its repressive aspects and still operates essentially on the basis of a colonial epistemology (Guha, 1983), inflicts on the rural poor, often in collaboration with the rural elite, political violence of exceptional brutality. While on the face of it, policy development for the rural poor has been receiving increasing attention at higher levels of policy-making, the contradictions of policy implementation as manifested in the increasing militancy of rural social protest movements and their violent repression by agents of the state and the rural rich have not been adequately addressed especially in the burgeoning technical literature on rural development.

The research and writing (including two major case studies) have brought into sharp focus the basic contradictions between the political-organisational characteristics of the inherited administrative structure and the constitutional imperatives of parliamentary democracy, federalism and development-oriented administration (Subramanian, 1986; 1987; 1988; 1992; 1993).

Due to understandable nationalistic assumptions, the study of bureaucratic behaviour in India has tended, by and large, to be in terms of civil service neutrality, independence and benevolence. (One may here contrast the situation in, say, Africa). Initially, well-worn themes were gone into such as the historical development of the bureaucracy, the history and role of the ICS, the role of the District Collector, the theory and practice of district administration, historical evolution of the administration and the police and so on. Subsequently, with the increasing role of the state in development in the context of parliamentary democracy, other themes were taken up such as the politician-civil servant relationship, the problem of 'political will' in the implementation of development policy and so on. In the latter context, it is not seen that when viewed from the bottom of the social structure there is no basic conflict of interest between the politician and the civil servant and that both of them appear as part of the same exploitative set-up. Similarly, it is not recognised that if there is a consistent record of failure in development policy say, in the sphere of land reforms, then that failure must be taken to be part of the policy itself. Traditional approaches in public administration, therefore, have not taken us very far in explaining bureaucratic behaviour today. Some of the analytical challenges before the specialists on public administration in India today would seem to be:

(i) How does one explain the explosive emergence of social conflicts of a most varied character in India today? What has been the role of the administration in all this?

(ii) How does one characterise the nature of the development process in India? Are the top public sector professionals one of the 'dominant proprietary classes' (Bardhan, 1984)? If so, what are the implications for public administration studies?

(iii) How does one explain the emergence of what has been

characterised as 'the massive growth of centralised police power' in India today?

(iv) How does the internal structure and process of the bureaucratic state apparatus relate to the external constraints and determinants of state power in India, much noticed in the literature? Does it have a 'relative autonomy' in the concrete Indian case?

(v) What is the nature of the phenomenon of 'governmental lawlessness', 'police atrocities', 'state-sponsored violence' and so on? Where does one locate it in the theoretical terrain of traditional public administration? Are they just unfortunate aberrations, not symbolic of some deeper structural problems?

vi) Under the Westminister model which we have adopted, the civil servant has the right to give disinterested policy advice to the political decision maker and has to follow the latter's orders only after the advice is rejected for good reasons. With so much going wrong administratively, how is it that we do not yet have many cases of civil servants taking strong stands on issues (say, in regard to the handling of communal riots) on which they can and should? On the other hand, civil servants often argue (perhaps self-servingly) that in a parliamentary democracy, the civil service has to do the politician's bidding, totally missing or eliding the point that the civil servant under the Westminster model has a specific and important role to play. What then is the theoretical strength of all the studies which postulate a conflict between the upright civil servant and the dishonest political master?

II

Although the focus of my own research has been on the administrative, managerial and policy challenges arising out of the violence against the rural poor and their resistance to it, it is useful to note 'the wide variety of social disturbances' that characterise the rural scene today. Balagopal (1988: 20) mentions the following:

> (i) struggles of the rural poor for land, wages and against social oppression;
>
> (ii) struggles of landed peasants for renumerative prices, cheap inputs and infrastructural facilities;
>
> (iii) booth capturing, assaults and other forms of physical

violence at the time of elections;

(iv) conflicts over rural co-operation and government contracts;

(v) organised assaults on the rural poor including atrocities and other forms of community-based oppression.

The case studies of emergent movements of the rural poor conducted by the present writer in selected districts of Bihar and Tamil Nadu confirm other studies on the pre-conditions for the emergence of social movements of this type (Huizer 1980; 1990). The important preconditions are well-formulated by Huizer:

> (i) the occurrence of a blatant case or situation of injustice or disadvantage, that is, a deterioration of the actual situation or the raising of false hopes of improvement;
>
> (ii) The availability of able, charismatic leaders who can voice discontent and initiate steps for correction of grievances and inspire the poor to action;
>
> (iii) some measure of tolerance by the state or active support by urban allies such as politicians, development workers and intellectuals in coping with the effects of the state's hegemony of law and order. (Huizer 1990; 9-10)

During field work in the Patna and Dharmapuri districts these conditions were generally found to exist but was found to exist to a greater extent in the Patna district than in the Dharmapuri district with a consequent greater intensity and severity of repression in the latter. Thus, while rural poor militancy in Patna and other south central districts of Bihar has remained unabated and has perhaps even intensified, the militancy in the Charmpur district to Tamil Nadu has been driven underground, for the moment at least.

As observed by Huizer and confirmed again by our field studies, social movements of the rural poor usually originate by articulating demands which correspond to the most concretely felt grievances and needs. When the elite/State machinery, instead of responding positively to the demands, tries to counter the growing movement, it becomes more radical; and even revolutionary, with attempts at violent suppression. When just and legitimate demands are sought to be violently suppressed the State tends to lose its legitimacy. Initially, such movements are non-violent and merely try to correct strongly felt grievances. When they gain some momentum and are sought to be violently suppressed through State intervention, they tend to become more militant and may start to use violence to counter State violence which is perceived as illegitimate (Huizer op.cit; Subramanian op.cit).

A number of studies have gone into the economic and social factors which inhibit the emergence of powerful organisations of the rural poor in India (see, for example, Huizer 1980). However, the impediments stemming from the nature of the legal-administrative system and the bureaucratic State power at the cutting edge level have not received serious attention. An experienced former civil servant has observed (Bandyopadhyay 1977:10) that the full implications of the role of the bureaucratic structure can never be realised fully by anyone who does not have an intimate knowledge of both the functioning of the Indian administrative machinery at the district level and the harassment and persecution that rural activists have to face in embarking on any direct action.

The position of the present writer, by and large, is that the concept of rule of law and the concomitant politico-administrative set-up established by the British which continued relatively unchanged into the post-colonial period constitute powerful obstacles in the path of development of organizations of the rural poor in India. In comparison, the situation in China was vastly different and relatively more favourable for the intervention of the rural poor in the political process. It is not that the colonial administrative structure has not undergone any qualitative changes at all in the post-independence period in India. There have, in fact, been such changes. But they have not powerfully shaken or undermined its basic structure as yet (Rao 1989). The role of this structure has to be viewed in conjunction with the economic weakness and social disabilities which inhibit the emergence and consolidation of organizations of the rural poor.

The political-organisational characteristics of the powerful colonial State apparatus built by the British in India have been brought into focus (Potter 1986; Arnold 1986;1988). Nehru himself admitted that one of his major failures was not to have changed this apparatus after independence (Potter 1986: 2).

Potter stresses the strength of the administrative structure in maintaining order, unity, integrity and stability and its relative lack of innovation, responsiveness, expertise and the accountability to the people. The institutional structure of government in the states as well as the Centre, is highly centralised and administrative power is concentrated in the hands of small groups of elite civil servants strategically located in districts, state secretariats and the Central government. A marked orientation to order is built into the overall fabric of administration. The value of this frame to political leaders at the Centre was repeatedly demonstrated after independence whenever there were political crises involving the imposition of President's Rule or a national Emergency (1975-77). A single group of political administrators in a national frame controllable from the Centre was a most useful mechanism (Potter 1986:242). As Potter observes:

> Indian revolutionaries perhaps tended to under estimate the strength of the state bureaucracy. Inefficient in implementing development programmes they may have been but that was never their strong point. What the bureaucratic structure of state power in India continued to be good and what the ICS tradition emphasized, was maintaining order and dealing with any serious internal opposition to their rule. (Ibid.1986: 245)

Potter goes on to make a useful analysis of the fundamental contradiction between this administrative structure and some of the essential features of the Indian Constitution framed in 1950 (1986: 150-79). These features are (i) the 'formal provision for a parliamentary system of democratic government and the consequent spread of democratic politics with politicians increasingly involved in administration at the district, state and central levels'; (ii) 'the Directive Principles of State Policy and all the steps taken subsequently in the Five Year Plans to pursue in an active manner the economic and social development the principles called for'; and (iii) 'the federal structure of government – which, in combination with the democratic feature did set in motion forces opposed to an all-Indian administrative service'.

A crucial but less often noticed feature of the Indian administration which inhibits the emergence of organizations of the rural poor, is the police structure. There have been many studies of the development of the Indian Police but the most important of them (Bayley 1969; Gupta 1979) are unable to see it as part of 'a deeper trend that spans Indian history from early colonialism to the present day – the creation, evolution and consolidation of powerful state apparatus with the police as one of its primary agencies' (Arnold 1986: 4). Arnold notes that in the history of the Indian Police '1947 marked no major watershed or hiatus' (ibid: 5), a point also conceded by Bayley (1969: 51) who, however, misses its real significance in relation to the rural poor in particular (see Arnold 1986: 98-149; 230-36). Arnold further observes that 'the massive growth of centralised police power since 1947, especially the intelligence and paramilitary police may be new departure but their origins lie in the natures and functions of the colonial police' (Arnold 1986: 236).

While stressing the colonial character of the Indian Police structure, Arnold especially notes its express functions as state servants and not public servants; its coercive disposition and strength together with the frequent use of state violence; its close identification with properties interests and so on.

It is in this overall context that we must examine the interface of the state apparatus at the cutting edge level with the ongoing struggles of the rural poor in different parts of the country to organise themselves for the assertion of their human, social and legal rights.

As noted by a former civil servant (Bandyopadhyay 1977: 7-11) historically the prime objective of district administration has been maintenance of order and tranquility in the countryside. The general administrative procedures and traditions, criminal and civil laws, judicial pronouncements and practices are centred around the preservation of the status quo and the prevailing property structure. If a conflict occurs between the implementation of a social legislation which might upset the social status quo and the maintenance of law and order, the weight of administrative culture and tradition favours the latter. The Indian Penal Code and the Criminal Procudure Code contain elaborate provisions for the maintenance of public order and tranquility and more than 33 per cent of the operational provisions of the Indian Penal Code relate to offences against property. The Criminal Procedure Code was overhauled in 1973 but still contains drastic provisions for the dispersal of unlawful assemblies by force.

The main demands of the rural poor centre around land, wages and struggle against social oppression. A large number of them are landless agricultural workers. And a landless person in rural India is a non-person. Any attempt at getting possession of land security of tenure, payment of minimum wages is seen as an attempt to disturb the social status quo and as soon as this happens public order and tranquility are threatened and all the relevant provisions of the Indian Penal Code and the Criminal Procedure Code can be invoked by the rural elite and the state machinery to proserve the status quo.

Bandyopadhyay cites several instances where land reforms laws which have bestowed some rights on share-croppers have been sabotaged through use of the provisions of Section 144 of the Criminal Procedure Code. Direct action by the rural poor to establish their rights have been met with punitive measures under the provisions of the Indian Penal Code and Criminal Procedure Code. In the face of the facility with which the legal and administrative set-up can be set in motion by the rural elites to defend their interests, Bandyopadhyay expresses some surprise as to how organisations of the rural poor could at all exist and develop.

Arnold's historically sensitive approach to the study of the Indian police enables us to perceive its role in the current social context very sharply indeed. The structure of police administration in the district as an inseparable part of the district administration as a whole serves to uphold the legal-administration set-up in relation to rural poor struggle as brought out in Bandyopadhyay's analysis.

As emphasised by Arnold (1986: 186) a political surveillance function has been implicit in the organisation and duties of the colonial Indian police right from its inception. The need for reliable information about the mood of the people and the causes of unrest and discontent led the colonial authorities to set up an intelligence agency at the centre in the 1980s which was to become the Intelligence Bureau. As already noted, Arnold brings out the colonial origins of the massive growth of intelligence and paramilitary police in the post-independence period. The system as it functions today has a continuous hierarchy of information channels from the local to the central level and forms an inseparable part of the highly centralised administrative structure from the district to the central government; it is a powerful instrument in the hands of the political authorities at the centre and plays a crucial role especially in times of political crisis (Potter 1986: 241).

The crucial role of the police information system in Indian government, in the realm of policy formation vis-a-vis the rural poor struggles required detailed examination but this is a task which can be carried out only by those, as noted in a different context by Bandyopadhyay (1977: 10) with detailed knowledge of the working of the Indian administrative machinery extending from the district to the centre.

I have documented the perceptions of intelligence authorities at the district, state and central levels in relation to rural poor struggles (Subramanian 1987; 1988). We may merely note here that, given the historically inherited organisational and political characteristics of the intelligence system in India, there is tendency to view struggles of the rural poor, especially those under radical political leadership, as attempts at 'incipient insurgency' threatening the existing political order. As we have noted, the intelligence machinery, composed mainly of police officers, tends to perceive social movements of the rural poor in terms of the security concerns of the organization (Subramanian 1987: 96). This leads to gap between the reality and its perception at the policy level. A more or less exclusive preoccupation develops in terms of the analysis of ideological differences that exist within political groups active in such movements, their areas of influences, organisational characteristics 'offences' committed by them, weapons seized from them, police requirements in terms of fire power, mobility, man-power etc.

A more significant line of enquiry from the administrative point of view would be to look at the systematic patterns of power and domination that arise in rural society and the injustice and exploitation that are associated with the unequal distribution of land and other productive assets. It would also be worthwhile to investigate the patterns of interaction of the administration at the cutting edge level with the rural power structure in the context of subsistence agriculture characteristic of most parts of rural India. It is this interaction which leads to such contradictions of administrative behaviours in rural India as are illustrated by the following examples:

(i) in the course of field work in one state, a case came to light in which a village landowner-cum-moneylender forcibly occupied a small plot of land belonging to a Scheduled Caste agricultural labourer who was indebted to him (the landowner). The agricultural worker attacked the landlard in anger and in return the latter had no difficulty in getting him arrested by the local police officer who belonged to the same caste;

(ii) in another case in the same state a village milk cooperative society was sought to be organised by some educated unemployed youths belonging to the Scheduled Castes. The local landlord who controlled the milk supply to the village could not tolerate this assertion of independence on the part of the Scheduled Castes and had them arrested by a local police officer who belonged to his caste alleging that they were involved in Naxalite activities.

(iii) in another case in another state, a local landlord was under attack by a group of Scheduled Caste activists for his exploitative practices. The official machinery extended assistance to him to organise a 'self-defence squad' against the so-called Naxalite activists of the Scheduled Castes. No similar initiative has been forthcoming for the enforcement of constitutionally guaranteed civil rights of the Scheduled Castes, enforcement of minimum agricultural wages, abolition of bonded labour, ending of atrocities and so on.

III

I have argued that quite apart from other factors including difficulties arising from internal contradictions in the Constitution itself (noted by scholars), the fulfilment of social justice objectives is powerfully hindered by the historically inherited limitations of the administrative structure. This historical continuity across 1947 was not just an accident but conscious and powerful forces worked behind it. (Potter, 1986 offers some fascinating insights. See especially chapter 3). Post-independence exercises in administrative reform have not been powerful enough even to raise this thorny issue, leave alone address it. The constitutional guarantees built into the document promulgated in 1950 for an outdated and all-India over-centralised structure seem to stand in need of serious re-examination but the political preconditions for such an exercise are not present yet.

The freedom struggle in India, despite its complexity (explored sensitively in Sarkar,1983) brought with it a certain vision of national objectives based on growth with social justice. A measure of social cohesion and solidarity essential for the fulfilment of these objectives also existed despite certain contra-indications. However, the judgement must be that the achievement has not measured up to initial expectations. One may paraphrase Amartya Sen and say that the Indian development strategy, in focussing far too closely on the means – namely, growth – has lost sight of the ultimate goal – namely, enhancing the capability of the Indian people to lead a better life "not battered by illiteracy, avoidable morbidity, escapable mortality and the slavery of pestilence and disease".

The processes of structural adjustment and globalisation in the Indian economy in the recent period, implying a sharp break with the earlier policies of state directed modernisation and reliance on administrative methods for resource allocation, mean a further retreat of the State from the social justice objectives of the Constitution. Despite rhetoric, the administrative machinery seems increasingly likely to discharge mainly law and order functions, the market being allowed to dictate the generalisation of social welfare benefits, such as they are. Democratic pressures from below will, of course, continue to play a crucial role in forcing social justice back on the agenda . . . witness the outcome of the recent Assembly elections in Uttar Pradesh and Madhya Pradesh. The liberal democratic state in India, while representing dominant interests in society does provide openings for the operations of dominated forces although the issue of how the latter play their cards remains highly problematic, even the revolutionary among them in danger of being coopted by the dominant interests in the system (Subramanian, 1989).

In the meanwhile, India has not been an exception to the emerging scenario of structural adjustment policies elsewhere leading to severe strains on the social fabric marked by increase in crime, violence, smuggling and trading in illicit goods, child labour, prostitution, intensification of female labour, the aggravation of social explosions and ethnic conflicts and growth of fundamentalist and extremist movements (Ghai 1992:14).

As Ghai (1992:17) remarks, rebuilding of social cohesion and solidarity can only come through a "strengthening and coalition of social groups committed to a better balance between collective needs and individual initiatives and between economic advance and social progress".

REFERENCES

Arnold, David, 1986, *Police Power and Colonial Rule: Madras, 1859-1947*, Oxford University Press, Delhi.

Balagopal, K., 1988, *Probings in the Political Economy of Agrarian Classes and Conflicts,* Perspectives Publishers, Hyderabad.

Bandyopadhyay, D., 1977, *External Impediments to the Growth of Organisations of the Rural Poor in India,* National Labour Institute Bulletin, New Delhi 10/77.

Bardhan, P., 1984, *Political Economy of Development in India,* Oxford University Press, Delhi.

Bayley, David H., 1969, *Police and Political Development in India,* Princeton University Press, Princeton, New Jersey.

Bures, T.J., 1988, 'A Chicago view of the Indian State : an oriental grin without an oriental cat and political economy without classes', *Journal of Commonwealth and Comparative Politics,* Vol. 26, No. 3, London, November.

Guha, Ranajit, 1983, *Elementary Aspects of Peasant Insurgency in Colonial India,* Oxford University Press.

Gupta, Anandswarup, 1979, *The Police in British India, 1861-1947,* Concept Publishers, Delhi.

Ghai, Dharam, 1992, *Structural Adjustment, Global Integration and Social Democracy* (DP 37), United Nations Research Institute for Social Development, Geneva.

Govt. of India, 1985, Ministry of Agriculture, Department of Rural Development, Government of India, New Delhi, *Report of the Committee to Review the Existing Administrative Arrangements for Rural Development and Poverty Alleviation Programmes,* December.

Huizer, G., 1980, *Peasant Movements and their Counter Forces in South East Asia,* Marwah Publishers, Delhi.

——, 1990, 'The State and Social Movements: A Comparative Perspective from Below,' paper for IDPAD Seminar on State and Society: Changing Relations Between State and Society in India and Trends Towards an Emerging European State, Nehru Memorial Museum and Library, New Delhi.

IDS Bulletin, 1986, *Developmental States and African Agriculture,* Vol. 17, No. 1, January.

IDS Bulletin, 1987a , *The Retreat of the State,* Vol. 18, No. 3, July.

IDS Bulletin, 1987b, *Politics in Command?,* Vol .18, No. 4, October.

IDS Bulletin, 1988, *Adjustment and the State: The Problem of Administrative Reform,* Vol. 19, No. 4, October.

Namboodiripad, E.M.S., *The Republican Constitution in the Struggle for Socialism: Selected Writings,* Volume One. National Book Agency, Calcutta, 1982.

Potter, David, 1986, *India's Political Administrators, 1919-1983*, Clarendon Press, Oxford.

Randhir, Singh, 1990, *Of Marxism and Indian Politics,* Ajanta Publishers, Delhi.

Rudolphs, Lioyd I. and Suzanne II, 1987, *In Pursuit of Lakshmi: The Political Economy of the Indian State,* Orient Longman, Bombay.

Rao, K.R., 1989, 'The State in India: A Historical Materialist Exercise', in R. Khan, Z. Hasan and S.N. Jha (eds), *Political Process and Identity: Reflection on Modern India,* Sage Publications, New Delhi.

Shah, 1990, *Capitalist Development: Critical Essays,* Popular Prakashan, Bombay.

Shah, Ghanshyam, 'Development, New Economic Policy and the Deprived Communities,' *Man & Development,* March, 1993.

Seminar No. 367, 1990, *The Politics of the State,* New Delhi, March.

Sarkar, Sumit, 1983, *Modern India, 1885-1947,* Macmillan, New Delhi.

Subramanian, K.S., 1986, 'Violence against the Scheduled Castes in India: Overview, Problems, Prospects,' Occasional Paper XIX, Nehru Memorial Museum and Library, New Delhi.

——, 1987, 'Administrative response to agrarian struggles in the context of Bihar: a public policy approach', Occasional Paper XXXIV, Nehru Memorial Museum and Library, New Delhi.

——, 1988, 'Administrative response to agrarian unrest: a report from Tamil Nadu', Occasional paper III (second series), Nehru Memorial Museum and Library, New Delhi.

——, 1987, 'Behind Rural Violence', *Frontline,* Madras, July 11-24.

——, 1989, *Parliamentary Communism: Crisis in the Communist Movement in India,* Ajanta Publishers, Delhi.

——, 1992, *Political Violence, Social Movements and the State in India,* DP 308, Institute of Development Studies, Sussex, U.K.

——, *The State and the Rural Poor in India Today: Some Contradictions,* Nehru Memorial Museum and Library, New Delhi.

Vanaik, A., 1990, *The Painful Transition: Bourgeois Democracy in India,* Verso, London, New York.

Language and Social Injustice

DEBI PRASAD PATTANAYAK

Social justice is written into the Preamble, Directive Principles and the main body of the Indian Constitution. The Preamble holds promises and the Directive Principles of State Policy are non-enforceable. Therefore one has to look into the enforceable Fundamental Rights enshrined in the body of the Constitution.

The Constitution assures all citizens social, economic and political justice, liberty of thought, expression and belief, equality of status and opportunity and fraternity ensuring the dignity of man. However since the adoption of the Constitution, until today, the country has moved in back gear. The gulf between promise and performance, privileged and the deprived, exploiters exploited, oppressor oppressed, rich poor, urban rural, strong weak has been reinforced and strengthened.

Inequality has many faces. Economic inequality, power inequality, status inequality, inequality of access to education and career opportunities are some of the faces. All of these are mutually reinforcing. For example inequality of access to education results in status inequality, power inequality, which in turn results in economic inequality. The reverse path is equally true. Economic inequality through power and status inequality results in inequality of access to education. Take for example the seesaw battle between Urdu and Hindi being eligibility condition for government jobs. When Urdu became recognised as one of the eligibility condition for goverment jobs in 1877, the 1877 order resulted in the declining number of students studying Hindi. In 1886 the order was rescinded. In 1890 Hindi was restored as an eligibility condition for jobs. The 1900 order gave a fillip to the study of Hindi. (Hans R. Dua, "Hindi language planning: A case study of status change", in Ulrich Ammon and Merlis Hellinger (eds.), *Status Change of Languages*, Walter de Gruyter, Berlin, New York, 1992). Similarly, Article 343 of the Constitution provided for the use of English beyond 15 years. But only in 1963, the Official Language Bill ensured that "the English Language may as from the appointed day, continue to be used in addition to Hindi". The Official Languages (Amendment) Act of

1967 forced English in the name of a compromise and this created unequal opportunity not only for Hindi speakers but also for all Indian language speakers. It created new inequalities.

The Indian Constitution incorporates Articles 120, 343, 344 regarding language use at the Union level; Articles 210, 345, 346, 347 regarding language use at the State level; Articles 348, 349 regarding language use in the judiciary; Articles 29, 30, 350, 351 regarding language use by the linguistic minorities. These Articles were not dictated by the multilingual reality of India. As we borrowed features of the Constitution from monolingual liberal democracies of the West, we saw ourselves through their tainted glasses. Although the Congress stated its objective of linguistic reorganisation of States in 1920, reiterated it in 1928, 1937, 1938, and 1945-46, the Dar Commission Report in 1948 and JVP Committee Report in 1949 were against it. Thus it will be seen that in the face of wavering political will, no systematic and consistent policy formulation is possible.

Much energy is dissipated on the question of whether English or Hindi should be the national official language. Hindi was expected to replace English and now English is threatening not only to replace Hindi, but also the Indian languages. Both these attitudes are products of dominant monolingualism. Our politicians and planners forgot that India is a multilingual pluricultural country and its problems cannot be solved by creating a single nation state in India nor by creating a number of mini regional nation states. Nation states in the West were created around unitary symbols, one language, one religion and one culture, and therefore that model is unsuitable for India. Acceptance of one among many confers privileges on the one and creates inequalities where there was none. Under these circumstances social justice was the first victim.

If the language of administration at the Union level is Hindi or English and Hindi, and in the regions it is the regional language, then this provision is blind to the reality that there exists areas with mixed population in the socalled unilingual areas and there are large bilingual belts at the junction of linguistic zones. Moreover, not only each language grew up with dialects, sociolects, styles and registers, but a language like Hindi is an overarching label encompassing in itself many languages such as Bhojpuri, Maithili, Magadhi, Braj and Avadi. Without these factors being taken into consideration, Hindi was perceived as blocking the socio-economic mobility of people. English, which was projected as of equal inconvenience to all and as a window to the outside world, gained importance. It created a privileged mini sector which controlled the administrative machinery, including administration of justice. As during the British days, people were punished without knowing what they were punished for. The same injustice was perpetrated in post-independence India.

Questions have been raised about Articles 29 and 30. It has been suggested that minorities have been conferred greater rights than the majority. Without getting bogged down with such questions; it is necessary to ask what is meant by "of its choice" in Article 30. A close reading of the Constitution would suggest that educational institutions run by the minority groups are meant to conserve their distinct language, script and culture. But many of the schools run by the minorities are meant to provide English medium education to the majority groups. This question has never seriously been raised, as it suits the elite mini sector.

That English brought through the back door has been the cause of the greatest social injustice needs some explanation. English language of 2 to 4 per cent of the population, is responsible for dividing Indian society into elite and masses, urban and rural, plus power and minus power. Since English is the language which ensures rank, status and wealth in society, there is bound to be clamour for it. But the catch is that people at one time were blamed for not learning English, now they are blamed for learning bad English. When they did not learn English they had their roots in their culture. With little learning of English, they suffer from anomie and alienation. Very fast they loose their roots. Under these conditions Article 350 providing for elementary education in the mother tongue is observed more in the breach.

Article 351 distinguishes between regional Hindi and development of Hindi as the national official language. This Hindi should be so developed that every Indian language would see its face in that mirror. It is stipulated that for its development Hindi should draw elements from Sanskrit and languages listed in the 8th Schedule. If Hindi is to be the national official language, then in its contact with all Indian languages, it must be enriched by elements from all and not restrict itself to the languages of the 8th Schedule. Even this limited provision has never been attempted to be implemented. Hindi would draw sustenance from other languages only if the Hindi region opens up to other languages. Bilingualism helps absorption of elements from those languages. No systematic effort has been made in this direction. Instead, the issue has been politicised.

Thus it will be seen that social injustice is written into the Constitution through its monolingual orientation. Whenever efforts have been made to mitigate social injustice, either through deferment of implementation, through non-implementation or through positive discrimination towards the elitist mini sector, such injustices are reinforced.

It is important to discuss here, the VIIIth Schedule of the Constitution. It does not require great insight to say that the VIIIth Schedule is based on an inadequate appreciation of the linguistic plurality in the country. It does not take into account the fact that the majority languages in states like Assam and Karnataka constitute 64 per cent of their population; in states like Nagaland no language is spoken by more than 20 per cent of the population; and the borders of all languages consist of bilingual belts. It has also not taken into account the fact that a major consequence of urbanisation is multilingualism. The schedule includes Sanskrit, a classical language, Sindhi and Kashmiri, non-state languages and lesser in numerical strength than Gondi and Santhali, which find no place in the schedule. Recognising one dominant language in a plurilingual milieu is denying equal opportunity of growth to the many unrecognised languages and cultures. The non-recognition triggers identity assertion movements. The Constitution, by selective recognition to languages bares itself open to pressures, which has resulted in periodic expansion of the schedule, the latest being the inclusion of Konkani, Manipuri and Nepali.

The VIIIth Schedule is a monolingual relic in our Constitution. By virtue of being state official languages and recognised by the Constitution, these languages not only enjoy special privileges and prestige, but become reference point for allocation of funds. The minority languages languish under majority tyranny and the minor languages and marginalised. The VIIIth Schedule has become anachronistic and irrelevant and needs to be scrapped.

The Rajmannar Report views language from the perspective of Centre-State relations. As it views the Centre and the states to be in perpetual adversary relation, the burden of the report is an argument for the retention of English as an official language for an indefinite period. This brings us to the question of language and state formation. The nation states were conceived around unitary symbols. One language, one religion, one culture in its extreme manifestation one party and one leader defined a nation state. That this was inadequate and inappropriate can be seen from the breakdown of the European nation states and formation of the EEC, European Parliament and the European Union. Experience has shown the inadequacy of the federal structure. Since it is power sharing between the national elite and the regional elite, it works well upto a point as long as the elitist bases in regions are broad and strong enough to withstand the identity assertion pressures from below.

Keeping the multilingual and pluricultural character of India in view Gandhi proposed Gram Swaraj, 'the autonomous village'. Lohia, taking into account the post-Gandhian political realities suggested the four pillar state. The panchayat, the district, the state and the Union must draw sustenance from the Constitution both in terms of power and finance. Thus the interests of diverse language and culture groups can be protected. The local and the regional can then participate in the developmental process as equal partners with the national and the international. A degree of social justice can only be ensured by making the Constitution accept the fact that the deprived sections and the marginalised sector was a fighting chance of survival with justice only if grassroot institutions are strengthened.

Official Language Vs Social Justice

PREM SINGH

I

The pledge to make "social, economic and political justice," that is 'social justice' available to all the citizens of the country, is the pledge expressed in the Preamble of the Indian Constitution. Constitution makers have made provisions to facilitate the availability of social justice to all people and groups, without "discrimination on the grounds of religion, race, caste, sex or place of birth". The intention behind this arrangement is the creation of an egalitarian society. Ideas of social justice witnessed on the international political scene contain sharper and revolutionary perceptions as compared to the Indian Consti-tution. The revolutionary parties within India itself are not completely satisfied with this constitutional delineation of social justice. The scope of this paper does not allow one to go into the details of the other concepts of social justice.

The deprived and the oppressed sections of Indian society for whom the Constitution's provision for social justice was specially formulated, really are the ones who are denied the same. The general opinion after forty-five years of the implementation of the Constitution is that the 'development' and the 'progress' which free India has made, has only resulted in making the rich, richer and the poor, poorer. The causes for this are complex and multifaceted. Significant among these is the constitutional acceptance given to English as the Official Language of the country. The Constitution makers obstructed the process of social justice in the very beginning by bestowing upon English the position of Offical Language in the country though after independence, Gandhi voiced his apprehensions about this: "Unless the government and their secretariats take care the English language is likely to usurp the place of Hindustani. This must do infinite harm to the millions of Indians who would never be able to understand English."[1] In free India, Lohia after Gandhi, argued consistently that the language issue has a direct bearing upon the social justice and democratic process.

A long 'Mahabharata' has been fought on the multifaceted language problem in the country. But the entire focus of the discussions gets suffocated and killed in limiting the argument to merely Hindi versus English, and Hindi versus other Indian languages. Like the monkey in the fable who devoured the loaf while meting out 'monkey-justice' to the quarrelsome cats, English has kept winning at the cost of Indian languages which are unable to arrive at any solution among themselves.

English was given the status of the Official Language of India for the first fifteen years of the country's independence. But the position has not changed till today. English has also achieved the position of a language which commands power and social status. Deeply responsible for this are those English-knowing elite who keep the common public away from socio- political processes. Also responsible for this are those who practice political games in the name of the language issue. Responsibility rests upon those 'progressive' thinkers too, who believe that English is necessary for the development of both capitalism as well as socialism. Commenting on such thinkers, Ram Vilas Sharma, the Marxist thinker and linguist, writes: "some progressive thinkers like to quote with pride Gandhi's ideas on the subject of state formation on language basis. But they very conveniently ignore what Gandhi said about doing away with English. These thinkers represent those middle class intellectuals who are hopeful of being admitted into official positions at all-India level by allowing English to continue at the Centre".[2] Gandhi and Ram Vilas Sharma, both advocate the use of Hindi- Hindustani in the place of English. The reference to them has been made not to prove the validity of their argument in favour of Hindi-Hindustani, but in order to underline the fact that they both consider English to be a weapon in the hands of a particular class which they use against the remaining common public.

II

It was argued at the time of Independence that the Indian languages were, for the time being, incapable of functioning as vehicles of communication and knowledge. And English 'as one of the major achievements made by the country during the foreign rule', was capable of building up national integration and bringing the country at par with the international scene of science and technology. The first two Education Commissions, the Radhakrishnan Commission (1947) and the Kothari Commission (1966) agreed that Indian languages should be the medium of instruction at universities, so that the chasm between the English knowing elite and the common masses is obliterated. The advocates of English however refused to believe that English could be the cause for this gap. The progressive writer, Mulk Raj Anand, considering English to be synonymous with knowledge itself, said that the "brown-sahibs" apart, the country has a "sincere English-knowing intelligentsia" which can make social justice and human dignity possible not only at the national level but also at the international level. The intellegentsia, committed to giving concrete shape to the India of Nehru's dream, cautions us against the usage of Indian languages, which they believe, confine us to being mere "suburbans, provincials and village idiots".[3] As per the wishes of this "sincere intelligentsia" consisting of scholars like Mulk Raj Anand and other supporters of the English language, most of the work in advanced education and research institutions (except the work being done in academies of Indian languages), is in the English language. Consequently, the maximum of research and scholarship in the country is done only in English language. The natural fallout of the situation is that English alone becomes the yardstick of excellence. Universities and institutions are laden with English texts and journals. This includes work done on the subject of social justice and revolution.

All the political parties in India committed to the ideology of social justice carry out their work in the English language. There is hardly any national or regional political party which has its manifesto, policy etc. written down originally in Indian languages. This includes the party led by Ram Manohar Lohia who had pledged to do away with English "today and now" because it hampered social justice in the country. The Marxist parties inspired by the revolutionary goal, the highest form of social justice, carry out all their official proceedings in English. English, already endowed with the responsibility of unifying the country as a 'nation state' is also burdened with the responsibility of organizing 'revolution' in the country. Prakash Karat maintains that after the formation of states on language basis "one of the obstacles to communist leadership links between states could be the gradual displacement of English..."[4]

The mere knowledge of English has come to be accepted as the touchstone of knowledge for achieving distinctive positions in the field of education, administration, judiciary and defence services. The same is true in the private sector as well. But what has been the outcome of all this? The result is simply the formation of a powerful and well-cushioned elite class on the one hand, and the deprived, oppressed common public on the other. The masses are unable to comprehend complex ideas regarding humanism, liberalism, socialism, communism, nationalism, pluralism etc. and the elite are victims of alienation unable to identify with the cultural roots and the common man.

Language is a medium of exchanging views. In India, the English language performs this function only within a very limited circle. For the remaining people, its role is that of a barrier which has a deep and long-term effect in delaying the process of social justice. English, from the very beginning has been present as a dark shadow between the common man and the constitutional promise of social justice. Viewed in the light of Lohia's words English divides the nation into "Two Castes" and to quote Rajni Kothari, into "Two Indias': English knowing elite India and the poor, oppressed masses.

The 'international language' thus accomplishes the job of keeping the majority of India's population away from the social and political processes. Since all projects, programmes and plans are drafted in English by English-knowing people, the non-English knowing public is unable to partake in the conception and implementation of any of these programmes and projects. Public opinion is limited to just elections. This, then, is the plight of the 'largest democracy' of the world – one, in which two to four perc ent people reign over the remaining ninty-eight per cent.

III

It has been assumed that the rich indigenous experience and institutions, distanced from the elitist India are worthless for the work of 'nation-building'. It is not merely a coincidence that Gandhi who supported the 'local' in form of village panchayats and Lohia upheld the same in the form of 'Chowkhamba Raj' were also opposed to English and those leaders who uphold 'universal' in the form of centralized governance also uphold the use of English in the country. Nehru maintained that "A village normally speaking is backward intellectually and culturally and no progress can be made from a backward environment. Narrow minded people are much more likely to be untruthful and violent".[5] Ambedkar too, wrote off the villages as "a den of ignorance and illiteracy, a habitat which perpetuates both physical and mental ill health".[6] Thus responsibility of nation-building was placed on the progressive intelligentsia whose minds have been illuminated by English. However the class interest which lies behind this apparent national interest is no more a concealed truth.

The acceptance of English as the Official Language by the supporters of the language and our Constitution-makers has proved to be the secret door from which the entry of the new imperialism has been made possible. The new economic policy, liberalisation, the GATT agreement etc. is a slap on the face of the same "sincere English-knowing intelligentia' who upheld the use of English in the name of social justice, human dignity, national integration, abundance of knowledge, international relations and so on. The extent to which English has contributed to the wisdom within the country, is proven by the fact that the larger section of the intelligentsia is content with simply circling around the synthetic-cosmetic socio-cultural and economic-political questions thrown up by the developed nations.

The documents regarding the blue-prints of the future of India is being prepared abroad by the officials in world institutions. The 'Bhagiraths' who claimed to flood India with the Ganges of wisdom brought in through the medium of English are now searching for their new roles in this new-fangled press-button technique of nation building. The country is endangered once again by the shadows of slavery. This time, tagging alongwith political servility is the threat of a sub-culture. Will the intellectuals who propound 'universal' ever pause and think about the possibilities of the 'local'? This is the area in which live crores and crores of people whose hands have not yet reached the basic requirements of life and whose feet have been uprooted from their soil. These are the people whose intervention and participation in the socio-political processes have been almost blocked.

If those who plead for the alternative ideology of 'humane governance' or those thinkers and leaders who strive towards the ideology of 'revolutionary democracy' actually wish to make people's participation in the socio-political processes a reality, then they must learn from the mistakes made in the past. The philosophy and politics of the liberation of the masses is possible only in the languages used by the masses. This is the bare, hard lesson of which history is the proof.

REFERENCES

1. Gandhi, *Thoughts on National Language,* Navjivan Publishing House, Ahmedabad, 1956, p. 168.
2. Ram Vilas Sharma, "Bhasha Niti aur Gandhiji", *Pratipaksh,* New Delhi, June 1990.
3. Mulk Raj Anand, "A Plea for English for Higher Education", *Language and Society in India,* Indian Institute of Advanced Study, Shimla, 1968.
4. Prakash Karat, *Language and Nationality Politics in India,* Orient Longman, New Delhi, 1973, p. 73.
5. Pyare Lal, *Towards New Horizons,* Navjivan Publishing House, Ahmedabad, 1959, p. 5.
6. Dharam Pal, *Constituents Assembly Debates on Panchayati Raj,* Award, New Delhi, 1961.

Ambedkar's Economic Thought

S. SESHAIAH

It is quite understandable why for a long time academicians and policy-makers have maintained silence over Ambedkar's economic thought, while his contribution, as an architect of the Constitution was acclaimed by all. It is, perhaps, the rising Dalit movement and the forces that are fighting for equality and human dignity that brought Ambedkar back into current discourse among academicians and intellectuals of various disciplines. That Ambedkar's phenomenal contribution in other disciplines such as law, religion, sociology and politics have overshadowed his contribution to economics is no excuse.[1]

This paper gives a brief account of Ambedkar's economic thought embodied in the Constitution regarding: (a) economic dimensions of the caste system; (b) notions about 'social scheme' or his conception of 'State socialism' and (c) the nature of the State and its role in the economy and polity. Since the objective is to find out to what extent his economic thoughts are embodied in the Constitution, the discussion is confined to the ideology of the Constitution and its relation to economic development. To study the interaction between the ideology of the Constitution and the problems of society, a critical legal theory's conception of the Constitution and system of rights is highly appropriate. Unger[2] says that a constitution denies, rather than reaffirms, social division and hierarchy, while a system of rights serves as a counter programme to maintenance or re-emergence of social divisions and hierarchy. He further says that they nurture a negative capability to dismantle or disenfranchise structures that support social division and hierarchy.

The constitution-makers clearly perceived the fundamental problem of poverty facing India. Nehru told the Constituent Assembly:[3]

> . . . at present the greatest and most important question in India is how to solve the problem of the poor and the starving masses. . . . The first task of the Assembly is to free India through a new constitution to feed the starving people and

clothe the naked masses. . . . This certainly is a great task.

While Nehru made it clear that the constitution of India should be purposive in nature, Ambedkar[4] highlighted the authoritative and inegalitarian characteristics of the Indian social structure:

> . . . democracy is only a top-dressing on the Indian soil which is essentially undemocratic . . . on the social plane we have in India a society based on the principle of graded inequality which means elevation for some and degradation for others. On the economic plane we have a society in which there are some who have immense wealth as against many who live in abject poverty.

In Ambedkar's view, democracy is meaningless in the absence of social and economic equality. He had a clear perception of caste and its role in perpetuation of poverty and inequality. Then, the proper question would be whether the Indian Constitution seeks to eliminate caste distinctions and promotes equality not only in social relations but also in relations of production.

Analysis of caste is crucial for proper understanding of poverty and inequality in the Indian context. Ambedkar looked at the caste system from the view point of justice. Agreeing with Bergson, he said that justice has always evoked ideas of equality, of proportion of "compensation". Equity signifies equality. Rules and regulations, right and righteousness are concerned with equality in value. If all men are equal all men of the same essence and the common essence entitled them to the same fundamental rights and to equal liberty. In short justice is simply another name for liberty, equality and fraternity.[5] From this point of view Ambedkar had criticised the caste system.

In his 'Annihilation of Caste' he came out with a hard-hitting critique of the rationalisation and justification of the caste system in different theories. He emphasised that what was implicit in the caste system was not merely the division of labour but also a division of labourers. Ambedkar argued that it is not occupation that was responsible for castes but it was the caste system that was the basis of assigning occupations. According to him, the theory of caste is that a Brahmin who is permitted to cultivate his intellect is not permitted to labour and is taught to look down upon labour. While the Sudra who is required to labour is not permitted to cultivate his intelligence. It is an ideology built up by Brahmins in the 'Holy' scriptures.[6]

Ambedkar believed that the caste system in India was a major obstacle to economic growth and development. He agreed with R.C. Dutt on how the caste system was disastrous for the growth of man. Caste devitalises man. It was a process of sterilisation. Education, wealth and labour were all necessary for every individual to reach full and free maturity. Education without wealth and labour was barren. Wealth without education and labour was brutal. Each was necessary for every one. They were necessary for the growth of man.[7] According to him, caste restricted the mobility of labour and capital. The immobility of capital, in turn, hindered optimal utilisation of investible resources.[8]

Ranking of caste groups was not validated only by ritual and social usage, but also by differential control over the production resources.[9] Caste was a system of 'cumulative inequalities' or a closed system, whereby the degree to which the given caste possessed command over property, and power corresponds within its ritual status in the local scheme of ranking.[10] Thus caste determined the status and dignity of the individual in society. It prohibited access to skills and means of production. Caste reinforced social discrimination and degradation. It legitimised the violation of human dignity.

As a champion of human rights, Ambedkar denounced untouchability. According to him untouchability is not only a religious system but also an economic system which was worse than slavery. In slavery, the master at least had the responsibility to feed cloth and house and keep a slave in good health, or else his market value might come down. In contrast, under the system of untouchability, the upper caste take no responsibility for the maintenance of the untouchable. Ambedkar observes in his work 'what Congress and Gandhi have done to the untouchables' that as an economic system (the caste system) permits exploitation without obligation. Untouchability is not only a system of unmitigated economic exploitation but is also uncontrolled economic exploitation.[11] In another book *The Untouchables,* Ambedkar argued that the caste system was a diabolical contrivance to suppress and enslave humanity. Its proper name would be infamy.[12] Thus, one could infer from Ambedkar's thought that caste is a system of inequality which in turn reinforces poverty.

Although the word 'poverty' is absent in the Constitution, its elimination had been the primary concern of the framers. There are in the very forefront of the Constitution comprehensive provisions on equality. To make these provisions purposive and functional, Ambedkar's interpretation of caste and its relation with inequality and poverty is necessary.

In the Indian context, caste is an index of poverty. Caste system is a means to maintain discrimination and hierarchy. Caste and class are conceptual associates to legitimise exploitation. Therefore, the Fundamental Rights to equality in the Constitution contemplates prohibition of social discrimination based on caste. Reflecting, probably, Ambedkar's perception of caste as 'anti-national' (CADIX. 980) Art. 15(1) and 16(2) prohibited discrimination on the basis of caste. As this may not be enough to emancipate the victims of caste from social degradation and economic exploitation, Art. 15 (4) and 16 (4) provides for preferential treatment within certain limits. Art. 17 outlawed untouchability. Art. 23 gave them a right against exploitation from forced labour as they formed the bulk of bonded labour. Ambedkar was clear in his mind that these negative rights, except 15 (2), 17, 23, would be of no use unless the State positively and actively intervenes in the economy. The reorganisation of the inegalitarian and inequitous social and economic order was an imperative for the modern State.

Ambedkar believed that the thrust of the strategy for India's economic development should be eradication of poverty, elimination of inequalities and ending the exploitation of the masses. In other words, he sought active involvement of the State in economic development.

The Directive Principles of the Constitution echo a clearer statement of social 'revolution'. They aim at making the Indian masses free from the passivity engendered by centuries of coercion by system (caste) and nature, free from the abject physical conditions that had prevented them from fulfilling their best selves. Although the Fundamental Rights and Directive Principles in the Constitution appear as distinct entities, they are inextricably and organically interlinked. The freedom movement had drawn no distinction between the positive and negative obligations of the State. Both types of rights had developed as a common demand and product of the national movement. Thus, Part III and Part IV of the Constitution are almost inseparable and reflect the intertwining character of Indian politics.[14]

The essence of the Directive Principles lies in Art. 38 which, echoing the preamble, reads:

> . . . the State shall strive to promote the welfare of the people by securing and protecting as effectively as it may a social order in which justice-social, economic and political shall inform all institutions of national life.

To foster these goals, the State shall ensure that citizens have an adequate means of livelihood, that the operation of the economic system and the ownership and control of the material resources of the country subserve the common good, etc., Part IV of the Constitution thus puts an obligation on the State to make laws to enforce them. As these principles are not justiciable, a court cannot enforce them, but they are nevertheless 'fundamental in the governance of the country.[15] Similarly, these principles have been the terms of reference to the Planning Commission in formulating Five Year Plans.

Thus, the equality provisions in Parts III and IV of the Constitution reflect an economic theory which recognises the role of inequality in poverty and treat poverty and inequality not as equivalent concepts but as associates. The equality provisions (Arts 14, 15, 16, 17, 23, 24 in Part III and Articles 38, 39 and 46 in Part IV) identify the inequalities based on caste, gender, income and property and render these inequalities illigitimate and proposes to dismantle them.

Many members in the Constituent Assembly were intellectuals and emotionally committed to some form of 'socialism'. According to Austin, "they ranged from Marxists through Gandhian socialists to conservative capitalists each with his own definition of 'Socialism'. Nearly every one in the Assembly was Fabian and Laski-ite enough to believe that 'socialism is everyday politics'. For social regeneration and a democratic constitution are . . . inseparably associated with the drive towards economic equality".[16] Probably, the success of the Russian revolution had a great impact on India.

In his book *State and Minorities,* Ambedkar advocated State-ownership of agricultural land with a democrative collectivised method of cultivation and limited control of industries (i.e., heavy industries and large public utilities). Ambedkar's concept of 'State Socialism' was based on three basic tenets:

(i) State ownership of agricultural land and key industries to meet the demands of the poorer strata of society.
(ii) Maintenance of productive resources by the State; and
(iii) a just distribution of the common produce among the different people without any distinction of caste or creed.

Ambedkar submitted the above scheme and programme to the Assembly for adoption as part of Fundamental Rights.[17] He believed that his draft provisions did not go beyond the proper scope of fundamental rights. In other words, what is called liberty from the control of the State is another name for the dictatorship of the employers. But his scheme of rights as well as many other provisions in his programme were rejected on several occasions in the Assembly on the ground that such provisions should be left to legislation and not to be embodied in the Constitution. From this position he retreated to the support of the Directive Principles. Some members supported Ambedkar and criticised these principles as mere pious wishes and window dressing unless made justiciable. The party in power, Ambedkar said, would certainly 'have to answer for these before the electorate at election time'. In Ambedkar's view both Fundamental Rights and Directive Principles should be justiciable. He was far ahead of his contemporaries in understanding that there is no trade off between equity and social justice. Only in the Fourth Five Year Plan did the planners realise the necessity of 'equity with social justice'. Previous Five Year Plans had emphasised the model of growth without justice or production first and distribution second, in other words the trickle down theory.

Ambedkar believed in 'casteless' society but not in a stateless society. He maintained that the State would continue to exist as long as human society survived. The State had a key role in the economy. It was obliged to plan the economic life of the people to lead to the highest point of productivity without closing every avenue to private enterprise, and also provide equitable distribution of wealth. He did not favour imposition of arbitrary restraints on economic process.[18]

But it is surprising to note that being an ordent supporter of human rights and the leader of Dalits, Ambedkar was party in conceding liberties for the sake of a strong state. His arguments for suspension of Fundamental Rights during an emergency, for reasonable restrictions on civil and political rights and for retention of preventive detention laws and denial of the right of states to secede from the Union indicates his preference for strong nation and state. If the creation of strong State apparatus was justified by the 'logic' of the nation-state, the justification of a strong State lay in the promise of transformation of Indian society, pre-eminently through the Constitution, law, planning and administration – all dominant spheres of politics. The Constitution of India provides abundant justification for the capitalist maturation of the Indian State and society.[19]

One cannot blame Ambedkar for inclusion of some negative aspects in the Constitution. The major responsibility lies with the Congress. The Constituent Assembly virtually followed the commands of the Congress party.[20] But Ambedkar's contribution to economic thought and constitutional law is significant. His analysis that the relation between caste based inequality and poverty still holds good for implementation of programmes of planned development. His conception of rights is very close to critical legal theory which says that the Constitution and system of rights must dismantle the inegalitarian and inequitable structure that perpetuate poverty and domination. It denies hegemony of ideology, hierarchy and divisions in society.

According to Baxi, the story of constitution-making is the story of the ascending of the ascendant classes. And, naturally, members of these classes will appropriate the part III freedoms to facilitate the pursuit of their own heterogeneous material interests. The State has to allow the process of accumulation to run its historic capitalist course. The text of the Constitution encoded this development.[21]

The issue of poverty was the background of the freedom struggle and continued in post-independent Indian planning. A discourse on planning and a discourse on upliftment of the poor were part of the process of legitimation of the demand for a state which would shake of colonial control. The post-colonial Indian State did not come into being as the result of a successful revolution elsewhere in the world and armed struggles in Telengana, West Bengal and Kerala. Therefore 'consensus' about the rhetoric of planning was not based only on the vision of an activist State. It was also based on agreement that the State would not interfere with the process of money making and power wielding in society. Probably this was the reason for not making the Directive Principles justiciable, and retaining the right to property as sacrosanct in part III, and avoiding to use the word 'socialism' in the Constitution.

Poverty is a result of long historical process of marginalisation of social groups; of inequality based on a position in the production system. There are institutional factors as well like family background, caste, sex, ethnic origin and geographical location. They are beyond the control of the individual. It is now recognised that peoples' intervention minimises the inequalities arising out of lopsided development. Such intervention demands strategies and programmes aimed at alterating relations of power and dominance. In this perspective one has to understand the doctrine of equality enshrined in the Constitution.

It may not be an exaggeration to argue that Ambedkar was the only member in the Constituent Assembly who conceived that caste is the antithesis of equality, freedom and fraternity. There could not be equality without freedom and without economic and social justice. The rights of equality embodied in the Constitution in Articles 14, 15, 16, 17, 23, 24 and 38 and 39 are restricted by the social order and social institution of caste and religion. Therefore, Ambedkar's critical understanding of Indian society and its dynamics would help legal scholars to dismantle the structures of domination and exploitation in society. Let us continue the legacy of Ambedkar in our struggle for emancipation of Dalits and cherish the value of equality without which social justice is simply a mirage.

NOTES

1. See Narendra Jadav, 'Neglected Economic thought of Baba Saheb Ambedkar', *EPW*, vol.xxvi pp. 980-82. Ambedkar was an edonomist by training and also the first Indian dalit who got Ph.D from abroad. In 1917, he earned his doctorate in economics at the Columbia University, U.S.A. Again the degree of Doctor of Sciences which the London School of Economics conferred on him in 1921 was for his research. His Ph.D. dissertation "The Evolution of Provincial Finance in British India" is a significant contribution to the history of Indian public finance. This book deals with centre

and state relations in British India during the period 1833 to 1921, a ground work on which rests the edifice of the the centre-state financial relations in modern India.

2. Unger, R.M. 'The critical legal studies movement', 96 *Harward Law Review* (1983,) pp. 567-85.
3. *Constituent Assembly Debates,* VII, pp. 317, 316 (4) (a) CAD vol.ix p. 979.
4. *Dr. Ambedkar's Writings and Speaches,* Vol.3. Government of Maharashtra, 1987, pp. 24-25.
5. Ibid., p. 67.
6. Ibid., p. 68.
7. Ibid., p. 68
8. Supra, note 1, p. 982.
9. P.G. Bailey, *Castes and the Economic Frontier,* Oxford University Press, 1985, p. 266.
10. Andre Beteille, *Caste, Class and Power,* OUP, 1966, pp. 6-7.
11. Ambedkar, *What Congress and Gandhi have done to the Untochables,* pp.196-97.
12. Ambedkar, *The Untouchables,* preface, p. ix.
13. Granville Austin, *The Indian Constitution, Corner Stone of a Nation,* OUP, 1966, p. 51.
14. *Ibid.,* p. 52.
15. See Art. 37, Indian Constitution.
16 Supra note, 13, p. 78.
17. Ambedkar, *States and Minorities,* Section II, Clause 4.
18. Supra, note 1, p. 982.
19. See Upendra Baxi, "Accumulation and Legitimacy. The Indian Constitution and State formation" in R.V. Chandrasekar Rao and V.S. Prasad (eds.), *Indian Constitution and Polity,* Sterling Publishers (1981), pp. 32-50.
20. Supra, note 13, pp. 8, 9.
21. Supra, note 19, p. 41.

Ambedkar's Idea of Social Justice

GOPAL GURU

Anyone who is attempting to write on Ambedkar would certainly agree that it is really a tough job to venture into analysing his complex but equally important social ideas, particularly his idea of social justice. Writing about Ambedkar, at least to me, is a tough challenge for two reasons. First, Ambedkar does not seem to have systematically worked out his concept of social justice in the entire writing and speeches that are now available both in English as well as in Marathi. Instead, what one comes across is that his idea of social justice is woven into single thread that is continuously running through his writings regarding equality, liberty, fraternity, human rights, his concept of socio-economic democracy and state and minorities. Secondly, it appears that Ambedkar's theoretical positions with particular reference to social justice are so close to each other that they might lead to misinterpretation if they are not carefully differentiated from each other in a dialectical fashion which is available in Ambedkar's writing.

Therefore, the purpose of this paper is four fold. First, to locate Ambedkar's idea of social justice on more visible and systematic terrain. Second, to bring out the essence of his idea of social justice which he seems to have developed through the dialectical negation of his earlier positions on social justice. Third, to outline the mechanism that Ambedkar suggested for meting out justice to the Untouchables. And finally, an attempt would be made to critically assess Ambedkar's concept of social justice in the modern context.

For discussing Ambedkar's concept of justice, it is necessary to discuss in the background various versions of social justice that the thinkers in India seem to have advocated from time to time both in pre-Ambedkar and post-Ambedkar period. Historically speaking, justice in Indian context was seen an important social value in as much as it consisted in the strict observance or enforcement of Hindu Law which was based on the four varnas and elaborated caste system. According to Ambedkar, "the Hindu Law is the law of the established order and was made by the Touchables. The Untouchables had nothing to do except to obey it and respect it. The Untouchables have no right against the Touchables. For them there is no equal right, no justice which is due to them, nothing is allowed to them. Nothing is due to them except what the Touchables are prepared to grant. The Untouchables must not insist on rights. They should pray for mercy and favour and rest content with what is offered."[1]

Ambedkar further maintains the view that the established order was based on graded inequality and was legitimised by Hindu Law which was the complete negation of equality, fraternity, liberty, democracy and human rights.[2] Ambedkar was of the view that the system of graded inequality was not national but it was legal and penal.[3] Thus, it can be argued that at the philosophical level, justice in the Indian feudal order had three characteristics: One, justice gave preference to hierarchy over equality. Second, this concept of justice underlined the importance of respecting traditional rights and performing traditional duties, and finally, justice in Hindu law meant different things to different castes and people. This concept of justice contained no notion of equal treatment to all men. In other words, the function of justice in this kind of situation was to preserve the existing hierarchy rather than to provide criterion for social reforms. Thus, the concept of justice has been used at the ideological level by the upper caste and upper classes just to deny the deprived sections the essence of justice. Justice in Indian context was depicted as the validation of societal stratification and the perpetuation of casteism.

Movement of the untouchables against this kind of injustice by the Hindu social order has a long history particularly in Maharashtra. The Dalit saints are found complaining to God about the injustice that was heaped on them by the exploitative social structure.[4] The idea of justice as viewed by them thus defined equality only in relation to God and not elsewhere and confined it to the devotees and not to the common man. Ambedkar, while criticising this rather theologico-religious concept of justice said this concept which was limited to only devotees and it failed to attack the "*chaturvarna* system" which was mainly responsible for perpetuating the structures of inequality and division of society into Touchables and the Untouchables.[5] He further argued that the Dalit saints, individually speaking, might have achieved the equality in the eyes of God and hence in the spiritual realm, but these saints failed to attack the social inequality that subverted the material life of the millions of Untouchables for centuries.[6]

In our time we have come across the position taken by Walter Kaufmann that the origin of justice has to be traced metaphysically to a kind of inherent moral sense in man, to his multiple emotive faculties.[7] Speaking about the multiple dimension of this unfulfilled promise, Kaufmann says: "The promise may concern reward or punishment, and this may be deferred or it may never come in our own sense or in that of others, and this non-event may be met with envy or compassion, with self pity or guilt feelings, with indignation or concern, with ardent hope or extreme anxiety".[8]

Ambedkar, like the overwhelming majority of liberal philosophers, has opposed this metaphysical concept of justice.[9] He was of the opinion that it was absolutely futile to except any compassion from the Touchables who were plagued with Brahminism.[10] He said that the Touchables lacked social conscience towards the Untouchables and his sense of obligation was restricted to a limited class of people, namely the members of his caste.[11] Ambedkar further argued that it is because of this that the Untouchables could not be said to belong to the society of the Hindus, and the Hindu did not feel that he and the Untouchables belonged to one society. According to him, this is the reason why the conduct of the Hindus is marked by a moralistic unconcernedness.[12] In his sharp attack on this metaphysical theory of justice, Ambedkar further says: "Not having conscience, the Hindu has no such thing in him as righteous indignation against the inequalities and injustices from which the Untouchable has been suffering. He sees no wrong in these inequities and injustices and refuses to budge. By his absence of conscience the Hindu is a great obstacle in the path of the removal of untouchability".[13]

On yet another occasion, Ambedkar linked up this lack of concern and the lack of righteous indignation to the spiritual and material interest of the Touchables. He was of the opinion that the Touchables are insensitive to the justice of the Untouchables due to a heavy impact of Hindu Dharma.[14] He further said that this impact is perpetuated by the material interest of those high caste Hindus who would not like a Untouchable sharing his material conforts.[15] Thus, Ambedkar, on very sound material ground, rejects this metaphysical deduction of justice from the concept of self-consciousness. However, he says that the

Touchables have become indifferent to the Untouchables because of their material interest.[16] Ambedkar maintains that Brahminical values are used by the upper castes to deny the Untouchables the social justice which otherwise directly threatens their material interests.[17]

It is this caste consciousness among the Touchables that makes Ambedkar suspicious about the validity of the legal concept of justice which involves punishment of wrongdoing and the compensation of injury through the creation and enforcement of a public set of rules.[18] In view of the fragmented and therefore discriminatory nature of Hindu Law during the feudal days, however, Ambedkar seemed to welcome the legal intervention of the Britishers who tried to standardise the legal system in India thus giving effect to the concept of equality before law. For example, Ambedkar desired the British legal injunction useful in declaring the practice of untouchability to be invalid.[19] He said that it was possible under the rule of law to declare untouchability invalid on the ground that it was opposed to morality and public policy.[20] But it was of no use, Ambedkar laments, unless it was declared to be so by a judicial tribunal. He was of the opinion that such a decision declaring the invalidity of the custom of untouchability would be of great help to the Untouchables in their fight for civil rights because it would seem illegal to import untouchability in civic matters.[21]

However, Ambedkar maintained the view that this legal justice at the formal or at the theoretical level could never do justice at the practical level. As he said, "It might have been thought that this principle of equal justice would strike a death blow to the established order. As a matter of fact, far from suffering any damage, the established order has continued to operate. It might be asked why the principle of equal justice has failed to have its affect. The answer to this is simple. To enunciate the principle of justice is one thing. To make it effective is another thing. Whether the principle of equal justice is effective or not must necessarily depend on the nature and character of the civil services who administer the principle. If the civil services are by reason of class bias the friend of the established order and the enemy of the new order, the new order can never come into being. That a civil service in tune with the new order was essential for the success of the new order was recognised by Karl Marx in 1871 in the formation of the Paris Commune and was adopted by Lenin in the constitution of Soviet Communism. Unfortunately, the British Government never cared about the personnel in the civil service. Indeed, it opened the gates of the administration to those classes who believed in the old established order of the Hindus in which the principles of equality had no place. As a result of this fact, India has been ruled by the Britishers but administerd by the Hindus."[22]

Ambedkar, while illustrating his point a little further said: "From the capital of India down to the village the whole administration is rigged by the Hindus. The Hindus are like the omnipotent almighty pervading all over the administration in all its branches having its authority in all its nooks and corners. There is no loophole for anyone opposed to the old order to escape. If the established order has continued to exist, it is because of the unfailing support it received from the Hindu officials of the state. The Hindu officials are not merely administrators administering the affairs on their merit, they are administrators with an eye to their parties. Their principle is not equal justice to all. Their motto is justice consistent with established order. This is inevitable. For they carry over into administration, the attitude towards different classes in society under the established order. This is well illustrated by the attitude of the state officials towards the Untouchables in the field of administration. As every Untouchable will be able to testify, if an Untouchable goes to a police officer with a complaint against the caste Hindu, instead of receiving any protection he will receive plenty of abuses. Either he will be driven away without his complaint being recorded or if it is recorded it would be recorded quite falsely to provide a way of escape to the Touchable aggressors. If he prosecutes his offenders before a Magistrate the fate of his proceeding could be foretold. The Untouchables will never be able to get Hindus as witness because of the conspiracy of the villagers not to support the case of the Untouchables however just it may be. If he brings witnesses from the Untouchables, the Magistrate will not accept their testimony because he can easily say that they are interested and not independent witnesses, or, if they are independent witnesses the Magistrate has an easy way of acquitting the accused by simply saying that the Untouchables did not strike him as a truthful witness. He can do this fearlessly knowing fully well that the higher tribunal will not reverse his finding because of the well established rule which says that an appellate court should not disturb the finding of the trial Magistrate based on the testimony of witness whose demeanour he had no opportunity to obeserve".[23] Thus, according to Ambedkar, the upper caste administrators have a Hindu bias and have an antipathy towards the Untouchables which results in the denial of protection and justice to the Untouchables.

Ambedkar, during the Mahad conference organised for establishing their right to take water from the Chawdar tank, proclaimed that the Untouchables wanted a complete overhauling of the Hindu social system. He further proclaimed that this reconstruction must not be on the foundation of Hindu Shastra but it must be consonant with justice and equality which he later on embedded into the philosophy of Buddhism. As is clear from the political practice of the Dalit movement, Ambedkar used all the just forms of protest from launching temple entry, boycott of Hindu practice to conversion for establishing social justice, preferential treatment to the Untouchables in the field of bureaucracy and political field, with intention of protecting the interest of the Untouchables from the hands the high caste- ridden bureaucracy and politics and finally conversion to Buddhism for establishing social justice. In this regard, it is essential to take into consideration Ambedkar's evidence before the South-Borough Committee and later on in the first All India Depressed Classes Congress held at Nagpur in 1930.

While advocating special treatment for the Untouchables in the services, Ambedkar said: "The power to administer laws is not less important than the power to make laws. And the spirit of the legislators may easily be violated if not nullified by the machinery of the administrators. This is not the only reason why the Depressed Classes should show special concern for securing power of control over administration. Oftentimes under pressure of work or under difficulties of circumstances one has to leave good deal of discretionary power in the hands of the heads of the administrative departments. The welfare of the people must greatly depend on how impartially this discretionary power is exercised. In a country like India where the public service is almost exclusively manned by people of one community, there is a great danger of this vast discretionary power being need for the personal aggrandisement of a class. The best antidote against it is to insist on a proper admixture of castes and creeds including the depressed classes in the public services of the country. We should demand a certain percentage in the public services to be preserved for the Depressed Classes and there will be no difficulty in guaranteeing this safeguard to us by a clause in the Constitution. Such protection you could have dispensed with if there was any chance of the Depressed Classes being represented in the future cabinets of the country. But there is not the remotest chance of this in view of the fact that the Depressed Classes will always remain in minority. This makes it all the more necessary why you should insist upon such a guarantee".[24]

Ambedkar, while stating the importance of political reservations for the Untouchables said: "The significance of suffrage or a political right consists in a chance for active and direct participation in the regulation of the term upon which associated life shall be sustained. Now the terms upon which the associated life between the Touchables and Untouchables is carried on today are the most ignominous to the former and highly detrimental to the latter. To make effective the capacities of a people, there must be the power to fix the social conditions of their exercise. If the conditions are too obdurate, it is in the interest of the Untouchables as well as the Touchables that the conditions should be revised. The Untouchables must be in a position to influence the revision looking to the gravity of their interest. They should get their representation as proposed in porportion to their population".[25] The mode of acquiring this political power in Ambedkar's scheme, however, has to be located in the pluralist framework where sharing of political power is the main assumption. But Ambedkar's concept of political power was aimed at enabling the Dalits to secure social justice on more equitable and honourable terms.

However, it is necessary to point out here that although Ambedkar started with the negation of the legal concept of justice on the ground that it cannot be realised because its implementation is in the hands of the upper castes, on this occasion he seems to be confirming this form of justice provided the implementation of the legal provisions is rested into the hands of the Untouchables. Therefore, in a way, what one finds is that Ambedkar's own concept of justice seems to be operating within the same liberal framework. In fact Ambedkar's idea of social justice is tantamount to the concept of social justice of Rawls who includes in his theory of distributive justice an element of difference principle while in Ambedkar's case it is the principle of special treatment. Both these principles of justice require a distribution of resources that would most effectively satisfy the needs of the worst off.[26] This distributive justice, according to another author, also involves the principle of equality. But in Ambedkar's case it also involves prestige and honour along with equality principle.

But the question that one can raise here is that does Ambedkar's concept of justice remain fettered within the narrow contours of liberalism? Does it imply the reconciliation of the conflicting interests in society? Or in other words, does it expose the limits of both legal and political justice that Ambedkar was talking about earlier? The answer to these questions can be given in the following body of material. In the beginning it is essential to mention that Ambedkar's concept of justice is not an abstract and a static one; on the contrary it is a concrete and a dynamic concept to be understood in terms of the changing social reality. As we have already seen, Ambedkar's concept of justice keeps developing out of the negation of his earlier position of justice. It moves in a definite direction away from the limits inherent in the liberal form of social justice. Though his concept of social justice involved a normative element in as much as it aims at the desirability or goodness in social life, yet he views rather objectively the limitations of liberal concept of justice which does not see the contradictions between how one lives and how one can live.

Ambedkar very clearly saw the conflicting interests that severely baffled the Untouchables, bureaucrats and the legislators while the latter tried to mete out justice to their own caste people. Ambedkar was painfully aware that even if adequately represented, Untouchables will not be able to mete out justice to their people because they would be working under terrible pressures and conditions of socio-economic insecurity dictated by the dominant forces in this country.[27] Regarding political leaders and the legislators, Ambedkar lost the hope that they would be able to do any justice to their people without the permission of their political bosses in the Congress Party.[28]

Therefore, it is clear that for Ambedkar political justice was not enough for the good of the Untouchables. In fact he gave more importance to social and economic justice. Nay, he considered socio-economic justice as the pre-condition for redeeming political justice. He said: "The third thing we must do is not to be content with mere political democracy. We must make our political democracy a social democracy as well. Political democracy cannot last unless there lies at the base of it social democracy. What social democracy means? It means a way of life which recognises liberty, equality and fraternity as the principle of life. These principle are not to be treated as separate items in trinity. They form a union of trinity in the sense that to divorce one from other is to defeat the very purpose of democracy. On the social plane, we have in India a society in which there are principles based on graded inequality which means elevation of some and degradation for others. On the economic plane, we have a society in which there are some who have immense wealth as against many who live in abject poverty. On the 26th January 1950, we are going to enter into a life of contradictions. In political life we will have equality and in social and economic life, we shall by reason of our social and economic structure, continue to deny the principle of one man one value. How long shall we continue to deny equality in our social and economic life? If we continue to deny it for long, we shall do so only by putting our political democracy in peril. We must remove this contradiction at the earliest possible moment or else those who suffer from inequality will blow up the structure of political democracy which this Assembly has so laboriously built up.[29]

It is also clear from the above that like other ethical philosophers who locate justice exclusively in moral terms, Ambedkar does not abstract the concept of social justice from its material base (that is social base). His concept of justice is firmly rooted in the synthesis of social equality involving freedom and liberty with economic equality. This is reflected in his under-standing of French revolution and Russian revolution. Ambedkar considers French revolution as the first stage and the Russian revolution as the second stage in human liberation.[30]

NOTES

1. *Writings and Speeches of Dr. B.R. Ambedkar, (WSBRA),* Maharashtra Govt. Publication, Vol. 4, 1989, p. 25.
2. Ibid.
3. *WSBRA,* Vol. 7, 1990, p. 27.
4. *Babasaheb Ambedkaranche Bahishkruit Bharatatil Agralekh* (Marathi),

Govt. of Maharashtra Publication, 1991, p. 228.
6. Ibid.
7. Ibid.
7. Shobhanlal Dutta Gupta, *Justice and the Political Order in India,* Calcutta: K.P. Bagchi & Company, 1979, p. 2.
8. Ibid.
9. Ibid.
10. Ratnakar Ganvir, *Ambedkaranchi Bahishkruit Bharatatil Sfut Lekh* (Marathi), Bhusawal: Ratnamitra Publication, 1987, p. 90.
11. *WSBRA,* Vol. 5, p. 99.
12. Ibid.
13. Ibid.
14. op. cit., Bahashkruit Bharatatil Agrealekh., 1991, p. 34(4).
15. Ibid.
16. Ibid.
17. Ibid.
18. Millar, David, *Social Justice,* Oxford: Clarendon Press, 1977, p. 277.
19. *WSBRA,* Vol. 5, p. 252.
20. Ibid.
21. Ibid.
22. Ibid.
23. Khairmode, C.B., *Bhimrao Ramji Ambedkar* (Marathi), Pune: Sugawa Publication, 1989, vol. 4, p. 265
24. *WSBRA,* Vol. 1, 1979, p. 265.
25. Ibid.
26. op.cit., Millar, p. 48.
27. Guru, Gopal, 'Ambedkar's concept of political power,' an unpublished paper submitted to Dept. of Political Science, University of Poona, Pune.
28. Ibid.
29. Keer, Dhananjya, *Life and Mission of Dr. Ambedkar,* Bombay: Popular, 1954, p. 412.
30. Khairmode, C.B., *B.R. Ambedkar* (Marathi), Maharashtra Sahitya Sanskruti Mandal Bombay, 1987, pp. 47, 48.

The Concept of Creamy Layer

MEENA DESHPANDE

The Government of India has adopted a policy of reserving some seats in professional colleges and in government services for those considered as Backward Classes. This policy is intended to provide social justice to those who were, it was thought, denied their due share in society due to the existence of caste. There is a long-standing controversy regarding the constitutionality and legality of caste as the sole criterion of social and educational backwardness while framing, implementing and interpreting reservation policy. In 1992 this controversy was given a new direction[1] with the inclusion of the concept of 'creamy layer'. This concept is not new. In fact the notion of reservation contains in itself the concept of creamy layer when it excluded some as forwards. Reservation policy is based on the presupposition that there is differentiation and variation in social and economic status among the members of society and creamy layer indicates the internal differentiation within a single caste, along with regional variations.[2] In this paper the main focus is on the concept of 'creamy layer' which brought to light the rule of exclusion among the BCs, as the judgement is confined to the SEBCs, the question of SCs is beyond the purview of this paper.

Some inherent drawbacks of caste as the sole basis of backwardness have played an important role in the origin, evolution and crystallisation of the creamy layer concept. Caste has been a necessary and sufficient condition while determining the forwardness or backwardness of a group. Caste was taken as an indivisible unit hence all the defects associated with it follow.[3] The presumption being that all those who belonged to a particular caste either belonged to the forward or backward group as a whole. Individual variations were not considered though from time to time suggestions flowed from different corners to that effect. The economic factor was never accepted independently,[4] though in some States where reservation existed for a sufficiently longer period, it started making its presence felt.[5] In different States, the Backward Classes Commission started suggesting a time limit for reservation and periodic revision of the list taking changes into consideration.[6]

The objective of this paper is to bring out the broad implications of the concept of creamy layer and point out the importance of economic factor in providing social justice. It is divided into five sections. In section I the concept is traced in Kalelkar's note. Section II deals with III Backward Classes Commission in Karnataka, 1990, where the concept of creamy layer gets a more detailed and systematic treatment based on empirical assessment of the situation. The judgement of the Supreme Court on creamy layer[7] is referred to in section III. In section IV the report of expert committee for specifying the criteria for identification of socially advanced persons among SEBC is briefly touched upon to show the relevance of the economic factor in solving the problem of social justice. Section V is a brief note.

I

Views of Kalelkar

In his letter to the President of India while forwarding the Report of the Backward Classes Commission (1953 to 1955) dated 30 March 1955, Kalelkar, the Chairman of Commission raised certain basic issues with regard to reservation policy, where one can notice the existence of creamy layer among the Backward Classes which he calls 'the dominants', a fact that seems to have been ignored by the Commission. Hence a dissent note.

The cause of backwardness has two interrelated elements, the subjective abstract element of domination that gets sustenance from the objective condition. In other words within the Backward Classes there is internal variation in terms of social and economic dominance that gets reflected in the larger social spectrum. Kalelkar views domination as a 'vice and curse' which exists all over the world and in India this vice exists with all its force even among the untouchables. The power to dominate emanates, according to Kalelkar, from 'the possession either of large tracts of land or money to lend or governmental power or the brain to create quarrel and factions among the people'. The first two factors indicate the dominance of economic factors, the third implies economic power and the fourth as the political acumen which leads to economic advancement. All these factors point towards the dominance of economic factors in determining the actual social status of a person. He further gives a list of dominating communities in 11 states of India to prove the presence of dominating groups/individuals within the designated backward castes. Kalelkar views with suspicion the leadership of dominant communities over others as it made 'an irony and mockery of justice'.

Two conclusions can be drawn from Kalelkar's note. First, the criteria for determining backwardness should be something other than caste in the presence of internal differentiation in each caste. Second, the unit should be individual and at the most family, not group. In other words BCs can't be and should not be indivisible units as there is variation within the group. He has noticed the contradiction between the religious hierarchy based exclusively on caste and social hierarchy depending on other variables other than caste. With the intrusion of economic factor along with its appendage of dominance the notion of social justice gets a different turn. Hence it needs to be handled differently.

II

THE REPORT OF THE THIRD BACKWARD CLASSES COMMISSION IN KARNATAKA 1990

The concept of 'creamy layer' exists in the report and its corollary 'the rule of exclusion' too is analysed at length. Creamy layer is referred to as 'pockets of privileged among the backward classes'.[8]

The rule of exclusion recommended by the Commission is based on the presumption that some among the BCs have reached a stage of 'sufficiency' or near sufficiency and hence do not need the help of the State in the form of reservation. Though the objective of the State is to make them self-confident and self-reliant not self-complacent, the reality is contrary to the objective due to continuous flow of benefits to the BCs. The implementation of a reservation policy based solely on caste and excluding other factors had led to the emergence of privileged pockets. These pockets have a tendency to perpetuate. How this process can be stopped? Can we depend on the goodwill of those who constitute this privileged pocket or is there a need for state action? How to clear the way for the really needy? The Commission has raised such basic questions and given a realistic answer based on an empirical study of the situation in Karnataka.

Two possible answers to the question raised above are: (i)

Voluntary withdrawal of the socially and educationally forward among the backward giving way to the really backward. (ii) State action debarring the privileged from enjoying the benefits.

The Commission gives an indication that the first solution is not workable. Human nature is unpredictable. In this connection the presumption is the 'privileged pockets' cling on to the facilities. The Commission has not clearly spelt out the futility of this solution. Instead it makes suggestion that efforts should be made to create a sense of competition among privileged BCs which seems impractical and unrealistic. The fact that the Commission has not given importance to this solution is proved by a detailed analysis of the second solution.

Four main presumptions underlying the rule of exclusion as presented in the report boil down to:

1. Privileged pockets exist among the backward classes which means all those in the castes/groups considered backward are not uniformly handicapped. There is differentiation.

2. As the reservation policy does not have a selfcorrecting mechanism it has led to the perpetuation of the solution along with the problem.

3. There is need for state action to prevent this process of perpetuation.

4. State action is manifested in the form of excluding the privileged sections from getting the benefits.

The report tries to answer the question as to who should be excluded from getting reservation benefits among the BCs and on what grounds? Who should be given the power to review and revise the list of backwards? Is reservation a proper solution for tackling the problem of backwardness?

The Commission recognises the need for a simple uncomplicated, periodic exercise to exclude those who have attained a 'fair degree of social educational standards'[9] and are ahead of other backward castes and tribes based on macro level assessment of all the castes/groups on certain empirical factors like education, profession, posts held, income, landholding, educational achievement of parents. Out of the six considerations five are directly or indirectly related to the economic test. One emphasises the educational factor, where a person both of whose parents are graduates is excluded from getting the benefit of reservation. Hence we can see the predominance of economic factor, making it a sufficient ground for exclusion.

Once the determinants are fixed the question is of preparing a revised list. To carry on this periodic exercise of revision, the Commission suggests the establishment of a permanent committee consisting of Chief Secretary to Government, Chairman of Public Service Commission and Secretary to Government (Backward Classes). This committee has to 'evaluate the progress of each caste/group included in the backward classes and decide before Feb. 15 every year whether the list needs any revision'.[10] The revision is made taking into consideration the educational performance (circumstance 1 and 2 as in p. 175 of the report) and employment (circumstance 3). The first consideration directly relates to educational standards and the second to the economic factor. Thus educational and economic advancement get precedence over caste status.

Further the Commission has also analysed the problems associated with the implementation of rule of exclusion. It suggests a 'stringent punishment' for those who obtain, help to obtain and issue false certificates regarding inclusion among the BCs. The same idea is upheld in the expert committee report.

In the concluding section, the Commission accepts caste degradation acquired at birth as original sin, the other two villains being 'economic underdevelopment and educational unawareness' which provide sustenance to caste. The overall standing of the Commission is in favour of economic and educational criteria as determinants of backwardness and not just caste factor. Hence the conclusion: 'the real key towards the solution of the problem of backwardness is the eradication of poverty and the removal of illiteracy and not mere reservation of few seats in professional colleges and few posts in government services'.[11] Reservation touches the fringe of problems of Social Justice.

III

Judgement of the Supreme Court on Creamy Layer

A nine judge bench was constituted to consider the issue of reservation in Central services for the SEBCs. This indicates the significance of the issue involved. The judges, too, unanimously agreed on the sensitivity and delicacy of the problem on hand. One of the judges, Justice Sawant, felt that the issue having economic, social and political overtones hyper-charged with emotions should be decided taking into consideration social realities and keeping in view the longterm interest of the society.[12] Hence Justice S.R. Pandian asserted that it required an objective, creative, pragmatic and realistic approach through discovering and enforcing dominant values.[13]

With a view to make the BCs compact and benefiting only the truly backward,[14] excluding the forward among them becomes 'obligatory'.[15] The argument 'once backward always backward' negates the policy of reservation.[16] Further the dynamic nature of society had a positive impact on the backwards making some of them in no way different from the 'forwards'. Therefore it is unjustifiable to continue the benefits at the cost of the really needy. This perpetuation will lead to enabling the forward among the backward to lap up all the benefits and pervert the objectives of the Constitution.[17] Once exclusion is accepted, the question of who should be excluded and on what ground arises.

This question was dealt with in the judgement as follows:

1. The majority of the judges felt that those whose economic advancement is so high that it means social advancement or those who have occupied posts of high social status should be excluded from getting the reservation benefits meant for OBCs. Once they are advanced socially, which also means economically and educationally, they no longer belong to the BCs.[18] The eminent jurist, K.K. Venugopal, called this advanced group among the BCs as 'pseudo-backwards masquerading as backwards'.[19]

2. Another justification in favour of exclusion came from Justice Sawant who felt that those who had attained 'sufficient capacity to compete with others' should be taken out of the BCs.[20] The qualitative representation in higher rungs of administration should be taken into account while deciding whether a person has reached the stage of creamy layer. Hence here the 'classification which places some section in each backward class internally above the other sections in the same class' can be made either on economic or other consideration. In this case too the judge is not much bothered about utopian criteria, but about the actual assessment based on empirical facts.

3. Justice R.M. Sahai called the continuation of protective discrimination even after the disadvantage has disappeared a 'mockery'. He felt the basis must vanish along with the problem. The creamy layer, he concluded 'must be excluded by fixation of proper income, property or status-criteria'.[21] The judge suggested the criteria of occupation, social acceptance, and income to

identify the creamy layer. He said, 'a wealthy man irrespective of caste or community needs no crutches. Not in 1990 when money more than social status and education have become the index'.[22] He even considered all legislative and executive measures in the removal of creamy layer either individually or collectively as 'constitutionally valid'.[23]

4. Justice Thommen assessed the creamy layer from the position of wealth and power. Those with the strength to join the mainstream of society, though educationally and socially backward, did not require to be protected. Educational and social backwardness lost their validity in the presence of financial strength. Therefore all those who had 'attained a predetermined economic level, must be weeded out'.[24]

The above views indicate the importance of economic factor in deciding the creamy layer. The acceptance of 'rule of exclusion' based on the creamy layer concept results in a change in the nature and content of reservation policy by modifying some of the existing notions and presuppositions. They are: (1) Caste though a necessary condition no longer remains a sufficient condition; (2) Economic test gets a predominance over the already existing identification yardsticks, (3) The unit is not BC as a single indivisible whole but demands internal categorisation.

IV

THE EXPERT COMMITTEE AND THE CONCEPT OF CREAMY LAYER

The expert committee took social and educational advancement leading to economic betterment as the test in identifying the creamy layer. The report made certain observations. The first observation related to the dwindling number of joint families among the upper strata of society. As persons in the creamy layer formed part of the upper strata a nuclear family was subject to the rule of exclusion. The second observation referred to the presumption that Indian society is male dominant; hence a woman who marries a Class I officer should not be excluded as she remains part of the weaker section of society. She is exempted from the rule of exclusion on the ground of 'lingering attributes of social backwardness' which is refuted in the judgement on many grounds.[25] This violates the rule that is laid down in para four of the report that if economic betterment flows from social and educational advancement, it should be taken note of. In this case there is no doubt about the woman's social and educational advancement but still she gets the benefit of exemption. The third observation is based on the presumption that women pursuing various professions as envisaged in category IV of the report get some concession i.e. their spouses' salary is not taken into consideration while subjecting them to economic test.

The Committee claims to be 'cautious' and to adopting a 'pragmatic approach' in identifying the creamy layer. It has given six categories with sub-categories.[26] Persons coming under them form this Creamy Layer of BCs and the rule of exclusion applies to their offspring. In some categories educational qualification becomes a necessary prerequisite for social and economic advancement, particularly in service category and professional class and some constitutional posts, except those based on elections.

V

The emergence of the concept of creamy layer to provide social justice to the really needy has reinforced the system with some kind of sensibility which was fast deteriorating in the face of politicisation. Exclusion of those who do not need the support of the State whould mean the inclusion of the really needy. The need base is more economic than social. It would be proper to use 'economic justice' in the place of 'social justice'.

NOTES AND REFERENCES

1. K.K. Venugopal, the jurist writes, 'the judgement not only puts brake on direction that the courts were taking in expanding the extent of reservation and benefits conferred on BCs but has significantly reversed the trend'. *Illustrated Weekly* dated 5.12.92.
2. Social and economic 'heterogeneity' exists in each caste. M.N. Srinivas, *Indian Bar Review*, Vol. 17 (3 and 4) 1990; Vol. 18 (1) 1991; p. 405; A.M. Shah, *Hindustan Times*, 13.02.1992.
3. Marc Galanter, *Competing Equalities*, OUP, 1984, p. 470.
4. Sawant J. writes, 'Economic consideration alone as the basis of backwardness was not only not intended but positively discarded.' The judgement, vol. II, p. 23.
5. Report of III Backward Classes Commission, Karnataka, 1990, p. 4; Marc Galanter, *Competing Equalities*, pp. 261-77.
6. *Report of Socially and Educationally Backward Classes Commission,*

Gujarat State, 1976, Vol. I, para 5.32.
7. 'Judgements', the Supreme Court Judgement (16-11-1992), Vol. I, II and III. Ministry of Welfare, Government of India.
8. III BBC Karnataka, p. 41.
9. Ibid.
10. Ibid., p. 175.
11. III BCC Report Karnataka p. 176.
12. 'Judgement', Vol. II, Sawant J., p. 1.
13. Ibid., p. 43.
14. Judgement, Vol. 1, para 86.
15. Judgement, Vol. II, para 82.
16. Ibid.
17. Ibid.
18. Judgement, Vol. I, para 86.
19. *Illustrated Weekly,* 5.12.1992.
20. Judgement, Vol. II, para 82.
21. Judgement, Vol. III, page 32.
22. Ibid., Vol. III, page 24.
23. Ibid., page 30.
24. Ibid., Vol. III, page 61.
25. Judgement Vol. I, para 84.
26. Six categories with sub-categories.
    1. Constitutional Posts
    2. Service Category: (a) Group A/Class I Officers of the All-India, Central and State Services (Direct Recruits); (b) Group B/Class II-Central Services and State Services (Direct Recruitment); (c) Employment in Public Sector Undertakings etc.
    3. Armed Forces including Para Military Forces (this will not include persons holding civil posts).
    4. Professional Class and those engaged in trade, business and industry.
    5. Property owners: (a) Agricultural Landholdings; (b) Plantations; (c) Vacant land and/or buildings in urban areas or urban agglomeration.
    6. Income/Wealth Test.

A View From Below

V.T. RAJSHEKAR

This is essentially a view from the bottom of the society. The city of Bombay may look wonderful from the top of Malabar Hill but go down to the Dharavi slum and you can't bear the stink. Go to its "Red Light area", you can see the ugly sex-exploitation, the living hell on earth. So ours is essentially a Dalit point of view which cannot hide the stink, the filth, the horrifying, agonising ugliness. After 45 years of so-called "independence", we the untouchables feel suffocated under upper caste rule. Babasaheb Ambedkar said on 26 January, 1950 while moving the new Constitution of India, as its first Law Minister and its chief draftsman, on the floor of the Constitutent Assembly: "On this day, we are going to enter into a life of contradictions. In politics, we will have equality and in social and economic life we will have inequality. We must remove this contradiction at the earliest moment, or else those who suffer from inequality will blow up the structure of political democracy which this Assembly has so laboriously built up".

We, the untouchables of India, are sorry to say that the upper caste rulers of India, whom we trusted, whose solemn promises we believed, have wrecked this constitution. Babasaheb predicted that those cheated of social and economic inequality would blow up political democracy. But what is happening today is that the rulers themselves are dynamiting the Constitution of India. Actually, it is the oppressed Bahujan Samaj masses of India, particularly the Untouchables and the Muslims, who should have done it. But it happened the other way.

The Constitution is meant for the people and not vice-versa. The existing Constitution is flouted not so much by the oppressed, over 85% of the Bahujan Samaj (BS), but by a minority of less than 15% constituting the Brahminical Social Order (BSO).

This is because the existing Constitution is opposed to the Constitution of Manu which governs the lives of this tiny BSO. Their war and violence over the Marathwada University, Mandal Commission Report, Punjab, Kashmir Babri Masjid demolition etc. prove that they are determined to enforce the Constitution of

Manu to promote their "jati" interests.

So what is going on today all over India is a war between the alien Manu dharmawadies and the peace-loving Bahujan Samajwadis, the producers of wealth, the original inhabitants of India.

That does not mean we are happy with the existing Constitution. A charge was made in the Constituent Assembly itself that Babasaheb being the "Architect of the Constitution" he should bear all the blame. Ambedkar immediately refuted this allegation and said he was totally dissatisfied with the Consitution and would be the first to burn it.

The BSO made use of Ambedkar and imposed a Constitution which could not enforce social justice to over 85% of the Bahujan Samaj, including upper caste women.

Forty-five years of our experience with the upper caste rulers has convinced us that they will never, ever implement any of the provisions of the Constitution. So what is the use of this Constitution? We admit there are so many thinking, concerned members of the BSO who are worried about this war and violence raging in the country and they too feel that a change is necessary.

The main defect of the Constitution is that it copied the Western model of democracy. Democracy itself is a Western concept. That doesn't mean we are opposed to democracy. We are opposed only to "parliamentary democracy", based on "majority rule". Western countries favour "democracy" because by and large they have a homogenous society or "nation-states". But India, Asian and African countries don't have nation-states (D. Smith, *State and Nation in the Third World,* 1989, Wheat, Shelf Book, Sussex, UK).

Whenever democracy goes against its interests, the West will not hesitate to destroy democracy. It destroyed a democratically elected government in Algeria (1992). The destruction of Soviet Russia is another example.

India is not a "nation" but a group of nations striving to be a nation, said Ambedkar. But every time we strive towards the nationhood, this Manuwadi upper caste nation strikes a blow and the nation-making process is delayed. That is why when every other Asian country is galloping, we have become a first-class beggar country.

So, under Indian conditions, the oppressed Bahujan Samaj, victim of Aryan brahminical aggression, can elect their genuine representatives only under an indigenous form of democracy after ensuring "three separations" as envisaged by Babasaheb Ambedkar (V.T. Rajshekar, *Textbook of Dalit Movement in India,* Dalit Sahitya Akademy, Bangalore, 1994).

That means self-determination within India.

The Bahujan Samaj includes six segments: (1) Scheduled Castes (20%), (2) Scheduled Tribes (10%) (3) Backward Castes (35%)-Total 65%, plus (4) Muslims (15%), (5) Christians, (2.5%) and (6) Sikhs (2%). In all 85%. To this, we have to include all upper caste women who are also victims of the BSO.

If every section of this multi-national country has to retain its identity and remain happy then a new constitution has to be framed based on "three separations": (i) *Political separation*: through separate electorate for Dalits, (ii) *Territorial separation:* through separate settlement for Dalits, (iii) *Religious separation*: through conversion to Buddhism for which Dalits need not depend on others.

This "three separations" may be extended to the other five segments and also the BSO. The principle behind "three separations" is to ensure that this "United States of India", comprises several separate but equal nations. What is separate in fact must be made separate by law.

SC/ST/BCs are India's indigenous people. Unable to bear the Aryan oppression, about 20% of them went over to egalitarian religions like Islam, Christianity and Sikhism. That means the so-called religious minorities – who are not minorities at all – are all our blood relations.

These six segments constitute the Bahujan Samaj. This Bahujan Samaj has remained together and jointly fought the BSO all through history. Since the country belongs to its original inhabitants of India, we love this country, our motherland, much more than the alien Aryans. So we are the only one who love the people of India and its country which includes Pakistan, Bangladesh and Sri Lanka also. All the people living in those countries are also our own people. It is possible to reunite them and forge the "United States of India" (Akhand Bharat) of our dream if the "Three separations" are assured not only to Dalits but all the sections including members of the BSO who are also Indians.

Only such a new political setup can ensure a healthy and happy India; else the existing tensions will increase and lead to more violence and eventual breakup which will further worsen the position of BSO.

Plays Express Dalit Anger

S.R. JALOTE

Dalit literature owes its inspiration to the writings of Babasaheb Ambedkar, and it is mostly written by socially, economically, politically and culturally deprived and disadvantaged people. Dalit literature truly blossomed in the post-Independence era and reached its peak in the mid '70s. In the early 1970s, two Maharashtrian movements achieved prominence – the Dalit Panthers and Dalit Literature. By substituting the word "Black" for "Dalit" the reader can immediately realise that a phenomenon comparable to the American Black Panthers and Black Literature has surfaced in the social and literary affairs of the Dalits. Like American movements, the Dalit Panthers and Dalit School of literature represent a new level of pride, militancy and sophisticated creativity. The word Dalit, like the word Black, was chosen by the group itself and is used proudly. Dalit implies those who have been broken, ground down by those above them in a deliberate and active way. There is in the word itself an inherent denial of pollution, Karma, and caste hierarchy.

Dalit writers are extremely interested in Black American Literature, and see their own movement as a parallel phenomenon. Gangadhar Pantawane began his major essay on Dalit Literature, *Mulyavedha* (the perception of value) published in 1974, with a quotation from James Baldwin, the black American novelist and playwright: "Our humanity is our burden, our life, we need not battle for it; we need only to do what is infinitely difficult – that is accept it".

Writing about the possible comparison between Black and Dalit, Janardan Waghmare points out that although the Black was brought to America from Africa, the Dalit was born in his own country. "He may have been an heir of this country but he could not claim his heritage." Waghmare holds:

> There is no difference between the place of the Negro in America and the level of the Untouchable in India. And so for a long time both were caught in the whirlwind of self-denigration and self-hatred. Both were confined in the prison of fatalism. To

prolong this imprisonment, the white found authority in the Bible's myths and symbols, and the clean castes in the Vedas and Manusmriti.[1]

Contemporary Dalit theatre has been portraying the struggles, the daily problems, the hopes and aspirations of the exploited masses. It is a demand for social and economic justice. It arises out of the cry of protest from the insulted and the injured. Mulk Raj Anand observes:

> The outcastes are crying against deaf gods, questioning God Brahma Himself. And their despair asserts itself in ringing triumphs of throwing off the yoke.[2]

Social themes, Buddhist legends, and historical incidents such as the reaction to Untouchable conversion to Islam at Meenakshipuram in Tamilnadu are subjects on which some of the Dalit plays have been written. In this paper I have scrutinised two Dalit plays, namely *The Village Without a Face* and *Beyond the Seven Oceans,* which reflect the Dalit's struggle to attain full equality and status in India and thereby regain his spiritual strength.

The play, *The Village Without a Face* (*Nav Nasalela Ganva*) written by Avinash Dolus, (published in *Nikaya* in 1977 and staged by Dalit Theatre, Aurangabad) represents the social injustice and atrocities inflicted on the Dalits in the post-Independence period. In this play Dolus expresses what it means to be a Dalit in India – the humiliation, the alienation, the despair and the rage. Dolus's play portrays emasculation of Dalits in symbolic language and multiple levels of interpretation. The play tells the story of a Dalit youth who perishes because he refuses to accept the subordinate position required for the Dalit, and dares to claim his economic social, and political rights and privileges. When the curtain rises and the play begins there is no one on the stage. Suddenly a few persons from among the audience rush onto the stage. Holding their prey in their hands they indulge in an increasingly wild dance. After having attained a trance-like state, they exeunt carrying their prey. The Sutradhar (the stage-manager) appears and comments that this wasn't merely a wild dance, instead it was a play being played by human beings ever since the ancient days.

The characters of *The Village Without a Face* are types; they belong to the village Eran. The Sutradhar addresses some of these characters who are sitting in the midst of the audience, and he calls upon them to come to the stage and introduce themselves. They are the Mukhia (the village Headman), the Patel, and the Mahars (the untouchables) of the village. The Sutradhar says that the Untouchables have been slaves for many centuries and their mere touch defiles the earth. They are inauspicious and are ordained to be born as Chandals (Untouchables) because of the sins of their past lives. The chrous sings:

> Deadly sin, deadly sin,
> We are the untouchables of the village,
> Our touch defiles,
> We are the Untouchables of Eran,
> We personify defilement![3]

The Village Without a Face tells the story of the Untouchable Mahars who have shaken the age-old yoke of servitude. It is about their struggles for equal rights, such as the right to education, the right to worship in the temple; also their struggle against scavanging and hauling dead animals. The protagonist of the play, Ramdas Nannavare, is an educated Dalit youth. He is the leader of the Dalits and won't say "Ram Ram", the expression of salutation, bacause the legendary king Ram beheaded Shambhuk and banished Sita. The Dalits have assembled at the place where Ramdas, their favourite leader, is going to deliver a speech. In his impassioned speech, Ramdas exhorts the Dalits to unite and to oppose untouchability. They should give up scavenging and they should not collect left-overs from the upper caste people of the village. They have to struggle for their rights and fight against social injustice, though this may mean poverty and hunger for them. They shouldn't cast their votes in favour of the upper caste people in the forthcoming Gram Panchayat elections. The meeting ends with the concensus that the Dalits will not cast their votes in favour of an upper caste man in the forthcoming Gram Panchayat elections. The chorus sings:

> The village is terror-stricken,
> The people are trembling and hesitating.
> Incredible things, are happening,
> The village is drowned in anxiety. (p. 158)

Though Ramdas is a social rebel, he rebels against the subservient position relegated to the Dalits in a peaceful democratic manner. In the village the cow of the Kulkarni has died, and the Patel wants it to be hauled away by the Mahars of the village. But the Dalits have abandoned the unclean profession. The dead cow has been decomposing and stinking obnoxiously for three days. This is considered a violation of the traditional norms and a challenge to the authority of the Patel by the Mahars. The dead cow is hauled by the upper caste people of the village including the Patel and the Mukhia. They feel that Ramdas, the leader of the Dalits and the prime force of the revolutionary spirit, should be eliminated. But the Mukhia and the Patel decide that since the Panchayat elections are at hand, they should refrain from the use of violence against Ramdas till after the elections.

In the Panchayat elections, Ramdas is a contestant and the rival of the Mukhia. The upper caste people are filled with revenge, because the Dalits are no longer humble and subservient. The Dalits know that Ramdas may not be elected, but they support Ramdas to further the cause of democracy. The Mukhia and the Patel win the Panchayat elections, yet, they despise Ramdas, because he instilled the love of democracy into the minds of the Dalits.

The upper caste people of the village are now looking for an opportunity to get rid of Ramdas. An epidemic breaks out in the village, and the people die of cholera one after another. The Mukhia invites the priest of the goddess Kali to exorcise the evil spirit from the village. Various items, such as lemons and coconuts, are placed before him for the performance of the ritual. The priest begins the ritual, and he is possessed with the spirit of Kali. He enters into a trance and makes wild movements:

The Mukhia: Mother! The people are dying in the village.
The Priest: I know.
The Mukhia: Help us, if we have sinned unknowingly.
The Priest: The people of the village have become dishonest.
The Mukhia: Pardon us now. In the next fair we will have twelve chariots, seated with your idols, pulled by devotees.... (p. 169)

The priest, in a state of trance, says that he has to eradicate the root cause of the evil. He further says that some one has buried a lemon as a device of witchcraft, somewhere in the eastern border of the village. That is why the people are dying of the epidemic, and no one in the village would survive.

The Priest:	In the east of the village. Beyond the boundary of the village – barring the first four houses – the fifth one . . .
A Villager:	Give us some clue
The Priest:	He is an opponent of the Mukhia, Anna. (The villagers begin their whisper– they are communicating through gestures)
The Patel:	What is the solution?
The Priest:	Will you have twelve chariots pulled in the fair by the devotees?
All:	Yes Mother....We will pull the chariots.
The Priest:	You will have to sacrifice.
The Mukhia:	We will sacrifice. Shall we sacrifice the one having two legs or four legs?
The Priest:	Two legs
The Patel:	A cock.
The Priest:	Not a cock (p. 170-71)

The Priest gets into a fit of rage; the villagers are shouting dreadfully. They rush towards the colony of the Untouchables. Ramdas is brought forcibly in front of the temple for his trial by the village Panchayat. The Patel, the Mukhia, and the Priest accuse Ramdas of practising witchcraft and sorcery for the annihilation of the village. The villagers beat him and the Priest threatens that the wrath of Mother Kali will fall on Ramdas if the lemon, which is used as a device of witchcraft, is not taken out. The villagers are shouting and laughing frantically. They accuse Ramdas of sole responsibility for the outbreak of the epidemic which has taken away the lives of many of their friends and relatives. The Patel orders the villagers to strip Ramdas of his clothes. The villagers get into an orgy, and the whole sky reverberates with "Ma Bhawani Ki Jai". Ramdas tries to run away, but the mob pulls him down and strips him of his clothes. The Patel orders to perform the rites of sacrifice. Loud cries of the youth rend the air. The mob holds him very tightly. The villagers burn incense to begin the worship and perform the sacrificial rites. At the instance of the Patel and the Mukhia, someone from the mob pulls and severes both the hands of Ramdas, one after another. Ramdas screams loudly; but the people, in a frenzy, are chanting the name of Mother Kali. The Patel, then, instigates the mob to pull Ramdas's legs apart and sever them. Ramdas's legs are plucked and his phallus is cut; he lies like a corpse. The ritual of sacrifice followed by Ramdas's castration suggests the efforts of the upper caste people to wrest from the Dalits the symbol of manhood.

Ramdas's wife comes along with her children. She beseeches the people to be merciful, but they kick her. Bending over her husband, she weeps bitterly. The mob, in an orgy, exeunts carrying Ramdas's corpse. His wife faints, but the younger child, who earlier was horror-stricken, is now filled with rage. The child's raising his fist in anger signifies that though Ramdas is dead, the invincible revolutionary spirit is a simmering.

Prabhakar Dupare's play *Beyond the Seven Oceans* (*Sat Samudra Palikade,* not dated) published by Prabhakar Prakashan, Nagpur and staged by Panthers Theatre Nagpur, (n.d.), is about the abject conditions of the Dalits in our contemporary society. Because of oppression, tyranny, exploitation and hatred received by the Dalits, their freedom is still beyond the seven oceans. Hence, the title of the play, *Beyond the Seven Oceans,* is an ironical title, meaning thereby that the desire of freedom of the Dalits in our contemporary society is an inaccessible object, a mirage. The plot of the play is loosely constructed, and the play constitutes of several stories. The purpose of the dramatist is to offer various glimpses of Dalit life, and the play ends when the playwright thinks that the audience has seen enough.

Beyond the Seven Oceans begins with a conversation between the mill owner and Manohar, the union leader. The setting is the cabin of the mill owner who is smoking a cigar; Manohar enters the cabin. He has come to meet the mill owner to find some way for the alleviation of the labourers' sufferings. The labourers of the mill have been on strike for the last two months, and the services of twenty of them have been terminated. Manohar points out to the mill owner that the labourers are neither free nor they have any kind of security. That is because those elected for the Legislative Assembly or to Parliament must be supported by the mill owner. Without his support one cannot become the Prime Minister or the President of India. The mill owner arrogantly admits that to fulfil his selfish ends he has been inflicting atrocities on the Dalits. His speech is illustrative of the age-old dictum that might is right.

The mill owner says that Manohar has joined the mill only an year ago; he, therefore, is full of the ideals of socialism, and that he is far away from the realities of life. According to the mill owner, Manohar cannot imagine the miserable plight of the labourers who haven't received their wages for the last two months.

As in the quick succession of scenes in a cinematograph, the setting of the play moves to the colony of the labourers. The Savaji (The Merchant) is beating and kicking Dinu, the labourer because he is unable to clear the merchant's bills. Lakshmi, Dinu's wife, enters screaming; she beseeches the Savaji and tells him that Dinu has been starving for the last two days. She offers her *mangalasutra* which the Savaji declines; he demands payment in cash only. The Savaji kicks Dinu in his stomach; Dinu screams and falls. The Savaji looks at Lakshmi's breasts with lustful eyes, and he holds her hand:

Dinu:	Savaji; Leave Lakshmi.
Lakshmi:	Leave me; mean, cur, shameless;
Savaji:	Dinya, don't come forward. I don't want money. Your wife will be my guest today.
Dinu:	Sa . . . Sava; Lakshmi. . . .
Lakshmi:	Leave me. Pig . . . Save. Dinesh . . . Save . . . Save . . . (p. 199)

The setting of the play, then, moves to the mill. The labourers and their families are broken, because of the long drawn strike. Manohar is adamant on the issue that the strike will continue till the labourers' demands are met. The deadlock continues and the labourers are obviously doomed. Dinu, drenched with blood, and his wife rush onto the stage in the midst of the mob. The Savaji enters chasing Dinu, stabs him in his stomach and runs away. Dinu is listless and dies soon after. Lakshmi sobbingly beseeches the mob to catch hold of the murderer. But the mob is helplessly watching the scene, and no one has the courage to catch hold of the Savaji. Manohar says that the Savaji belongs to a different world and "in our court of law there is no punishment for that murderer." (p. 201)

Manohar says:

> He is not a labourer. We labourers have a different world. Lakshmi, we don't have our own court of law. Whatever court of law is there, we don't get justice there. Because its doors are ever closed for us. But the doors of the temple of injustice are

ever open for us. (p. 201)

Lakshmi sobbingly tells the mob that the Savaji tried to force Dinu to be an accomplice in bootlegging. Dinu had no hopes to remain alive. In the morning he kissed his son and exhorted him to have courage and never to feel disappointed.

Three months have passed since the labourers' strike had started. The mill owner charges that Manohar, the union leader, is solely responsible for the misery, starvation and death of his brethern. But Manohar insists that the labourers are fighting for their freedom. In his impassioned speech addressed to the labourers, he says that though many of his brethern have died and many were injured during the long-drawn strike, their struggle to live a respectable life would continue. The procession of labourers marches peacefully towards the residence of the mill owner to give him a charter of demands. The procession is blocked by the police; but Manohar, violating the orders, marches ahead. The police begins a lathi-charge, the labourers run away, and Manohar is left alone. He is severely beaten by the police. He cries, but in vain, that all the ideals of freedom and democracy in our Constitution are sham.

Manohar comes to realise that though both he and Lila, his wife, are graduates, they have no jobs. He has to pull a rickshaw to earn bread for his family. He dreams of having a small house, his children going to a convent and his wife wearing a decent sari. But he knows that his dreams may never come true.

The next day Manohar is returning from the pub heavily drunk. His friend, Ramesh, informs him that his wife has committed suicide. She had gone to the house of the merchant to clean dishes. The merchant accused her of stealing bread, shut her in a room and tried to rape her. She killed the merchant and rushed to her house with her hands stained with blood. The police was after her and she committed suicide by taking poison.

The mob enters with Lila's dead body. Manohar laments and repents that his being out of the job and his utter poverty are the causes of the tragedy. He says that Lila had rightly killed the merchant, because the merchant had tried to implicate her on the basis of false allegations of stealing bread, and also tried to rape her. In the bonfire of the Dalits' injured dignity, the oppressors and tyrants like the merchant will be burnt to ashes one day. A day will come when the sweat and the blood of the labourers will engulf the palatial houses of the rich.

After a few days Manohar receives an appointment letter for the post of a clerk. He boards the train to join his new assignment. When he reaches the town, he confronts the stark reality that nobody is willing to rent an apartment to him. With a great difficulty he gets a place in a locality dominated by Brahmins. Soon after he occupies it, a throng of upper-caste people brandishing lathis swarm in front. They accuse the Brahmin owner of the house of polluting the colony by letting rooms to a Mahar. Someone in the mob drags Manohar out of his apartment, and he is beaten up severely. When he raises loud cries of protest, the people run away. Manohar feels that his freedom is still an illusory object for which he has been aspiring all his life; it is still beyond the seven oceans. But the sole aim of his life will be to reform the debased and degenerated society.

The plays discussed above and other contemporary Dalit plays graphically represent their resentment against the prejudice and discrimination prevailing against them in our society. In the post-independence period, the framers of the Indian Constitution made efforts to provide protective measures for the Scheduled Castes and Scheduled Tribes in order to bring them into the mainstream of life. Under these provisions, some of the benefits accorded by the Parliament for the advancement of socially and educationally backward classes of citizens are reserved seats in all legislative bodies, the reservation of government jobs, financial assistance to students through the college level, financial support for marriages in which one partner is an untouchable, support for housing projects, and legal machinery for suits against discriminative practices. In spite of these protective laws passed by the Parliament, however, the contemporary Dalit theatre reflects the continuing anger of the Dalits.

REFERENCES

1. Janardan Waghmare, "Black Literature", in *Poisoned Bread*, ed. Arjun Dangle, Bombay: Orient Longman, p. 307.
2. *An Anthology of Dali Literature*, eds. Mulk Raj Anand and Eleanor Zelliot, New Delhi: Gyan Publishing House, p. XIV.
3. *Dalit Rangamanch*, eds. Kamlakar Gangawane and Tryambak Mahajan, Ajmer: Krishna Brothers, p. 151. All the subsequent page references to this book have been absorbed in the text itself.

TABLE 1

Annexures of Bihari Muslim Other Backward and Most Backward Classes 1951 - 1993 *

Names	1951	1955	1976	1978	1980	1992	1993
Bhat			O&M	O&M	O	M	O
Bhathiara	M	M	O&M	O&M	O	M	O
Chik	M	O	O&M	O&M	O	M	O
Churihara	O	M	O	O	O		O
Dafalange					O		
Dafale	M	M	O&M	O&M	O	M	O
Dhobi	M	O	O&M	O&M		M	O
Dhunia	M	M	O&M	O&M	O	M	O
Faqir					O		
Gadihar				O			
Hima, Karanjia, Qassar					O		
Ibrahimi		O					
Idrisi	O	O	O	O	O	O	
Kassab	M	O	O&M	O&M	O	M	O
Mehtar, Lalbegi Halalkhor, Bhangi	M	M	O&M	O&M	O	M	O
Madari	M		O&M	O&M	O	M	O
Miriasin	M		O&M	O&M	O	M	O
Mirshikar	O	O	O&M	O&M	O	M	O
Momin	O	O	O	O	O	M	O
Mukero	O				O	O	O
Nalband	O		O	O	O	O	
Nat	M	M	O&M	O&M	O	M	O
Pamaria	M	O	O&M	O&M	O	M	O
Rangrez	O	O	O	O	O	O	O
Rayeen	O	O	O	O	O	O	O
Sayee	O	O	O&M	O&M	O	M	O
Thakurai					O		

Key: O : Other Backward classes; M : Most Backward Classes.

Note: There was a common list in the years 1980 & 1993 i.e. there was no O and M classification in these years.

**Source*:

1. 1951 & 1976: Mungeri Lal Commission Report, pp. 114-5 and 118-9 respectively.
2. 1955 : GOI Report of the Backward Classes Commission (1955), vol ii, pp. 16-23.
3. 1978 : Govt. of Bihar, Dept. of Personnel & Administrative Reform: Circulars etc. upto 1988, (10 November, 1978)pp.118-23.
4. 1980 : GOI Report of the Backward Classes Commission (1980), vol vi, pp. 178-9.
5. 1992 : Govt. of Bihar Gazette, 10 March 1992, pp. 9-12.
6. 1993 : GOI, Extraordinary Gazette, 13 September 1993, pp. 40-3

Contributors

Y. RAFEEK AHMED is Chairman, Post-Graduate Department of Political Science, University of Mysore. He has published widely in professional journals and his papers have also appeared in important anthologies. His area of interest is political organization – both national and international.

AJIT BHATTACHARJEA is a noted columnist. He has edited the *Hindustan Times* and the *Indian Express* as well as Jayaprakash Narayan's weekly *Everyman's*. His publications include *Kashmir, the Wounded Valley; Jayaprakash Narayan, a Political Biography; Dateline Bangladesh,* and several pamphlets. He has been a Fellow of the Institute of Advanced Study and is currently Director, Press Institute of India, New Delhi.

MEENA DESPANDE is Visiting Fellow at Institute for Studies in Industrial Development (ISID), and is engaged in research in policy-making processes in India.

KIRPAL S. DHILLON, has been a member of the Senior Directing Staff in the National Academy of Administration, Director General, Central Bureau of Police Research and Development and Director General of Police, Punjab. He has also been a Fellow of the Indian Institute of Advanced Study.

PAPIYA GHOSH teaches History at Patna University and is working towards a book on *Community and Nation: Bihar in the 1940s*. She has also done research on the South Asian partition diaspora.

GOPAL GURU, teaches in the Department of Politics and Public Administration, University of Poona. He has written extensively on various, what might be called, subaltern movements in the country: the dalit movement, the peasant movement and the sugar workers' movement. His work on the political thought of Ambedkar has been greatly influential.

G. HARGOPAL is Professor of Political Science at the Central University of Hyderabad. Besides research papers on public policy, development administration and political economy, published *Public Policy and Rural Poor* (conjoint), *Grassroots Planning for Development* (conjoint) and *Administration Leadership.*

S.R. JALOTE is a Reader in the Department of English, Banaras Hindu University. He was a Fellow of Indian Institute of Advanced Study during 1993-94.

AMARJIT S. NARANG is Associate Professor of Political Science at Indira Gandhi National Open University. He has been a Fellow of Brock University, Canada and Indian Institute of Advanced Study. His publications include *Storm Over the Sutlej: The Akali Politics, Indian Government and Politics, Democracy, Development and Distortion,* and *Ethnic Identities and Federalism.*

C.D. NARASIMHAIAH was Professor of English at Mysore University until 1979 when he retired and set up Dhvanyaloka, a resrearch centre for Literatures. He has edited *The Literary Criterion* since 1952. Professor Narasimhaiah was awarded the Padma Bhushan in 1990.

V.K. NATRAJ is Professor of Development Studies at the Institute of Development Studies in the University of Mysore. His publications include *Decentralization of Planning in India*; *Land Reforms in Karnataka* and *Regional Planning and National Development.*

JAKKA PARTHASARATHY is a Senior Lecturer in Cultural Anthropology in the Tribal Research Centre of Tamil University, Tamil Nadu. His research papers have appeared in professional journals.

JAGANATH PATHY is Professor of Sociology, South Gujarat University, Surat. A recipient of the UGC Career Award for the Social Sciences, he has published widely in professional journals. He has also authored the following books: *Tribal Peasantry, Anthropology of Development, Ethnic Minorities, Underdevelopment and Destitution.*

V.S. PRASAD is one of the Directors of Indira Gandhi National Open University. He is the author of several books and articles on public administration and distance education.

PREM SINGH, former Fellow of Indian Institute of Advanced Study, teaches Hindi in Delhi University. He is a poet and a critic.

V.T. RAJSHEKHAR is a noted journalist and writer with over 25 books to his credit.

K. RAGHAVENDRA RAO has taught English literature and Political Science in several universities of the country. He is a poet, a critic and a much acclaimed translator.

AMAL RAY has taught at the Institute for Social and Economic Change, Bangalore. His publications include *Political Change and Constitutional Development, Federal Politics and Government, Tension Areas in India's Federal System* and *Inter-Governmental Relations in India.*

B.K. ROY BURMAN has held several important academic and administrative positions. His is one of the authoritative voices on matters relating to the tribes of our country.

S. SESHAIAH teaches Law in the Department of Law, S.K. University, Andhra Pradesh. He is actively associated with the Civil Liberties Movement in Andhra Pradesh and is a regular contributor to *Swecha.*

SANDEEP SHASTRI teaches Political Science at Bangalore University. His fields of specialisation are legislative and electoral behaviour and Indian federalism.

K.S. SUBRAMANIAN is a senior member of the Indian Police Service. He has also held several academic and research positions in various organizations in India and abroad.

R.C. VYAS, has taught Law at Lucknow University. He has also held several visiting assignments in research institutions and universities abroad.